DIESELS FROM EDDYSTONE: THE STORY OF
BALDWIN DIESEL LOCOMOTIVES

BY GARY W. DOLZALL AND STEPHEN F. DOLZALL

Photogra ... ise credited.

Editor: Bob H ... wrence O. Luser

"The diesel locomotive has great possibilities, especially on long hauls, where the diesel engine will be supreme. It will cost from two to three times the price of steam locomotives, but its operations will be cheaper and will offset the original cost."—Samuel Matthews Vauclain, April 6, 1925

PREFACE

THIS BOOK documents the diesel locomotives constructed by Baldwin Locomotive Works and associated models built by that company's successor, Baldwin-Lima-Hamilton (Baldwin was merged with Lima-Hamilton Corp. in 1950). This includes 3209 diesel locomotives constructed between 1925 and 1956. Diesel locomotives built under the "Baldwin-Westinghouse" name (Westinghouse Electric & Manufacturing Co. controlled Baldwin from 1948 to 1954) are included.

The following subjects are not included: (1) Westinghouse diesel locomotives. From 1928 to 1937 a number of Westinghouse diesels were partially constructed at Baldwin's Eddystone (Pennsylvania) facility. However, responsibility for the marketing and final construction of these locomotives fell entirely to Westinghouse. (2) Locomotives produced by Lima-Hamilton. In 1949, prior to its merger with Baldwin, Lima-Hamilton began production of a line of diesel switcher and transfer units at Lima, Ohio. This line was competitive with Baldwin's diesels and was dropped following the merger. (3) Whitcomb diesel locomotives. After 1931 Whitcomb Locomotive Works of Rochelle, Illinois, was controlled by Baldwin Locomotive Works, and from 1940 Whitcomb was a division of Baldwin. In February 1952 production of Whitcomb industrial locomotives was transferred to the Eddystone plant and the line became known as the Baldwin-Lima-Hamilton "Industrial Line." We leave the Whitcomb/B-L-H industrial line to future authors. The relationships of Lima-Hamilton and Whitcomb (and their locomotives) to Baldwin are further discussed in Chapter 3.

The first chapter outlines Baldwin Locomotive Works' origins, its growth into one of the world's largest locomotive manufacturers, and the construction of its Eddystone (Pennsylvania) plant. The second chapter describes Baldwin's entry into the diesel age, documenting the company's earliest experimental diesel locomotives and its preparations to begin production of commercial diesel locomotives. Chapter 3 is a synopsis of Baldwin production — from the introduction of non-experimental units in 1936 through shipment of the last diesel in 1956. Chapter 3 also describes the development of Baldwin diesel power plants, Baldwin's role in the market for diesel railroad locomotives, and Baldwin's corporate structure, including its control by Westinghouse Electric & Manufacturing Co., and its merger with Lima-Hamilton.

The remaining chapters document Baldwin diesel yard switchers, streamlined passenger-service models, dual-engine transfer diesels, heavy road-switchers, streamlined freight-service models, light road-switchers, and models built strictly for export (units of domestic design sold outside the U. S. are described with those delivered to U. S. roads). Each chapter includes detailed information on all models constructed, plus information on many individual locomotives' service careers, retirements, and, in some fortunate cases, preservation. A complete production list of Baldwin diesels can be found at the end of the book.

ACKNOWLEDGMENTS

In the preparation of this book, the authors have received the aid of scores of individuals and organizations. John F. Kirkland, retired Baldwin Regional Manager, Pacific Coast, provided assistance of an extraordinary nature; without him the process would have been much more difficult, if not impossible. The authors also owe heartfelt thanks to these Baldwin employees: H. L. Broadbelt (who supplied hundreds of Baldwin photos), Charles A. Brown, Fred Cave, Albert Hoefer, William Kellow, Matthew Gray, Burt St. Vincent, and Robert Van Valkenburgh Jr.

We would also like to single out for their repeated assistance TRAINS magazine Editor David P. Morgan and Managing Editor J. David Ingles, Ken Douglas, Bill Volkmer, Morley J. Kelsey, and Warren Calloway. And the authors thank Howard W. Ameling, Herbert H. Harwood Jr., Alan R. Cripe, George M. Leilich, Frank A. King, Jim Scribbins, J. H. Price, Robert C. Anderson, William A. Gibson, Margaret Morgan, Thomas Lawson, Louis R. Saillard, the late Alfred E. Perlman, and G. W. Jacobs.

The aid of various individuals from the following railroads is appreciated: Atchison, Topeka & Santa Fe, Bessemer & Lake Erie, Burlington Northern, Elgin, Joliet & Eastern, Illinois Central Gulf, Missouri-Kansas-Texas, Missouri Pacific, and Union Pacific. Representatives of the New York Central Historical Society and the New Haven Railroad Historical & Technical Association, Inc., also provided useful information.

An invaluable reference for any study of diesel motive power is *Extra 2200 South*, and this book project was no exception. We wish to thank publisher Don Dover not only for providing data, but also for the loan of several photographs from the *Extra 2200 South* files. The authors heartily recommend a subscription to *Extra 2200 South* as a means to update and supplement the material in this book. Thanks are due, also, to all the photographers who generously provided material to illustrate this volume. Their names appear throughout the book with their work.

Finally, both authors thank their families for the patience they have shown and the support they have offered during the preparation of this book. This especially applies to our wives, Lana and Donnette. We are also grateful to Donnette (Gary's wife) for her aid in editing the final manuscript.

Gary W. Dolzall, Waukesha, Wisconsin
Stephen F. Dolzall, Brownsburg, Indiana
January 1984

DEDICATION

This book is dedicated to those who designed, built, sold, operated, maintained, or were intrigued by the diesel locomotives of Baldwin.

CONTENTS

4 BALDWIN — THE MAN, THE COMPANY
A locomotive company grows to maturity

7 THE DIESEL COMES TO EDDYSTONE
Grand experiments and troubled times

11 BALDWIN AND THE DIESEL
A synopsis of Baldwin's diesel years

26 EDDYSTONE'S FINEST
Baldwin diesel yard switchers

52 FROM A GIANT TO A LIGHTWEIGHT
Streamlined passenger-service diesels

**70 TALES OF THE "GOLDEN GOOSE"
AND THE "BLUEBIRD"**
Heavy transfer units

80 EDDYSTONE'S TRIPLETS
Heavy road-switchers

98 NEW TRIPLETS
The 1950 standard line heavy road-switchers

118 THE "HAULING FOOL"
Streamlined freight-service diesels

130 YARD GOATS WITH ROAD-SWITCHERS' SHOES
Light road-switchers

138 BOUND FOR FOREIGN SHORES
Baldwin export-model diesels

143 PRODUCTION LIST

BALDWIN — THE MAN, THE COMPANY

A locomotive company grows to maturity

MATTHIAS W. BALDWIN, born in Elizabethtown, New Jersey, in 1795, was a jeweler, an inventor, an industrialist, and a philanthropist. Above all else, though, "Matty" Baldwin was a builder of locomotives. In 1827, Baldwin built his first steam engine, a tall, stationary, five-horsepower creation constructed for his own machine shop on Minor Street in Philadelphia. The engine was a success, and soon Baldwin was constructing stationary engines for other firms.

In 1830, Franklin Peale of the Philadelphia Museum asked Baldwin to build a miniature operating steam locomotive, and in April 1831 the little machine first came to motion on a tight circle of track at the museum. Later that year, the Philadelphia, Germantown and Norristown Railroad Company — impressed by Baldwin's miniature handiwork — contracted for the construction of one full-sized steam locomotive. History was made.

On November 23, 1832, a diminutive four-wheeled, horizontal-boiler, 30-mph steam locomotive christened *Old Ironsides* turned its 54″ drivers for the first time. It was months after the debut of *Old Ironsides* before Matty Baldwin received another steam locomotive order, and his second locomotive — the six-wheeled *E. L. Miller* constructed for the Charleston & Hamburg Railroad — was not completed until February 18, 1834. But by the end of 1834, Baldwin had completed four more locomotives, three for the

Matthias W. Baldwin, 1795-1866.

state of Pennsylvania's "State Road" and one for the Philadelphia & Trenton. Baldwin was in the locomotive business to stay. From the little shop in Philadelphia's Lodge Alley where these early locomotives were constructed, Baldwin's company grew, eventually moving to an L-shaped, three-story, brick edifice at Broad and Hamilton Streets in Philadelphia.

In 1866, Matthias Baldwin died at age 71. Before his death, the company — although saddled with a myriad of partnership and name changes — had constructed 1500 locomotives. The growth of Baldwin's enterprise continued after 1866, paralleling the rapid expansion of the railroads. By the end of 1889 the company had turned countless tons of iron and timber into more than 10,000 locomotives; by the final day of the nineteenth century that quantity had grown to more than 17,000. From the primitive *Old Ironsides* that Matthias Baldwin had assembled with his own hands the list of the company's locomotives had grown to include 2-4-2s and 4-4-0s, 4-6-0s and 4-8-0s, 2-8-0s and 0-10-0s, and the first 2-8-2s (for Japan's Nippon Railway, in 1897).

THE BIRTH OF THE EDDYSTONE WORKS

At the dawn of the twentieth century Baldwin occupied 19 acres bordered by Broad and Spring Garden Streets in Philadelphia. In 1902 the company completed its 20,000th locomotive. With business continuing to expand and locomotives growing ever larger, the Philadelphia works could little longer accommodate either the volume of Baldwin's business or the increasing bulk of its products.

In 1906 Baldwin acquired 184 acres of land on the west bank of the Delaware River in Delaware County, Pennsylvania. First to be constructed were a new foundry and smith shop, then a huge new erecting shop was begun; when completed in 1912 the erecting shop covered 7½ acres. Baldwin's new facility took its name from the community around it — Eddystone, Pennsylvania. Legendary Eddystone was being born.

It took Baldwin 22 years to complete its move from Philadelphia to the new facility, but long before its completion Eddystone began playing a significant role in Baldwin's growth. In 1918 Eddystone was Baldwin's chief instrument as the company constructed a record 3580 locomotives. That year, with Southern Railway 2-8-8-2 No. 4009, Baldwin marked its 50,000th locomotive. In 1926, Baldwin's 60,000th creation — a great 3-cylinder, watertube-firebox experimental 4-10-2 — rolled out of the Eddystone Works.

When the finishing touches were applied to the grand main office building in mid-1928 Eddystone was deemed complete. The facility had grown to 590.95 acres, 108 acres under roof. There were 90 major buildings, including two separate erecting shops. Twenty-six miles of Baldwin-operated track linked the buildings to one another and to the outside world, and the plant had rail connections to three railroads — the Pennsylvania, the Reading, and the Baltimore & Ohio; the Pennsylvania's Philadelphia-Washington, D. C., main line actually bisected Eddystone from north to south. And on the bank of the Delaware River stood Wharf 251, Baldwin's tidewater dock where locomotives were loaded on oceangoing vessels for shipment all over the world. Matthias Baldwin's company had grown to greatness.

On the morning of Thursday June 28, 1928, the company simultaneously closed its Philadelphia shops and formally dedicated Eddystone. In addition to Baldwin employees, nearly 4000 guests attended the event. A special train was operated to Eddystone from Atlantic City, New Jersey, and BLW experimental 4-10-2 No. 60000 stood on hand for inspection. During the ceremonies U. S. Secretary of Labor James J. Davis took the podium and described the greatness that Baldwin Locomotive Works had attained: "There is one thing . . . which is known to all Americans who have any knowledge whatsoever, namely that on all the great railroads, not only in America, but throughout the world, trains are drawn by locomotives built by the Baldwin Locomotive Works. A Baldwin locomotive is a guarantee of soundness of construction and efficiency."

Baldwin's Philadelphia plant, bordered by Broad and Spring Garden Streets, covered 19 acres in the heart of the city. The works were formally closed on June 28, 1928, the same day that Eddystone was ceremoniously opened.

DIVERSIFICATION — AND THE DIESEL

While Eddystone was constructed to ensure Baldwin's continued position as one of the great locomotive builders of the world, that was not its sole purpose. As Baldwin looked toward its centennial year in 1931 the company prepared to diversify, and the Eddystone facility was intended to manufacture a variety of heavy industrial products. The "Baldwin Group" was soon formed and included three divisions at Eddystone: the Locomotive & Ordnance Division, which

At left is Baldwin's first stationary steam engine of 1827, and above is a replica of Baldwin's first full-sized steam locomotive, *Old Ironsides* of 1832.

Magnificent Eddystone: In the foreground is the original erecting shop (later the Southwark Division) and boiler shops (later the fabricating shops). In the center of the scene is the main office building. Across the Pennsylvania Railroad main line which bisects the photo stands the main erecting shop and adjacent machine shop. In the far left-hand corner stands the tender shop, which later became the diesel shop.

This 1918 artist's conception of Eddystone is dominated by Wharf 251 on the shore of the Delaware River.

constructed locomotives, locomotive parts, diesel power plants, and military hardware, and provided special heavy machining; the Southwark Division, which built hydraulic machinery, testing machines, mill equipment, hydraulic turbines, and hydraulic valves; and the Cramp Brass and Iron Foundries Division, maker of ship propellers, bronze valves, and castings and forgings. The Baldwin Group also

evolved to hold firms not located at Eddystone, including the Standard Steel Division at Burnham, Pennsylvania; the Pelton Water Wheel Company at San Francisco, California; and the Whitcomb Locomotive Works at Rochelle, Illinois.

As a part of this growth it was only natural that Baldwin should consider expanding its line of locomotives beyond its staple of steam locomotives and a lesser number of straight electrics (usually built in cooperation with Westinghouse Electric & Manufacturing Co.). By the ceremonial opening of Eddystone, one step had already been taken. Among all the machines borne by flanged wheels that Baldwin had built since *Old Ironsides* — the 4-4-0s and 2-8-0s, the 2-8-8-2s, the 25-ton electrics, the New York Elevated Railroad steam-dummies, the steam cars, and the gasoline-powered locomotives (Baldwin built its first such internal-combustion locomotive in 1910) — there stood one creature unlike all its kindred. Assembled at Eddystone in the spring of 1925 and bearing builder's number 58501, on its flanks it wore the Baldwin Locomotive Works name. It was a homely, squarish, six-axled creature that had nothing to do with coal or steam or overhead catenary. Instead, it relied upon the internal combustion of fuel oil and air to move its pistons and to generate electrical current to turn its wheels. Baldwin serial number 58501 was a diesel-electric, and although steam would rule supreme in the halls of Eddystone for another score of years, days of change were coming.

THE DIESEL COMES TO EDDYSTONE

Grand experiments and troubled times

BALDWIN LOCOMOTIVE WORKS stood among this nation's pioneers in diesel locomotive development. In 1925, when the company's first diesel was built at Eddystone, oil-burning internal-combustion locomotives were curiosities in American railroading. Of 1055 locomotives ordered for domestic use in 1925, only 13 were to be diesel-powered, and America's "first commercially successful diesel-electric," a diminutive 60-ton, 300-h.p. boxcab built jointly by Alco, General Electric, and Ingersoll-Rand, was but a few months into its career as Central Railroad of New Jersey 1000.

Despite the commercial insignificance of diesel-electrics in the mid-1920s, Baldwin forged an entry into the great experiment with fervor: Eddystone's first diesel — BLW 58501 — was a ponderous, 275,000-pound, 12-cylinder, 52'-1¾"-long, A1A + A1A boxcab rated at 1000 h.p., the might of more than three CNJ 1000s. The rail trade was impressed: *Railway Age* heralded BLW 58501 as possessor of "the largest horsepower capacity of any internal combustion locomotive yet built in this country . . . ."

The size and strength of 58501 could be ascribed to Samuel Matthews Vauclain. A grandfatherly figure with a penchant for wearing string ties and derby hats, Vauclain had left the Pennsylvania Railroad in 1883 to join Baldwin. Looks aside, Vauclain was a strong-willed man, a company man, and in 1919 he had become Baldwin's president. This story about Vauclain and BLW 58501 was told to TRAINS magazine Editor David P. Morgan by an ex-Baldwin employee: "Vauclain was making the rounds of the drafting offices in the 1920s when he chanced upon a side elevation of the firm's first diesel. Informed that the proposed design was rated at 300 h.p., he ripped the blueprint off the drawing board and told the surprised draftsman, 'Young man, Baldwin never builds horsepower in hundreds, we build in thousands.' "

In 1925 coaxing 1000 h.p. from a single locomotive-sized diesel power plant was no everyday task. The engine Baldwin selected was a two-cycle, solid-injection, 12-cylinder machine with a 9¾" bore and a 13½" stroke, designed by Knudsen Motor Corporation of New York. The 12-cylinder configuration was actually fabricated at Eddystone by mating twin, inverted V-6 cylinder A-frames (the equivalent of cylinder-block assemblies). Adjacent cylinder pairs shared a common cylinder head, combustion chamber, and fuel injector. The cylinders drove parallel crankshafts geared together at the generator end to drive a single power shaft which turned at a maximum 450 rpm. A second gear set turned a final drive shaft — and a 750-volt d.c. Westinghouse main generator — at 1200 rpm. An extension of the generator shaft was geared to a 3600 rpm centrifugal blower which provided scavenging air to the engine.

To harness the power of the Knudsen V-12 and its generator, Baldwin set four Westinghouse Type 353-D-3 200-h.p. traction motors into a pair of A1A trucks. To prevent operational stresses from damaging the locomotive frame or power plant the trucks were linked together and the unit's drawbars were mounted directly to the trucks. The base of the locomotive was a multi-piece cast frame, and crew cabs, with Westinghouse controls, were set at both ends. The unit was equipped with three electrically driven air compressors; one of these compressors was also linked to a 4-cylinder gasoline engine and was used to start the Knudsen diesel. Unlike most boxcabs of the period, BLW 58501 featured end platforms, which were mounted on the trucks. When completed in June 1925, 58501 stood with 180,000 pounds of its 275,000 pounds total weight on drivers, and was reported to be capable of 52,200 pounds of tractive effort. Baldwin gave its first diesel this designation: Class 12 (OE) 1000-1-CC, 1.

BLW 58501 began trials on the Eddystone test track in mid-1925, then ventured onto the Reading Railroad. During much of the summer and fall of 1925 the 58501 worked road and switching assignments between Reading and Tamaqua, Pennsylvania. On this 40-mile stretch 58501 pulled trains of 1000 tons out of Reading, working grades of .7 percent at speeds of 16 mph; out of Tamaqua the 58501 handled 2000-ton trains. While these results were far from disappointing, the Knudsen engine was an overly complex piece of machinery to maintain, and worse, it failed to attain the 1000-h.p. rating Vauclain had prescribed. Quietly, 58501 retreated to Eddystone, where it was used as a plant switcher until at least 1933 and where it was scrapped in 1941. Baldwin put its diesel experiments aside, awaiting a time when it could acquire a more sound diesel power plant.

1000 H.P. — FROM SIX CYLINDERS

In 1929 Baldwin turned its attention back to diesel-electrics. Although the market for diesels had grown only moderately since 1925 (in 1929, 68 of the 1230 locomotives ordered for domestic use were diesels), there was increasing builder activity. General Electric and Ingersoll-Rand jointly built a modest number of boxcabs, while Alco — the third member of the partnership that had constructed CNJ 1000 — was developing its own diesel line. Working with

TRAINS collection

BLW President Samuel M. Vauclain.

New York Central, Alco had constructed a 750-h.p. 2-D-2 diesel (NYC 1550) in June 1928, and a 900-h.p. 2-D-2 locomotive (NYC 1500) in July 1928. Westinghouse Electric & Manufacturing Co. had also started marketing low-horsepower boxcabs (many with carbodies constructed by Baldwin), and was preparing a line of "visibility cab" diesels. Baldwin considered it time for another step.

Baldwin's second diesel carried on in the tradition of BLW 58501 — after a fashion. The new locomotive was to be a 1000-h.p. unit, and once again it would be a

Baldwin Locomotive Works' first diesel-electric, BLW 58501, was completed in June 1925. The big A1A + A1A boxcab was invested with 1000 h.p. at the instigation of Baldwin President Samuel Matthews Vauclain.

bidirectional boxcab. The trucks would be linked, with pilots and drawbars attached, and like 58501 the new Baldwin would wear its construction serial number. This time that number was 61000.

There were also differences — major ones. While 58501 had been tested both as a road engine and switcher, Baldwin conceived the 61000 purely to test the abilities of a heavy-duty diesel switcher. For this slow, start-and-stop duty, instead of six axles the 61000 was equipped with four,

in a B + B arrangement that placed all the weight on powered wheels. Maximum speed was to be 25 mph. The most important difference was the power plant; the 61000 was built around a German-built Krupp 6-cylinder, four-cycle, solid-injection inline engine with square 15″ x 15″ bore and stroke. With its huge pistons, the Krupp yielded 1000 h.p. using but half the cylinders that the Knudsen engine in 58501 had required. The Krupp weighed 47,000 pounds and developed its rated horsepower at 500 rpm.

An imposing creation, BLW 58501 weighed 275,000 pounds and was 52′-1¾″ long. The power plant was a Knudsen 12-cylinder diesel engine.

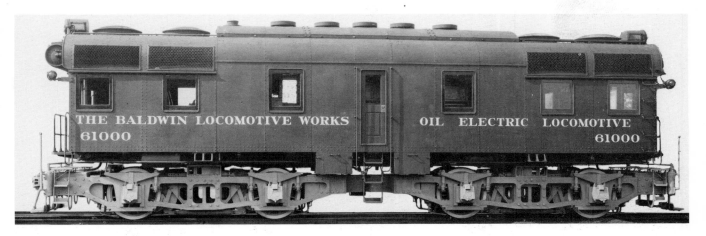

Baldwin's second diesel-electric (actually an "oil electric" in the popular terminology of the period) was BLW 61000, completed in May 1929. The B + B locomotive relied upon a 6-cylinder Krupp diesel for its 1000 h.p. With a weight of 270,000 pounds, the unit produced 67,500 pounds of tractive effort.

For the 61000, Eddystone used a one-piece cast frame. Westinghouse again supplied the electrical gear, including a Type 478-A main generator and Type 355 traction motors. Cooling system radiators were placed at each end of the locomotive, directly above the cabs, and in a bit of advanced thinking (for 1929), electrically driven rooftop cooling system exhaust fans were installed. Large air reservoirs enclosed in the carbody provided air for braking and to start the diesel.

In May 1929 an Eddystone painter stenciled "61000" on the flanks of Baldwin's second diesel and the machine was complete. From coupler to coupler it measured 51' even; from railhead to headlight it stood 15'-8¾" tall. With 270,000 pounds of weight on drivers, 61000 stood ready to exert 67,500 pounds of tractive effort. Baldwin's second diesel was both shorter and lighter than its first, but because 61000 had its entire weight on powered drivers, it exerted 15,300 pounds more tractive effort than its predecessor. Like 58501, the new diesel received a mouthful of designation: Class 8-OE-1000-1-CC, 1.

Between May 1929 and the fall of 1931 BLW 61000 was tested on at least seven Class 1 railroads — the Pennsylvania, Nickel Plate, Illinois Central, Milwaukee Road, Rock Island, Santa Fe, and Northern Pacific — and proved itself a capable journeyman. The locomotive was also dispatched for a two-month trial on the open-pit mine trackage of the Oliver Iron Mining Company in Minnesota. On one Class 1 road the diesel worked at a 45 percent fuel-cost savings over the line's steam locomotives.

The success of 61000 could have launched Baldwin into diesel locomotive manufacturing during the early 1930s. While the locomotive was not considered a prototype for a new standard line, building the unit — together with 58501 — had developed the expertise to create such a diesel line. But fate had dealt Baldwin a bad hand. While 61000 was only beginning its test runs the great stock market crash of October 29, 1929 — "Black Tuesday" — had occurred. By 1931, as 61000 completed testing, the nation was in an economic abyss. Domestic motive power orders placed that year dropped to 174 locomotives — one-ninth what

W. W. Nugent Co.; H. L. Broadbelt collection

BLW 61000 operated on at least seven Class 1 railroads, as well as ore-hauler Oliver Iron Mining. Here, on August 12, 1931, the pioneering diesel nosed out of the Milwaukee Road roundhouse at Bensenville, Illinois.

Historic Baldwin diesels 61000 (left) and 58501 stand face to face at Eddystone in 1930.
BLW 58501 served as a plant switcher until at least 1933; both were scrapped in 1941.

railroads had ordered per year in the late 1920s. Baldwin, solidly in the black when it had constructed No. 61000 in 1929 (net profits of $2.3 million on $42.7 million in sales, including non-locomotive products), was by 1931 just as solidly in the red. Total sales plummeted to $20.4 million, with a net loss of $4.1 million. By 1932 demand for new locomotives was non-existent (13 were ordered), Baldwin's diverse industrial products were suffering equally poor sales, and the company was sliding deeper into financial trouble. From 1932 through 1934 Baldwin posted losses totaling more than $11.1 million. Then, on February 25, 1935, Baldwin was forced to file for reorganization under Section 77 of the National Bankruptcy Act.

AMID DARK DAYS COMES THE VO

While the Great Depression extinguished any hope of in-

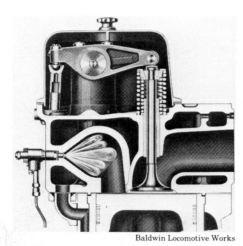

This cross section of a VO cylinder head reveals the unusual combustion chamber design. The horizontal fuel injector is at left, the 4″-diameter valve and exhaust port at right.

troducing a diesel line in the early 1930s, Baldwin was still able to take steps toward that end. In retrospect, they were major steps. In 1931 Baldwin purchased I. P. Morris & De La Vergne, Inc., and moved its assets to Eddystone. The De La Vergne section of the company had long been involved in power plant construction; its experience with oil engines dated to 1893 and it had built its first diesel in 1917. With De La Vergne came the basic knowledge Baldwin needed to design and build its own line of diesel locomotive power plants. (An additional plus to the acquisition was that Bald-

win acquired De La Vergne's existing line of stationary and marine diesel engines, some of which, in updated form, remained in production into the 1950s.)

After De La Vergne became part of the Baldwin family plans for a new diesel locomotive and suitable power plant proceeded, albeit slowly. Initial planning for an endcab switcher began in 1933, and a medium-sized, low-speed engine designated "Model VO" took shape. Testing of the VO power plant, in 6-cylinder form, took place in 1935. The engine was an inline, four-cycle, solid-injection, normally aspirated diesel with a 12½″ bore and 15½″ stroke. The 6-cylinder version produced 660 h.p. at 600 rpm. An 8-cylinder, 900-h.p. version was also placed on the drawing boards but would not be produced until 1937.

The VO used a one-piece cast A-frame with an underslung crankshaft (meaning the crankshaft bearing supports were within the A-frame). The oil sump and engine subbase were separate. The cylinder liners were lapped into the engine block to create a metal-to-metal fit designed to eliminate the need for potentially troublesome cylinder-liner seals. Each cylinder head was an individual casting which could be removed separately. Upper and lower main bearings were removable through crankcase doors on each side of the block.

An unusual feature of the VO engine was its spherical combustion chamber offset from the center of the piston bore and connected to it via a "throat" passageway. This design was thought to offer a number of advantages over standard combustion chambers. First, it improved compression turbulence in the cylinder, and provided a more controlled and slower-burning combustion cycle. This meant improved performance and fuel economy, as well as cleaner engine exhaust. The offset combustion chamber allowed Bosch fuel injectors to be mounted horizontally on the side of each cylinder rather than directly above the piston, permitting the use of larger injectors. The larger injectors were suitable for use with low grades of fuel oil and less prone to clog, and since the injectors did not compete for the limited vertical space above the piston bores, there was room for large, 4″-diameter valves. The VO had one intake and one exhaust valve per cylinder, and flat pistons were employed. Offsetting the combustion chamber also allowed the chamber to be fully surrounded by a water jacket, which effectively lowered operating temperatures of the valves, pistons, and cylinder liners.

The railroad industry began to recover from the Great Depression in 1936. Locomotive orders that year totaled 533, more than the previous five years combined. Although Baldwin would not return to profitability until 1937, it was time for the diesel locomotive to return to the halls of Eddystone.

The De La Vergne VO power plant was Baldwin's first building block for production diesel locomotives. During 1938, Baldwin redesigned the VO, with the result shown here. A fabricated A-frame replaced cast, and cylinder bore was increased by one-quarter inch.

BALDWIN AND THE DIESEL

A synopsis of Baldwin's diesel years

BALDWIN'S intent to produce diesel locomotives was renewed by the improved economic conditions of late 1936. This time, armed with the De La Vergne VO engine, Baldwin's purpose was not to experiment, but to produce a line of standard diesel locomotives.

There would be competition. The diesel marketplace had evolved considerably by late 1936. Unencumbered by the huge facilities and the resulting fixed costs of the steam builders (such as Baldwin), a new locomotive manufacturer — Electro-Motive Corporation — had risen up during the depression. By the end of 1936, Electro-Motive, in conjunction with Budd or Pullman-Standard, had furnished mainline, Winton-diesel-powered, streamlined passenger trains to the Burlington, Union Pacific, Boston & Maine/Maine Central, and Illinois Central. Diesel-electric motor cars built by EMC and St. Louis Car Co. operated on the Seaboard Air Line, and burly boxcab diesels built to EMC standards by General Electric and St. Louis Car led Baltimore & Ohio's *Royal Blue* and Santa Fe's opulent new *Super Chief*. Electro-Motive also offered a line of 600-h.p. and 900-h.p. endcab switchers, and on May 20, 1936, the company marked the beginning of diesel production at its own

Baldwin Locomotive Works

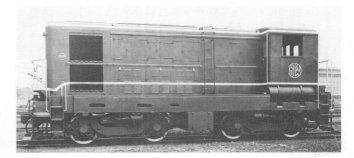

At left, when 6-cylinder VO power plant serial number 1600 was placed on the cast frame of BLW 62000 it marked the first locomotive application of the VO engine. The 660-h.p. engine featured a 12½″ bore and 15½″ stroke and achieved rated horsepower at 600 rpm. When BLW 62000 rolled out of the shops in the fall of 1936 (above), Eddystone made the transition from diesel experimenter to manufacturer.

Baldwin carried on development of its 408 engine from 1939 through 1943. In September 1943, one of the Roots-blown V-8, 750-h.p. engines stood on the test stand at Eddystone.

plant in La Grange, Illinois, with Santa Fe switcher No. 2301. Baldwin's nemesis among steam locomotive builders, Alco, meanwhile had offered a standard 600-h.p. endcab switcher, and, with American Car & Foundry, had constructed two diesel streamliners — the *Rebels* — for the Gulf, Mobile & Northern (a third was built in 1937).

Baldwin had not forgotten the favorable economics that experimental diesel 61000 had displayed in yard service, and chose to inaugurate its commercial offerings with an endcab yard switcher. As early as 1933 Eddystone had de-

veloped its preliminary design for an endcab switcher, and in July 1935 a 6-cylinder VO engine — serial number 1600 — had been brought to the erecting shop in anticipation of constructing a locomotive. Eddystone outshopped BLW 62000, a 39′-6″-long, 212,000-pound switcher powered with the De La Vergne engine, in the fall of 1936. Given the model designation 8OE 660/1, the 62000 served as both a test-bed and a sales demonstrator.

With the introduction of BLW 62000 Eddystone made the transition from experimenter to diesel manufacturer. While

Completed in April 1939, BLW VO-660 No. 299 was the first standard VO-model switcher. Here No. 299 lugs flat cars carrying another Eddystone product, ship propellers.

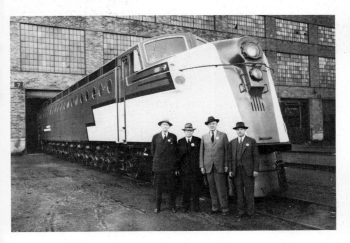

Baldwin's great 2-D + D-2 diesel, BLW 6000, noses out of the erecting shop on May 28, 1943. At left is Charles E. Brinley, who had become Baldwin's chairman of the board the previous month. At right is Baldwin President Ralph Kelly.

Completed in December 1944, BLW 0-6-6-0 1000/2 DE No. 2000 stands in the scale house at Eddystone.

extensive improvements in manufacturing techniques and refinements in design would come in the years that followed, No. 62000 introduced many of the design principles and mechanical elements that would mark Baldwin's diesel locomotives for years to come. Further, No. 62000 was the first Baldwin diesel to go to work — full-time — for a common carrier railroad. In April 1937, BLW 62000 began service in Chicago, Illinois, for the Santa Fe Railway. Renumbered AT&SF 2200, the unit went to the Santa Fe under a conditional-purchase agreement: The 660-h.p. switcher would have to meet with Santa Fe's favor before the sale would become final. In June 1937 AT&SF signed on the dotted line.

THE VO SPUTTERS, THEN COMES TO LIFE

BLW 62000 was not the only good news at Eddystone in early 1937. Even before Baldwin's premiere 660-h.p. diesel switcher began its service on Santa Fe, Eddystone had locked up its first outright sales agreement for a diesel locomotive. In January 1937 Baldwin secured an order from the New Orleans Public Belt for three diesel switchers, each to be equipped with the De La Vergne 8-cylinder, 900-h.p. VO engine. When the trio — NOPB 31-33 — was delivered in December 1937 it might have seemed that Baldwin's diesel switcher line was off and running. Unfortunately, that was not the case; problems with the VO engine were becoming apparent.

The first problem with the VO power plant was cost. With its cast A-frame the VO engine was an expensive machine to produce, and there were early signs that the engine's rigid cast A-frame, unable to flex even slightly, would crack under the rigors of rail service. In 1938 the decision was made to redesign the VO with a less expensive, more-durable, fabricated A-frame. At the same time the bore would be increased from 12½″ to 12¾″ so the 8-cylinder VO engine could attain 1000 h.p. (in normally aspirated form). During the VO redesign program sales efforts for Baldwin's new diesel locomotives were deliberately restricted.

Throughout 1938 Eddystone developed its second-generation VO engine. In addition to the new welded A-frame and subbase, the crankshaft bearings were incorporated into the engine base, which also included an extension to support the main generator. As a result, the engine and main generator could be installed in or removed from a locomotive as a complete unit. Modified VO cylinder liners consisted of removable sleeves, with rubber rings employed to form water jacket seals. The camshaft was a two-piece unit designed for ease of maintenance. Individual cast cylinder heads were again used. The injector system was supplied by

Bosch, with injector pumps for each cylinder. Engine speed was controlled by a Woodward hydraulic governor. An overspeed stop was also incorporated.

The engine changes required a new switcher frame as well. Baldwin did not cast frames itself; instead, the task was handled by the General Steel Castings plant adjacent to Eddystone (along with Alco, American Steel Foundries, and Pullman, Baldwin held a one-quarter financial interest in GSC). Baldwin's new switcher frame from GSC would be easier to build and more stylish as well, and along with it Eddystone gave its entire switcher design a facelift. Based on its experience with BLW 62000 and NOPB 31-33, Baldwin produced blueprints for a standard switcher that would be more stylish, more reliable, and more economical to produce.

COMES PRODUCTION — AND THE WAR

In April 1939, Baldwin took the wraps off its redesigned diesel switcher line. BLW 299, an attractive 660-h.p. switcher painted in baby blue with gold lettering, rolled out and Baldwin assumed a legitimate position in the diesel marketplace. The 660-h.p. VO power plant inside No. 299 gave the unit its model designation: VO-660; the 8-cylinder VO engine would power a sister model: the VO-1000. For both, Westinghouse would supply the main generator, traction motors, and electrical gear. Baldwin took the first or-

Baldwin Locomotive Works

As early as 1936, Eddystone experimented with turbocharging the VO power plant, but the engine's unique combustion chamber design and the need to strengthen the A-frame precluded further development of a turbocharged VO.

Heavy road-switchers began taking form at Eddystone in the summer of 1946. DRS-6-4-1500s for the Columbus & Greenville Railway and French North Africa were first. A massive 608SC engine rests on the frame of a unit for French North Africa in August 1946.

ders for the VO-1000 in 1939 and for the VO-660 in early 1940. The trials and tribulations were over; diesel standardization and full-fledged production had finally arrived at Eddystone.*

---

* In June 1939 a 660-h.p. switcher was delivered to the Reading Co. It had been ordered in December 1938, and was used to test new equipment and evaluate manufacturing techniques. Because it was begun before BLW 299, it employed the first fabricated A-frame VO engine, but otherwise the unit had little in common mechanically with Baldwin's new standard line. See page 28 for details.

Hulking 363,300-pound Elgin, Joliet & Eastern DT-6-6-2000 No. 100 eased out of Eddystone in 1946. Production-model DT-6-6-2000s would first be ordered the following year.

Production of the VO-660 and VO-1000 seemed to place Baldwin in a position of some strength. With Eddystone still very much in the steam locomotive business — witness an order for 28 Southern Pacific cab-forward 4-8-8-2s received in 1939 — Baldwin could now effectively tap the diesel market as well. For the short term, the VO-660 and VO-1000 gave the company the ability to compete for most diesel orders (since a high percentage were for switchers), but the stakes in the diesel race were quickly being raised. Electro-Motive's E units, debuted with B&O EA No. 51 in 1937, were proving that diesels were well suited — and salable — for everyday, mainline passenger service. With its 567-series-powered E3 of March 1939 EMC moved the E unit ever closer to being a production-line offering. Then, in November 1939, EMC unveiled a four-unit, cab-and-booster, 5400-h.p. freight diesel — FT No. 103 — a locomotive designed to defeat steam at its best trade — mainline freight duty. In January 1940 Alco introduced its first standard road diesel — the DL109 — a twin-engined, 2000-h.p., A1A-A1A passenger diesel similar to EMC's E units. If Baldwin was to remain competitive in the diesel marketplace, Eddystone could not rest on the laurels of its new switcher line.

By 1939-40 Baldwin was ready to commit to development of a full line of diesels. The company began to gradually convert Eddystone's tender shop into a diesel-building facility, and also established an independent diesel support group and hired experts to aid in diesel development. In 1939, Baldwin began development of an all-new engine — the 408. The new power plant was a modern design — a four-cycle V-8, with square bore and stroke dimensions of $9\frac{1}{2}''$. By using a gear-driven Roots-type blower, the 408 en-

In 1946 the DS-4-4-1000 replaced the VO-1000 as the 1000-h.p. switcher in Baldwin's line. Seaboard Air Line DS-4-4-1000 No. 1418, placed in service in July 1946, was among the first of the new 608NA-powered switchers delivered.

gine would attain up to 750 h.p. (at 1050 rpm). Concurrently, Baldwin applied for patents on two huge, 4000-h.p., single-unit locomotives, each to be powered by six diesel engines: a 1-D+D-1 and a 2-C+C-2. By early 1940, plans for an even more uncommon creation, an eight-engined 6000-h.p. 2-D+D-2, were also taking form.

Baldwin decided to build the most massive design — the 6000-h.p. 2-D+D-2. Although Samuel Vauclain had died in 1940 (he had served as chairman of the board from 1929 until his death), his predilection for building the unprecedented lived on at Eddystone. The leviathan diesel would be powered by eight 408 engines mounted crosswise in its huge carbody. Conceived primarily as a high-speed passenger locomotive, it would also be readily adaptable to freight service.

Designated the 4-8-8-4 750/8 DE, Baldwin's great diesel began taking shape in July 1941. Less than six months later America was at war, and with the war, all the rules in the diesel race changed. In January 1942 the U. S. Supply, Priorities and Allocation Board granted priority through April 1942 for continued construction by all builders of 620 diesel locomotives which were either on order or being built for stock, but on April 4, the War Production Board (successor to the Supply, Priorities and Allocation Board) placed severe limitations on locomotive construction. Locomotive-building regulations were set up, and because of their requirements for generous amounts of copper and other critical war materials, diesels were particularly restricted. In addition to steam locomotives, Baldwin and Alco were restricted to building diesels of 660 to 1000 h.p., while Electro-Motive was given the nod to construct only 5400-h.p. FT freight diesels (EMD had begun production of the FT in February 1941). Construction of passenger-service diesels was discontinued.*

Just as the Great Depression had delayed Baldwin's diesel development in the early 1930s, the war strangled the program Baldwin had planned in 1939-41. In its place, Eddystone put forth one of the great industrial efforts of World War Two. The shops were filled to bursting with construction of thousands of tons of critical war material. In June 1942, Baldwin President Charles E. Brinley announced that production was at a record level for the 111-year-old firm. Eddystone's contributions to the armed services alone included 1119 2-10-0s, 847 2-8-2s, 611 2-8-0s, 98 VO switchers, 624 diesel power plants, 2399 M-series tanks,

and 60 million pounds of ship propellers. For all buyers, Eddystone provided a total of 397 diesel switchers in the years 1942-44.

While continued development of the 6000-h.p. diesel was officially allowed, progress was delayed by shortages of time and raw materials. It was not until the spring of 1943 — nearly two years after construction began — that the huge machine was ready for testing. Even then, due to limits on supplies and the necessity of using improvised tooling, only four of the eight 750-h.p. V-8 engines could be installed. The mammoth diesel — Baldwin road number 6000 — began testing in June 1943, and by November the grand experiment was over. Management's patience with the creature had run out. Given the conditions — especially a war of which the conclusion could be years away — Baldwin chose to turn away from the uncertainties (and excessive costs) of the great 2-D+D-2 and its V-8 engines and concentrate instead on preparing a conventional road diesel using standard components.

Baldwin's interest in a more modest road diesel began in 1943 because management believed — rightfully so — that the 4-8-8-4 750/8 DE would not appeal to all customers, and Eddystone began planning a 2000-h.p. A1A-A1A design

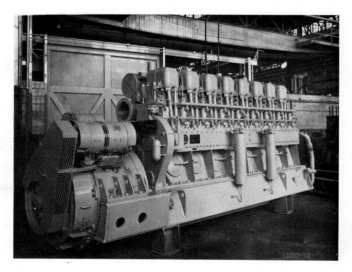

The heart of Baldwin's postwar diesel-electric locomotive line was the 600-series power plant. This normally aspirated 608NA produced 1000 h.p. from eight cylinders.

* Based on the premise that the DL109 was a dual-service diesel, Alco was given permission to build a small number of these units during the war, primarily for the New Haven.

DR-12-8-3000s under construction: Following its debut on the Seaboard, Baldwin's giant 3000-h.p. diesel attracted the attention of National Railways of Mexico and the Pennsylvania Railroad. Here, in 1947, baby-faced Pennsy DR-12-8-3000s are assembled in the "tender shop" at Eddystone.

Charles A. Brown

Seaboard Air Line 4500 was the first locomotive powered by Baldwin's 600-series power plant, the first unit to employ the babyface carbody styling, and the first DR-12-8-3000. Number 4500 was delivered to the Seaboard in December 1945.

based on a pair of standard 8-cylinder VO engines. Work on the 2000-h.p. locomotive began in earnest in early 1944, and the result — BLW demonstrator 2000 — was completed in December 1944.

Designated the 0-6-6-0 1000/2 DE, No. 2000 toured alone, then was joined by a mate — BLW 2001 — in spring 1945. The timing was critical for Baldwin's diesel plans, because even though World War Two would not conclude until August 1945, the industrial strength of the U. S. had rebounded to the point that passenger locomotive production was allowed to resume in February 1945.

PREPARING FOR A NEW ERA

As WWII neared its end, the railroad industry speculated on the potential size of the postwar locomotive market. Or-

ders of 1000-plus locomotives a year, typical during the war, were expected to continue, and with the end of government regulation the market would again be open to all comers. Performance of diesels during the war had left no doubt as to their worth — or to their sales potential. Even with restrictions on construction from 1941 through 1944, the railroads had ordered 3313 diesels (versus 1152 steam locomotives). As the war wound down all builders prepared to implement new designs (during the war, the designs of standard locomotives were frozen; no production changes could be made), and Baldwin was no exception.

Paramount at Eddystone was the matter of the VO engine. In service, the VO's cylinder heads sometimes cracked. This was due to a manufacturing problem; successfully casting the VO's complicated combustion chamber and providing adequate cooling area within the heads was difficult. The shape of the VO combustion chamber was also causing another problem for Baldwin. As early as 1936, Eddystone had experimented with turbocharging the VO, but the full power increases of a turbocharger could not be attained because of the combustion chamber design. Subsequent experiments also revealed that the VO A-frame lacked the structural integrity to withstand the added stresses of turbocharging. These factors led to another redesign of the De La Vergne engine; the VO evolved into an improved engine — the 600 series.

At the top of the 600-series power plant was a new cylinder head configuration: a vertically mounted fuel injector, two intake and two exhaust valves per cylinder, and six symmetrically placed hold-down studs. To accommodate the new cylinder head, the flat-top VO pistons were replaced with crowned pistons. (Later, Baldwin would develop a five-stud version of the 600-series cylinder head to retrofit to VO engines.) Internally, the 600-series engine retained the bore and stroke of the fabricated A-frame VO along with its 8¾" crankshaft main journals and 8⅜" crankpins. To strengthen the A-frame, vertical ribs were added between the crankcase access ports, and the engine base was similarly strengthened.

Baldwin developed three versions of the 600-series power

The carbody hovers overhead as an NYC DR-4-4-1500 booster takes shape in 1948. A turbocharged 608SC power plant and the electrical equipment have been installed.

plant: the 606NA, a normally aspirated 6-cylinder engine rated at 660 h.p.; the 608NA, an 8-cylinder normally aspirated engine rated at 1000 h.p.; and the 608SC, a turbocharged 8-cylinder engine rated at 1500 h.p. The turbocharger applied to the 608SC was the Elliot model BF-44. All three versions of the 600-series power plant were built to turn at the traditional 625 rpm (maximum).

The 600-series engines were not available for installation in locomotives until December 1945 (which is why demonstrators 2000-2001 employed the VO), and not available in numbers for some months after that, so the VO had a few final days in the sun. The most significant occurred in June 1945, when Eddystone exported 30 VO-powered, 1000-h.p., streamlined diesels (in essence a single-engine version of the 0-6-6-0 1000/2 DE) to the Soviet Union. This, Baldwin's first venture into building export-model diesels, was sponsored by the U. S. armed services in an effort to rebuild Russia's war-torn railroads. At home the VO engine was used exclusively to power Baldwin's standard switchers until May 1946, then came a transition period in June and July 1946 when both VO and 600-series engines were installed in 1000-h.p. switchers.

In August 1945 BLW 0-6-6-0 1000/2 DE passenger cabs 2000-2001 ended their demonstration tour and were turned over to their new owner, the National Railways of Mexico. NdeM placed an order for a third identical unit, and in August 1946 NdeM 0-6-6-0 1000/2 DE No. 6002 entered service. It was the last new VO-powered locomotive Baldwin built.

THE SHAPING OF A STANDARD LINE

The new 600-series engines powered a varied line of locomotives, all of them equipped with Westinghouse electrical gear. The VO-660 was retired in favor of the 606NA-powered DS-4-4-660, the VO-1000 was replaced by the 608NA-powered DS-4-4-1000, and the 0-6-6-0 1000/2 DE was transformed — with a pair of 608NA engines — into

the DR-6-4-2000. In addition there were all-new offerings.

Baldwin's first road-switcher — the DRS-6-4-660 — was delivered in April 1946. An A1A-A1A locomotive powered by the 606NA engine, the DRS-6-4-660 was an export model built for France, but it was a precursor of Baldwin's plans for a domestic road-switcher. Alco's 1000-h.p. RS1 of 1941 had shown immediate popularity with the railroads and Baldwin intended to counter with a heavier, more powerful road-switcher. As early as 1944 Eddystone had developed initial designs for such a locomotive, but could not proceed until a turbocharged engine was developed. With the 1500-h.p. 608SC available, Baldwin offered a trio of related road-switchers, the A1A-A1A DRS-6-4-1500, the B-B DRS-4-4-1500, and the C-C DRS-6-6-1500. Construction of heavy road-switchers began in the summer of 1946 with DRS-6-4-1500s bound for the Columbus & Greenville Railway and for French North Africa. Columbus & Greenville No. 601 (completed in September 1946) was America's first 1500-h.p. road-switcher.

The 608SC engine which was so crucial to Baldwin's road-switcher effort also provided the basis for a 1500-h.p. streamlined freight locomotive. The success of the Electro-Motive FT had left no doubt that postwar sales of streamlined freight diesels would be brisk. In 1945, EMD began production of its 1500-h.p. F3, and Alco — after testing its "Black Maria" freight unit in 1945 — introduced the FA1/FB1 series in January 1946. Baldwin's entry was the 1500-h.p. DR-4-4-1500, and the first order for it came from Central Railroad of New Jersey subsidiary Central of Pennsylvania in September 1945.

Two postwar creations resulted from the preferences of particular customers but later flowered into standard models. At the end of the war the Elgin, Joliet & Eastern was ready to dieselize its road and transfer operations — duties then performed by large 2-8-2s. The EJ&E, in cooperation with Baldwin, developed a design for a bidirectional, twin-engined, 2000-h.p., six-axle (C-C) diesel capable of replac-

ing the EJ&E's powerful steam locomotives on a one-for-one basis. In April 1945, EJ&E issued an order for a prototype, and in May 1946 the result — EJ&E No. 100 — entered service. A hulking, 363,300-pound beast, EJ&E 100 carried the model designation DT-6-6-2000. The first orders for a modified production version were received in 1947.

Surpassing even EJ&E 100 in size was the mammoth unit completed for the Seaboard Air Line in December 1945. Although Eddystone's great 6000-h.p. diesel — BLW 6000 — never operated after 1943, it remained at Eddystone throughout the war. On a visit to Eddystone, SAL motive power officials viewed the great beast, and were impressed by such a locomotive's potential. In June 1945 SAL issued an order for a scaled-down version. By scrapping BLW 6000 and using its running gear for a new twin-608SC-powered locomotive, Baldwin created SAL 4500 — the first DR-12-8-3000. The 3000-h.p. machine, proudly proclaimed as "America's most powerful single-unit diesel locomotive," was then offered as a standard model in the Baldwin line. National Railways of Mexico and the Pennsylvania were interested almost immediately.

SAL 4500 was the first 600-series-powered locomotive that Baldwin built (delivered in December 1945), and it introduced a new cab styling — nicknamed "babyface" for its low-nose, wide-eyed look — that would be employed on the DR-6-4-2000 and DR-4-4-1500 as well. In fact, on the first locomotives of the DR-6-4-2000 class — delivered to the

Central Railroad of New Jersey in late 1946 and early 1947 — the "babyface" would receive double-billing: Intended for commuter service, CNJ's units had dual cabs for bidirectional operation. Because of this option they carried the designation DRX-6-4-2000.

LIMITED SUCCESS

The new standard line of 600-series-powered diesels began to produce orders immediately in the booming postwar market. In 1945, when U. S. operators ordered 691 diesels and foreign concerns added 210 more, Baldwin took orders for 187, 20 percent of the total. In 1946 orders grew to 989 in the U. S. and approximately 169 for export, and Eddystone's cut grew to 328, 28 percent.

With a lag of approximately one year between orders and deliveries, Eddystone's diesel production began showing marked growth in 1947. Baldwin delivered 106 diesels in 1946, 183 in 1947. Such figures were encouraging, particularly in the face of rapidly declining steam orders. In 1945, Baldwin received orders for 691 steam locomotives; by 1947 the number had fallen to 134 (in both years the vast majority were for export; in 1947 only 79 steam locomotives were ordered for U. S. domestic use from *all* builders).

But Baldwin's surge of diesel sales did not continue; in fact, in 1947 the company's share declined to 12 percent of the market. That year, Eddystone received orders for 281 diesels — 47 less than in 1946 — as total U. S. diesel orders

In 1948 the turbocharged, 6-cylinder 606SC replaced the 608NA as Baldwin's basic 1000-h.p. engine.

At left, Baldwin 6- and 8-cylinder 600-series engines are readied for installation in locomotives in 1948. The massive size of the power plant is easily gauged by the relative size of the workers.

During the late 1940s, Baldwin performed development work on a new diesel power plant — the 2000-series. Of four-cycle, V-design, the 2000-series engines would have included 8-, 12-, and 16-cylinder versions. In late 1948 the program was terminated. The 2-cylinder test engine shown at right was constructed before development ceased.

reached a stunning 2149 units and export orders added approximately 140 more. Baldwin was in third place in the diesel sales race, well behind Electro-Motive and Alco. Switchers and road-switchers proved the staples of the line (although even switcher production suffered a short-term lull); sales — and production — of passenger and streamlined freight units were uncertain.

Through 1947, Eddystone had delivered only 33 DR-6-4-2000s and DR-12-8-3000s. The lead Electro-Motive had gained in the 1930s and early 1940s with its E units would be extremely difficult to overcome, or even to significantly dent. Many railroads were firmly committed to the E unit, and among those not bound to EMD, many favored Alco. In an attempt to make further headway in the passenger market Baldwin offered a third streamlined passenger model — the DR-6-4-1500 — in early 1946. The first such unit rolled out of Eddystone in November 1947, a vest-pocket A1A-A1A diesel powered by a single 608SC engine.

Baldwin took its worst whipping in streamlined freight unit sales. Electro-Motive, by virtue of early development of the FT and the resulting exclusive right to build mainline freight diesels during the war, had attained a tremendous lead. Before Baldwin had taken even one order for the DR-4-4-1500, EMD had already *built* approximately 1000 streamlined freight units! To compound the problem, the prototype CNJ DR-4-4-1500s took longer than expected to build and were not delivered until November 1947. This

was a period of material shortages (which plagued all builders) and labor problems at both Baldwin and electrical supplier Westinghouse, and in the case of the DR-4-4-1500 technical difficulties cropped up as well. Had Eddystone successfully introduced its DR-4-4-1500 promptly after the war, the model might have enjoyed substantial sales (as did the Alco FA1/FB1, at 682 units), but the delays with CNJ's units further weakened Baldwin's position. The sale of streamlined freight locomotives represented a huge segment of the overall diesel market (between late 1945 and the end of 1950, EMD and Alco would build more than 2500 such units).

Baldwin's sales during this period were also adversely affected by a round of teething problems suffered by the 608SC engine (mostly piston and turbocharger failures), and by some customer dissatisfaction with haphazard design and workmanship, particularly in plumbing and electrical installations.

As 1947 closed Baldwin engineers were once again busy improving the company's diesel locomotives and streamlining production methods. Two power plant programs were ongoing. The first involved the 6-cylinder 600-series engine. By applying an Elliot BF-34 turbocharger, Baldwin produced the 1000-h.p. 606SC engine. The benefits were immediate; the new 606SC could replace the 1000-h.p. 608NA used in the DS-4-4-1000 switcher, DR-6-4-2000 passenger unit, and the prototype DT-6-6-2000. The turbocharged 6-

Pennsylvania DR-6-4-2000s debuted the famous Baldwin sharknose in 1948. Here three-unit Pennsy set 5771A-5770B-5770A stands before the main office building at Eddystone.

A light road-switcher, the DRS-4-4-1000, was unveiled in July 1948. Tennessee Central No. 75 was the first.

cylinder engine would offer better fuel economy than the 608NA, would be lighter and shorter, and would develop full horsepower at high altitudes (which the 608NA could not do). The 606SC was less expensive to produce, would allow the use of a common frame for the DS-4-4-660 and DS-4-4-1000 switchers (since both models would now employ 6-cylinder engines), and it would help balance out production demands for 600-series 6- and 8-cylinder power plants. (Previously, the 6-cylinder engine had been used only in the DS-4-4-660 and DRS-6-4-660, while all other models employed the 8-cylinder engine.) The 606SC made its debut in the DS-4-4-1000 switcher line in January 1948, and by mid-year was also in use in the DR-6-4-2000, production model DT-6-6-2000 transfer units (first delivered in March 1948), and a pair of new light road-switcher models — the export DRS-6-4-1000 and the domestic DRS-4-4-1000.

Baldwin's second, more ambitious, engine program was to develop an all-new line of power plants, the 2000 series. The new engine was to be a four-cycle V-design with 10″ bore and 11″ stroke. Four versions were on the drawing boards: 8-cylinder normally aspirated, 700 h.p.; 8-cylinder turbocharged, 1000 h.p.; 12-cylinder turbocharged, 1500 h.p.; and 16-cylinder turbocharged, 2000 h.p. All would attain rated horsepower at 1000 rpm. Development of the 2000 series was in progress in mid-1948 when a major corporate change occurred.

THE WESTINGHOUSE CONNECTION

Baldwin Locomotive Works and Westinghouse Electric & Manufacturing Co. had long been closely associated. They had cooperated to construct electric and diesel-electric locomotives, and every diesel locomotive Baldwin had built — with the sole exception of BLW 62000 — employed Westinghouse electrical gear. In August 1948, upon the recommendation of Baldwin President Ralph Kelly, Baldwin sold Westinghouse 500,000 shares of authorized but unissued stock. Together with previous holdings (around 15,000 shares), the purchase gave Westinghouse control of 21.68 percent of Baldwin's outstanding stock. Although technically a minority stockholder, Westinghouse immediately took control of Baldwin. Westinghouse Vice-President, Engineering and Research, Marvin W. Smith became Baldwin's executive vice-president and a director of the company. Ralph Kelly took a leave of absence, for all intents and purposes placing day-to-day control of Baldwin in Smith's hands. Smith formally became Baldwin's president on May 5, 1949.

Effective with the Westinghouse stock purchase Baldwin's diesel offerings became known as "Baldwin-Westinghouse" locomotives. Westinghouse influence brought other changes; many new employees with new ideas came over from Westinghouse to Eddystone. A casualty of this transition was the Baldwin 2000-series power plant. In late 1948 the 2000-series program was dropped in favor of another new prime mover design — the 547 series. The replacement design (which derived its designation from the cubic inch displacement of each of its cylinders) was a far different breed from the 2000 series. First, it was an opposed-piston (OP) engine, with pistons turning crankshafts placed at both top and bottom of the engine A-frame. Consequently

Lehigh Valley No. 239 was among the first S-12 switchers constructed. Before painting, the 1200-h.p. switcher posed for the camera outside the shop with its hood removed, revealing its shiny new 6-cylinder 606A power plant.

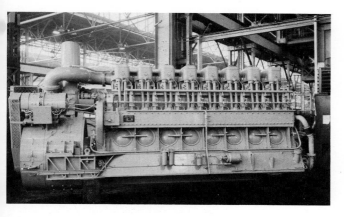

The ultimate development of the 600-series power plant came in 1950. The turbocharged 608A actually produced 1750 h.p., but it was promoted by Baldwin as a 1600-h.p. engine.

there were no cylinder heads. (The OP was not new to railroading; the design had been successfully introduced by Fairbanks-Morse, which by 1948 was offering a 1000-h.p. switcher, 1500- and 2000-h.p. road-switchers, and a 2000-h.p. dual-service streamlined unit.) The 547-series OP engine was planned as a two-cycle machine, with 6½" bore and 8¼" stroke, in two versions: 6-cylinder 1100-h.p., and 9-cylinder 1650-h.p. Both would achieve rated horsepower at 1200 rpm. The 547-series engine was favored over the 2000-series in part because the U. S. Navy was at the time interested in a new two-cycle OP engine, and partially sponsored the 547's development. But the change in direction meant that an all-new engine for the locomotive line was several years away, at best. The 600-series power plant would continue as the prime building block for diesel locomotives.

Even with the corporate uncertainties of 1948 and the obstacles Baldwin faced in selling certain of its diesel models the year turned out relatively successful. The diesel marketplace had been bullish, with 2822 orders placed. At year end Baldwin reported total corporate sales of $126.4 million, with 70 percent coming from sales of locomotives and locomotive replacement parts (new diesel sales accounted for $59.1 million). Eddystone had taken orders for 385 diesels (approximately 13 percent of the market) and 291 steam locomotives. Diesel deliveries ran to a record 416 units, with all categories showing production increases over 1947. Switcher deliveries climbed from 35 in 1947 to 217 in 1948, and passenger diesels increased from 34 to 62 in the same period, boosted by construction of 27 DR-6-4-2000 units for the Pennsylvania. The Pennsy's tuscan-clad DR-6-4-2000s unveiled a new Raymond Loewy carbody styling based on the lines of the PRR's Baldwin-built T1 4-4-4-4 duplex steam locomotives of 1942 — the famous "sharknose" had joined Baldwin's diesel line. There was also a curiosity among the passenger diesels: On a special order from the Chicago & North Western a half-locomotive, half-baggage car, driven by a single 606SC engine, was built and given the designation DR-6-2-1000.

In 1949 Baldwin took additional steps to enhance sales of its 600-series-powered locomotives. In February, with the delivery of the first of 68 DR-4-4-1500 cab and booster units to the Pennsylvania, the streamlined freight diesel underwent the same styling change as had the DR-6-4-2000 — to a sharknose carbody. A four-unit DR-4-4-1500 sharknose demonstrator set, BLW 6001, hit the road.

Locomotive sales softened nationwide in 1949 (a total of 1888 orders to all builders, 67 percent of the 1948 total) and in reaction, the builders cut prices. Baldwin dropped its prices by 5 percent. On a DS-4-4-1000 selling for $100,000 this decrease amounted to $5000; on a DT-6-6-2000 in the $200,000 range the savings were $10,000. In mid-1949 Baldwin boosted the horsepower rating of its 606NA engine

to 750 h.p. to improve the competitive position of its junior switcher. This horsepower increase was accomplished by changing the stop on the fuel rack to allow more fuel flow into the cylinders. The DS-4-4-750 switcher, first placed in service on the Santa Fe in July 1949, and the export DRS-6-4-750 light road-switcher (only one was built) were the results.

Despite these efforts 1949 concluded as a sobering year. Baldwin's new diesel orders for the year fell to 178 units, less than half the number received in 1948, and market share dipped below 10 percent. Diesel deliveries, meanwhile, totaled 398 units based on the solid sales of 1948. Gains were made in the switcher line (251 units delivered in 1949 versus 217 in 1948), the DR-4-4-1500 (56 in 1949 versus 30 in 1948), and heavy road-switchers (57 in 1949 versus 54 in 1948), but shipments of other models declined. Passenger diesel production had ceased altogether for lack of orders. Meanwhile, in September 1949, Eddystone delivered the last of 10 2-6-6-2s built for the Chesapeake & Ohio. The original order of 1947 for 25 had been cut to 10, largely because of a protracted miners' strike. These C&O Mallets were the last standard steam locomotives Baldwin produced for an American railroad.

1950: A NEW LINE, A NEW PARTNER

The year 1950 brought tremendous change, both for the locomotive industry and for Baldwin. It became apparent that the sluggish diesel sales of 1949 had been only temporary. Now, many American railroads rushed to replace steam; in 1950, 4473 diesel locomotives were ordered for domestic service alone, and approximately 220 more were ordered for export. Baldwin was ready. Working hard to overcome its poor showing in 1949, in early 1950 the company was preparing to introduce a complete new line of standard locomotives. The opposed-piston 547-series engine was still not ready for locomotive application (although it had progressed to prototype form, with a 9-cylinder engine undergoing stationary testing at Eddystone); instead, the new line would again be based on the venerable 600 series.

A number of refinements were applied to the 600-series engines. The 8-cylinder version received an Elliot H-704 turbocharger, while the 606SC engine had an Elliot H-503 applied. Transverse web plates were added to the subbase of all versions to increase rigidity and ensure improved alignment for the crankshaft and main generator. Heavier A-frames, made of a special alloy steel, were adopted. The crankshaft was increased in diameter, counter-weighted, and dynamically balanced for smoother operation. To accommodate the revised crankshaft, new thin-shell copper-lead main and connecting-rod bearings were developed. Connecting rods were designed with a heavier cross section and manufactured to a weight tolerance of plus or minus one pound to facilitate engine balancing. Numerous changes were made to prevent lube oil contamination and leakage. To reduce operational shocks to the power plant and generator assembly, a new four-point mounting system was developed. With these modifications came horsepower increases and new engine designations. The old 606NA would be upped to 800 h.p. and become the 606; the 606SC would be rated at 1325 h.p. and be designated the 606A; and the 608SC would be boosted to 1750 h.p. and become the 608A. Officially, however, the 606A was listed at 1200 h.p. and the 608A at 1600 h.p. This was apparently done to correspond with the competition's horsepower ratings.

Ten new models were offered with the improved 600-series engines. The 606 engine powered the S-8, an 800-h.p. switcher. The 606A engine was employed in the S-12, a 1200-h.p. switcher; the RS-12, a 1200-h.p. light road-switcher; and the RT-624, a dual-engine 2400-h.p. transfer unit. The 608A engine powered the RF-16, a shark-nosed streamlined freight unit; the AS-416, an A1A-A1A 1600-h.p. road-switcher; the AS-16, a B-B 1600-h.p. road-switcher; and the AS-616, a 1600-h.p. C-C road-switcher.

Here Baldwin's first batch of 1600-h.p. AS-616 heavy road-switchers takes shape in the summer of 1950. At the front of the line, with its 608A engine already in place, is Southern Pacific No. 5229, which would enter its owner's service in September 1950.

No new versions of the DR-6-4-1500, DR-6-4-2000, or DR-12-8-3000 were offered since none had been delivered since 1948. For the export market, the AS-412E, a six-axle 1200-h.p. road-switcher, and the R-616E, a streamlined six-axle (C-C) 1600-h.p. unit, were offered.

The new "Baldwin-Westinghouse Standard Line" was officially unveiled in June 1950. With the booming demand — and a strong marketing push by Baldwin — results were immediate. At the end of August 1950, Baldwin held orders for all eight domestic models; by September, the first S-12 switcher and AS-16 and AS-616 road-switchers were rolling out of Eddystone. Year-end production numbered only 280 because of the poor sales in 1949, but new orders received in 1950 totaled 442 units (including DRS-series units).

As important as the new line of standard locomotives was, it only shared the limelight in 1950. In August 1950 Baldwin Locomotive Works and the Lima-Hamilton Corporation announced plans to consolidate. The new corporation would be named Baldwin-Lima-Hamilton, and Eddystone became the "Eddystone Division."

Lima-Hamilton was the descendant of Lima Locomotive Works, the third of America's "Big Three" steam builders along with Baldwin and Alco. Lima had stayed with steam until the end, building its last steam locomotive — Nickel Plate 2-8-4 No. 779 — at the company's Lima, Ohio, shop in 1949. Not until 1947, when Lima merged with Hamilton Corporation of Hamilton, Ohio, a maker of diesel power plants, had Lima taken a step toward producing diesel loco-

motives. In May 1949, Lima-Hamilton built its first diesel — a 1000-h.p. switcher demonstrator later sold to the Toledo, Peoria & Western — and by 1950 the company offered switchers ranging from 750 h.p. to 1200 h.p., a light 1200-h.p. road-switcher, and a twin-engined 2500-h.p. transfer unit.

Lima-Hamilton was another step in Baldwin's continuing diversification, and although L-H had its own railroad heritage, it was not locomotives that drew Baldwin into the merger. Orders for Lima-Hamilton diesels were no longer sought after the merger (the last L-H order taken, from the Pennsylvania, was for 11 2500-h.p. transfer units in August 1950; the last unit — PRR 5683 — was delivered in September 1951). Instead, Baldwin was attracted to Lima-Hamilton's other products, which included machine tools, mechanical presses, crawlers, rubber-mounted cranes, shovels, and draglines. Shortly after the merger was consummated on November 30, 1950, Baldwin-Lima-Hamilton announced that it was acquiring all 303,945 outstanding shares of the Austin-Western Co. of Aurora, Illinois. Austin-Western constructed power graders, street sweepers, shovels and cranes, road rollers, and crushing plants. Baldwin was particularly interested in both Lima-Hamilton and Austin-Western for their road-building products, because the U. S. stood on the eve of construction of the great interstate highway system.

HALCYON DAYS

The halcyon days of Baldwin as a diesel builder came in

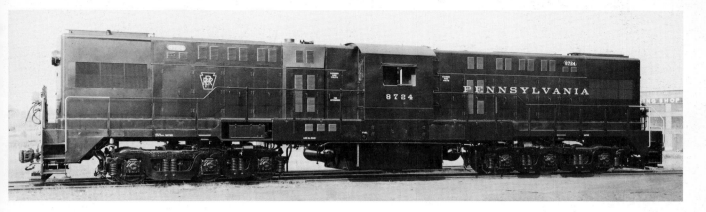

Baldwin's final refinement of the dual-engine center cab transfer locomotive was the 2400-h.p. RT-624. Pennsy 8724 was shipped from Eddystone in October 1952.

1951. By February of that year Eddystone had finished the final DRS-series units ordered prior to June 1950,* and construction of the new locomotives was moving smoothly ahead. The RT-624 was the final member of the new breed to enter service, that occurring in August 1951 with a unit for the Pennsylvania. With the diesel marketplace still booming (4413 units ordered, including 342 for export), Baldwin sales even topped 1950, ending at 474 diesel locomotives ordered. Eddystone delivered 398 new diesels in 1951, and Baldwin-Lima-Hamilton's year-end financial results showed sales of $197.6 million, with locomotives and locomotive parts responsible for 45 percent of the total. Overall, B-L-H showed a net profit of $4.5 million.

But there was a sobering side, even to 1951. After its initial surge of diesel sales immediately after the war, Baldwin's share of the total diesel market stayed in the range of 9 to 13 percent each year; 1951 sales were about 10.7 percent of the market. The introduction of the 1950 standard line had arrested the decline in Baldwin's market share apparent in 1949, but by standing pat with a minority share Baldwin was actually losing ground. The ever-growing numerical advantage EMD or Alco units enjoyed on any particular railroad meant that road would continue to lean toward EMD or Alco unless a clearly superior product were offered by someone else.

Baldwin's 1950 standard line was undoubtedly its best yet. Combining the high-torque, four-cycle 600-series engines with rugged Westinghouse traction motors and main generators, Baldwin diesels had very early earned a reputation for unmatched low-speed lugging power. Many were placed in services where that ability could be used to its fullest — coal and ore hauling, slow drag freight duty, hump service, and, of course, yard switching. It was within yard limits that Baldwin diesels gained a reputation of excellence. With the 1950 line, Eddystone had made strides in improving electrical and plumbing layouts, placing electrical conduits and fluid piping on opposite sides of the locomotive wherever possible, and installing oil sumps in strategic locations. Refinements to the 606/606A/608A-series of engines had improved dependability and fuel economy, but despite all the improvements made to it the 600-series was still a design of the early 1930s. It was still relatively expensive to maintain, and had difficulty competing with the more modern engines offered by other builders. While the Westinghouse heavy traction equipment (traction motors and main generator) was rugged, it was also expensive to replace when problems did occur. Furthermore, the electrical controls Westinghouse provided to Baldwin were not as advanced as those from General Electric (for Alco) or Electro-Motive. Simply put, Baldwin's 1950 standard line

included good locomotives, but not necessarily great locomotives — and to overcome the company's ever-increasing numerical disadvantage, Baldwin needed great locomotives.

At Baldwin, 1952 was a year of contrasts. Fueled by the record number of orders received in 1951, diesel production remained high. By year-end, 382 locomotives had been delivered, only 16 less than the previous year. Switcher shipments actually increased, from 159 in 1951 to 205 in 1952. But the explosion of orders in the diesel marketplace had subsided. In 1952, orders were placed among all builders for 1829 diesels to serve in the U. S., and approximately 182 more for export — still a respectable market, but only 45 percent of the 1951 total. Baldwin's orders plummeted to 164 worldwide (106 by U. S. operators), about 8 percent of the total. Baldwin's U. S. sales during this period depended on a few good customers, among them Southern Pacific, Reading, and Pennsylvania. Foremost was the Pennsylvania: From 1946 through 1952 PRR took delivery of 628 Baldwin diesels, 28 percent of Eddystone's total diesel production in that period. But in 1952, Pennsy did not order a single diesel from any builder. Eddystone's export sales, meanwhile, were boosted primarily by an order from the Argentine State Railways for 51 R-615Es — a 1500-h.p. derivative of the R-616E.

To better utilize Eddystone, B-L-H transferred production of Austin-Western side dump cars and Whitcomb industrial diesels to the plant. Whitcomb diesels had previously been constructed at Rochelle, Illinois; now that they were built at Eddystone the Whitcomb name was soon dropped in favor of the "Baldwin-Lima-Hamilton Industrial Line." Meanwhile, Baldwin's traditional line was still known as the "Baldwin-Westinghouse Standard Line." With B-L-H's other industrial projects showing an upturn, the company had total sales in 1952 of $268.9 million and a net income of $7.2 million, both up dramatically from the consolidated results of 1951. Eddystone's locomotive business accounted for only 30 percent of the corporate giant's sales dollars in 1952.

THE BEGINNING OF THE END

Baldwin-Lima-Hamilton's 1952 report to stockholders carried a message of optimism for 1953 from President Marvin Smith and Chairman George A. Rentschler: "While a number of roads have practically completed their [diesel] conversion programs, there are still many diesel locomotives to be purchased, particularly for freight service. With a substantial replacement potential still ahead, it is expected that the railroads will increase purchases in 1953. . . ."

The prediction was marginally correct — U. S. diesel orders did increase slightly over 1952 levels, to 1923 units sold for domestic service and 143 ordered for export — but Baldwin's share declined, to 107 units sold in the U. S., and 20 for export to Mexico, a mere 6 percent of the total. With

---

* At special request, DRS-6-4-1500s were delivered to Morocco through 1952. See page 93 for details.

In June 1953, Pennsylvania placed its final diesel order with Baldwin for 14 units — five S-12s, six RS-12s, two AS-616s, and one RT-624. All 14 units were shipped from Eddystone in February 1954; AS-616 No. 8111 was among them.

The light road-switcher replacement for the DRS-4-4-1000 in the new 1950 Baldwin-Westinghouse "Standard line" was the RS-12. Kaiser Bauxite RS-12 No. 102, equipped with special dual head lamps, was dispatched to Jamaica in 1952.

total orders less than half of what they had been just two years before, the delivery times of the major builders were shortened, and some railroads that had ordered minority makes — such as Baldwin or Fairbanks-Morse units — because they could take delivery earlier did so no longer. With steam already swept from their rosters, many roads began to standardize their diesel fleets, and on all but a handful of roads that meant standardizing toward EMD and Alco locomotives.

With 1953 marking two years of lackluster sales, Eddystone's production of diesel locomotives was only 185 units, less than half of the 1952 total. And 1953 also marked the first year when no steam locomotives were ordered in the U. S., either for domestic use or export.

There were other problems, too. The Navy dropped its interest in the 547-series OP engine, and with company locomotive sales struggling, B-L-H discontinued the project altogether. Westinghouse (which even after the consolidations of Baldwin, Lima-Hamilton, and Austin-Western still held more than 10 percent of the company's stock) was seriously contemplating dropping production of heavy railroad electrical apparatus.

Baldwin contacted General Electric and GE developed main generators specifically suited for the 600-series engines. The GE GT-590 was designed for use with the 608A engine and the GT-591 was developed for 606 and 606A. Standard GE 752-series traction motors could be employed, but the attendant traction motor blower equipment required additional frame length and, as a result, Baldwin's road-switchers and S-12 switcher were eventually redesigned with frames six inches longer. (Baldwin intended, however, to continue to use Westinghouse equipment as long as it was available.) Eddystone redesigned the heavy road-switcher line, primarily to improve its adaptability to optional equipment (see page 108), and this resulted in a new carbody design, first seen on Baldwin AS-616 testbed/demonstrator No. 1601 in early 1953. The AS-616, along with the initial R-615E for Argentina, was publicly unveiled at the 1953 Atlantic City Railroad Exhibition.

Meanwhile, with locomotive production decreasing at Eddystone, sales of construction equipment accounted for 40 percent of Baldwin-Lima-Hamilton's $276.2 million in sales in 1953.

The locomotive situation worsened in 1954. Total U. S. orders for new diesels fell to 1108 (958 for domestic use), and Baldwin's sale of new standard-line diesels slipped to only 30 units in the U. S. (3 percent), 33 worldwide. Pennsylvania, which had again purchased Baldwin diesels in 1953 (14 units ordered in June), bought no locomotives in

1954, and although it was unknown at the time, PRR would never again place an order for B-L-H locomotives. B-L-H delivered 99 units, most of them on orders taken in 1953. Steam made a minor comeback at Eddystone as Baldwin constructed a massive steam-turbine-electric — the *Jawn Henry* — for Norfolk & Western, and received an order from India for 50 2-8-2s.

Whatever question remained about Baldwin's fate as a locomotive builder was answered in June 1954, when Westinghouse publicly announced its intention to cease building heavy railroad electrical gear. At the same time, it was announced that Baldwin-Lima-Hamilton had arranged to re-acquire from Westinghouse its 515,000 shares of B-L-H stock for $4.6 million. Ominously, Baldwin-Lima-Hamilton Chairman Rentschler pointed out that B-L-H's diversification had reached the point that 80 percent of the company's business consisted of heavy machinery, while locomotives and locomotive renewal parts accounted for less than 20 percent. In 1954 the decision was made to prepare for the closeout of diesel-electric locomotive production.

In 1955, a year which saw a moderate increase in U. S. diesel sales (more than 1400 units), Baldwin sold only 20. Delivery of standard-line diesel units tallied but 27 units, with only the heavy and light road-switcher and switcher models represented. For lack of further orders, the last RF-16 had been constructed in 1953 and the final RT-624 and S-8 were shipped in 1954. Although B-L-H had prepared for installation of General Electric gear in its locomotives, only 22 sets each of the GE GT-590 and GT-591 generators were purchased to augment the remaining Westinghouse supply. As it turned out, the GE main generators (and traction motors) began arriving at Eddystone in 1955-56 just as locomotive production was concluding. Only 2 GT-590 and 11 GT-591 main generators were utilized in new locomotive production (through 1956). The last AS-616 and AS-416 departed Eddystone in 1955, and steam made its farewell with shipment of the Indian Mikados.

A DREAM OF SALVATION, THEN DEMISE

While B-L-H had made the decision to drop its current line of locomotives, a new diesel-hydraulic line offered Eddystone some hope for salvation. By 1953, Baldwin had prepared preliminary designs for these diesel-hydraulics, and B-L-H held the U. S. license for the Mechydro hydraulic transmission developed in Germany by Maybach A.G. of Friedrichshafen and was licensed to build the Maybach power plant in the U. S.

Among B-L-H's locomotive orders in 1955 were two for diesel-hydraulics. These orders were the realization of a

Shark-nose styling gave NYC RP-210 No. 20 a decidedly Baldwin appearance. The 1000-h.p. diesel-hydraulic posed in 1956 with Electro-Motive Aerotrain locomotive No. 1001.

dream. Since 1947 Robert R. Young, first as chairman of the Chesapeake & Ohio, then New York Central, had championed the idea of "Train X" — a lightweight passenger train meant to revitalize America's declining passenger service. In conjunction with the C&O and NYC, Pullman-Standard developed the rolling stock for "Train X." Talgo of Spain (through American Car and Foundry) and General Motors also developed lightweight passenger train designs at the time. In 1954, NYC President Alfred E. Perlman called together a committee of eastern railroad officials with the aim of establishing standard requirements for lightweight trains. The roads were NYC, New Haven, Pennsylvania, C&O, and Baltimore & Ohio. These were the results: In 1955, New York Central and New Haven each issued orders to Pullman-Standard for construction of lightweight trains, and orders to B-L-H for 1000-h.p. diesel-hydraulics to power them. NYC ordered one unit, while the New Haven — taken with the idea of bidirectional operation — ordered a unit for each end of its train.

Before constructing the hydraulics for NYC and New Haven, B-L-H constructed a 52-ton diesel-hydraulic switcher for the U. S. Army in September 1955. This unit, powered by a Caterpillar D-397 engine, was in essence a hydraulic version of the diesel-electric RSC-4T, a Whitcomb/B-L-H design built during the Korean War (examples were also manufactured by Davenport). The diminutive diesel provided B-L-H some hands-on experience with the Mechydro hydraulic transmission and allowed Eddystone to hail construction of the "first hydraulic transmission locomotive built in the United States."

The mainline diesel-hydraulics for the NYNH&H and NYC took shape in early and mid-1956. Given the designation RP-210, the units were low, sleek creatures measuring just 11' from railhead to roof. Each was powered by a Maybach V-12 engine imported from Germany, which developed rated horsepower at 1200 rpm (a far cry from Baldwin's traditional slow-churning 600-series). The power plant was linked to Mechydro transmissions, also imported from Germany. The NYC unit — NYC 20 — featured shark-nose styling, while the New Haven units had more squarish lines. The New Haven units were equipped with traction motors and third rail electrical pickups so that they could operate into New York's Grand Central Terminal. Eddystone was actually more of an assembly station for the RP-210s instead of a true manufacturer. The NYC unit, for example, was built with components supplied by more than 25 companies. NYC 20 was completed and delivered in May 1956; meanwhile, New Haven's pair was also completed, but remained at Eddystone through October 1956 while

tests were conducted on their complex d.c. electrical systems.

As the hydraulic program progressed, delivery of standard-line locomotives was coming to an end. In 1956, no orders were taken for diesel-electrics, and at least one order — from the Southern Pacific for 22 S-12 switchers — was declined by B-L-H. A total of 18 diesel-electrics were delivered in 1956. From January through July, four AS-16s and six S-12 switchers were shipped to Pennsylvania-Reading Seashore Lines, a pair of RS-12s departed for Kaiser Bauxite of Jamaica, and two S-12s were dispatched to Rayonier Lumber. That left but four units — four S-12s — to be accounted for. On August 6, 1956, Eddystone shipped Columbia Geneva Steel S-12s 33-35, the last diesel-electric locomotives of Baldwin's standard line built. Columbia Geneva Steel 35 was the final example; it wore the highest construction number (76140) and carried the highest power plant serial number (6870) assigned to any 600-series-powered locomotive.

Columbia Geneva Steel 35 was to share the notoriety of being the last with a sister: Erie Mining S-12 No. 403. Built in December 1955, the S-12 remained at Eddystone to aid in the testing of the New Haven RP-210's electrical systems. For those tests, Eddystone needed a source of d.c. power, and the Erie Mining S-12's main generator provided it. After New Haven's hydraulics were delivered, Erie Mining 403 was shipped west to Minnesota on October 30, 1956. It was the last Baldwin diesel of common carrier size to leave the halls of Eddystone.

PRODUCTION POSTSCRIPT

In its year-end report to stockholders, Baldwin-Lima-Hamilton described 1956 as "a difficult and trying year," and the once-magnificent Eddystone complex had been the cause of much of the company's discomfort. The huge facility — expensive to heat, maintain, and operate — had, in the face of declining locomotive production, become a financial albatross. B-L-H referred to it as the "Eddystone problem," and addressed the problem by selling 300 acres of Eddystone's land and buildings, including virtually all holdings east of the Pennsylvania Railroad. The diesel facility was included. (Along with the standard line of diesel electrics, the B-L-H "Industrial Line" was also discontinued. Marble Cliff Quarries No. 28, a two-axle, 30-ton switcher was the last of these, delivered in December 1956.) The great main office building on the west side of the PRR tracks was also sold. B-L-H retained 81 acres of Eddystone property which included buildings the company felt could be modernized at reasonable cost and operated on a profitable basis. Products of the retrenched Eddystone Division included locomotive renewal parts, 600-series diesel engines, Austin-Western dump cars, weldments, and ship propellers.

Even this skeletal remnant of Eddystone was still large enough to serve as an erecting hall for B-L-H diesel-hydraulic locomotives, if the company could make progress in that field. But the hydraulic project never bore fruit. The great lightweight passenger train experiment that had spawned the RP-210s was flawed — the concept (whether the trains were built by Pullman-Standard, AC&F, or GM) did not adapt well to American-style railroading. The ride of the lightweights was rough and noisy, and they were not accepted by the traveling public. Neither NYC nor New Haven considered additional purchases of the RP-210, and the locomotive creations conceived by all builders for the lightweight craze passed into obscurity. Baldwin-Lima-Hamilton undertook a limited amount of further diesel-hydraulic engineering, and in March 1957 announced its plans for an "all-purpose" diesel-hydraulic to be powered by a Maybach 1800-h.p. engine. But while the 1800-h.p. B-L-H diesel-hydraulic received a fair amount of attention from the rail industry press, it never garnered the enthusiasm of top B-L-H management, and eventually the program was abandoned. The last locomotive had, indeed, departed Eddystone.

Baldwin fielded two VO-1000 demonstrators, BLW 307 and 332, in 1940. BLW 307, shown here in the tender shop at Eddystone, demonstrated on the Pennsy, then was sold — along with its mate, No. 332 — to the Spokane, Portland & Seattle.

EDDYSTONE'S FINEST

Baldwin diesel yard switchers

THE DIESEL-ELECTRIC switcher configuration which became an industry standard — one power plant, four axles, an end cab, and a narrow hood with side walkways — was formulated at the dawn of the 1930s. Westinghouse had come within a whisker of the design with its "visibility cab" switchers, which replaced the boxcab style that had characterized earlier offerings with one crew cab set high on the end of the carbody (centercabs were also offered). The top of the Westinghouse carbody was narrower than the full-width lower portion, providing good visibility in either direction.

But it was left to one of the steam builders — Alco — to establish the endcab design with 300- and 600-h.p. diesel switchers in 1931. From the 600-h.p. unit (Alco demonstrator No. 600, which became New Haven 0900), Alco developed a new production model — the HH600 — and built 78 of them through 1939. The Alco HH-series switchers went on to attain 1000 h.p. per unit (in the HH1000 of 1939), and construction of the line did not conclude until 1940.

Electro-Motive Corporation, aglow with its successes in lightweight diesel streamliners, followed Alco's lead in switchers in 1935. EMC's offering was constructed at General Electric's Erie, Pennsylvania, plant (EMC's La Grange facility would not open until May 20, 1936), and was powered by a Winton 201-A 8-cylinder 600-h.p. engine. Two units for the Lackawanna were completed in February and March 1935. At the same time, EMC sponsored a 12-cylinder, 900-h.p. switcher built at Bethlehem Steel in Wilmington, Delaware. It was not an endcab design and was never repeated, but it set the precedent for the line of EMC 900-h.p. switchers to follow. With the opening of La Grange, EMC began production of its 600-h.p. model SC (the model SW followed in December), and in 1937 Electro-Motive began construction of standard 900-h.p. endcab switchers (the NC and NW series). Between 1931 and 1940, Alco sold approximately 184 diesel switchers and Electro-Motive accounted for 174 more.

BALDWIN AND THE SWITCHER: NO. 62000

During these formative years for the diesel switcher Baldwin was mired in its financial problems, and it was not until mid-1936 that the company's first endcab switcher — BLW 62000 — began to take form. Designated 8OE 660/1, No. 62000 was powered by the De La Vergne 660-h.p. 6-cylinder VO engine. General Steel Castings supplied the cast steel frame, which featured built-in reservoirs for sand (2200 pounds) and diesel fuel (500 gallons). Also integral with the cast frame were the battery compartment, cab steps, and traction motor air ducts. A cork cushion separated the engine subbase from the frame casting. Electrical equipment was supplied by Allis-Chalmers Manufacturing Company, but Baldwin was prepared to offer any manufacturer's equipment in production switchers.

BLW 62000's four traction motors were permanently connected in parallel, with no electrical switching (called "transition") necessary as locomotive speed or horsepower output increased (this lack of transition became a standard Baldwin feature). Electric motors for radiator fans, traction motor blower, and air compressor were all powered from an auxiliary generator. The rigid-bolster trucks were cast by

J. C. Seacrest collection

GSC and incorporated cast-in passages through the center pin and bolster to the traction motor cooling air inlets. The truck was designed to permit the traction motor and axle assembly to be removed as a unit, and could accommodate either friction journals or roller bearings. Timken roller bearings were applied to No. 62000.

When completed, the switcher weighed in at 212,000 pounds (loaded) and measured 39'-6" long. Width overall was 10'-2", but the hood measured only 5'-6", providing excellent visibility for the crew. At 30 percent adhesion, BLW 62000 offered 63,600 pounds of tractive effort, and its continuous rating stood at 29,900 pounds (at 5.7 mph); maximum speed was 45 mph. Eddystone proclaimed the unit in keeping with "Baldwin traditions of simplicity, ruggedness, and reliability."

Completed in October 1936, 62000 was built with a commitment from the Santa Fe for purchase — if the unit proved satisfactory. Baldwin's plan was to demonstrate the new diesel on several eastern roads, then dispatch it to Chicago and the AT&SF. The unit arrived on the Santa Fe — and was renumbered AT&SF 2200 — in April 1937. In June 1937 came the seal of approval from Santa Fe.

NEW ORLEANS WELCOMES THE 8DE 900/1

By the time workmen put the finishing touches on No. 62000 Baldwin had found the customer for its first outright diesel switcher sale — New Orleans Public Belt. In 1936 the NOPB had undertaken a study to determine what motive power could best lug tonnage over New Orleans' new Public Belt Bridge spanning the Mississippi River (the structure is better known as the Huey P. Long Bridge). Negotiating the bridge and its approaches in either direction meant dealing with a compensated grade of 1.25 percent for more than two miles, and the total length of the bridge run — from West Bridge Junction to East Bridge Junction — was 5.1 miles. NOPB considered 0-8-0 steam switchers with reversible boosters, 0-10-0s, and diesels — and diesels won. The study concluded that a pair of 240,000-pound

Measuring a stubby 39'-6" long, AT&SF 2200 is less than half the length of the observation car it hauls at Dearborn Station, Chicago in the photo above. Below, Baldwin 62000 marked the original application of the De La Vergne VO power plant in a locomotive. Completed in 1936, the historic switcher stands in the steam erecting shop at Eddystone. At the bottom of the page diesel pioneers meet at Chicago's Dearborn Station. Here the premier VO-powered diesel, which had become AT&SF 2200 in April 1937, has coupled onto a heavyweight observation car, while EMC E1A No. 4 awaits its next call, quite possibly on the *Super Chief*.

J. C. Seacrest collection

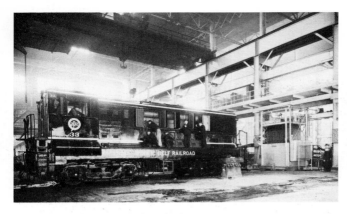

In the view above workmen tend to the construction of New Orleans Public Belt 33, one of the three 900-h.p. switchers built for the railroad in 1937. At right, an overhead view of the same locomotive reveals several differences between the unit and BLW 62000. Exhaust stacks are evenly spaced and twin radiator fans are utilized. Not so obvious is 6′ additional length of the 8 DE 900/1 over the earlier 8OE 660/1.

diesel switchers could handle the heavy transfer service on the bridge, yet could be split up to work flat yards and to venture down lightly built industrial sidings where no large 0-8-0 or 0-10-0 would dare. A third unit was prescribed for backup duty, and in January 1937 NOPB placed its order with Baldwin. At a cost to the railroad of $250,000-plus, Eddystone would construct three 900-h.p. endcab switchers, each with multiple-unit capability.

The three units — Baldwin designation 8DE 900/1 — were similar to 62000. A cast frame — again with built-in reservoirs for sand and fuel — was set atop two-axle trucks (this time without roller bearings). Length was increased to 45′-6″ (inside coupler knuckles) to accommodate the longer, 8-cylinder VO. Electrical equipment was supplied by Westinghouse. Each switcher weighed 246,000 pounds, stood 14′-3″ tall, and was 10′-2″ wide. At 30 percent adhesion starting tractive effort was 73,800 pounds; continuous tractive effort at 8.94 mph was 29,500 pounds. The units could operate around a 130-foot radius curve with train. Wearing road numbers 31-33, the trio departed Eddystone in December 1937, and in the following year worked NOPB's 117 miles of main line, yards, and sidings at an average per-hour cost of $3.17 each, which included enginemen's wages, fuel, lubricants, enginehouse expense, and maintenance.

AN OFFSHOOT IN THE EVOLUTIONARY CHAIN

After BLW 62000 and the three NOPB units, Baldwin's budding diesel switcher program halted abruptly due to the problems with the cast-A-frame VO engine. Eddystone revised the VO for fabricated-A-frame construction, increased the bore from 12½″ to 12¾″, then redesigned the switcher to accommodate the revised power plant. While this was going on the Reading Co. placed Baldwin sales order No. 38510 in December 1938 for a single 660-h.p. switcher. The result was a hybrid unit — an offshoot in the evolutionary chain of Baldwin switchers — which was used to test new manufacturing techniques and mechanical assemblies.

An ungainly creation, the Reading diesel was the first locomotive with a fabricated-A-frame VO engine. Its backbone was a massive — and unsightly — fabricated frame, which provided Eddystone a cost comparison with cast frames. On top of the frame was the welded-A-frame 6-cylinder VO — but with the old 12½″ bore. (For this locomotive this was insignificant, since the bore increase was intended to boost the 8-cylinder version to 1000 h.p. The old bore size was probably a result of Eddystone not having the

tooling for the larger bore ready at the time.) In a departure from previous practice, the power plant was oriented with its generator end facing away from the cab. Modine radiators were force cooled by mechanically driven fans placed at the top and front of the carbody, another break in pattern from BLW 62000 and NOPB 31-33.

Underneath, the Reading unit boasted yet another innovation: a new two-axle switcher truck. Cast by Baldwin's Standard Steel Division, the truck was called the "Baldwin switcher truck" at Eddystone (today, it is generally referred to as the "Batz" truck), and quite possibly should have been called the "Santa Fe" switcher truck. By this time, Santa Fe had more than a year of experience with its No. 2200, and had developed ideas on truck design which Baldwin transformed into steel. In the steam era, it was common for railroad mechanical personnel to design various mechanical features and then specify their use on new purchases. The Baldwin truck was a large, rather unsightly design with an 8′-4″ rigid wheelbase and 40″ wheels. Future AT&SF units from Eddystone would employ the truck, but while Eddystone's new standard switcher line was being prepared it was left to the Reading locomotive to introduce it.

When completed in mid-1939 Reading No. 36 tipped the scales at 194,000 pounds and measured 43′-8″ inside coupler knuckles. The switcher was capable of 58,200 pounds of tractive effort (at 30 percent adhesion), its continuous tractive force rating was 28,000 pounds at 6.5 mph, and its maximum speed was 45 mph.

COMES THE VO SWITCHER

While Reading 36 was taking form (it was not turned over to the Reading until late June 1939), Baldwin made progress on its revised standard line of switchers, the 660-h.p. VO-660 and 1000-h.p. VO-1000. (Baldwin at first classified both simply as "Model VO"; for clarity we use the more descriptive designations.) Few of the concepts tested on Reading 36 were employed. Both the VO-660 and VO-1000 had cast frames, and power plants again were placed with generator end toward the cab. An all-new radiator sys-

Above, two of the three 900-h.p. New Orleans Public Belt switchers pose for the camera at Eddystone. Designated 8DE 900/1, the units were powered by 8-cylinder VO engines. At left a pair of the units are shown in the service for which they were intended, handling a train on the Public Belt Bridge over the Mississippi River. Two units usually worked this assignment while the backup diesel tended to switching chores.

tem was introduced which included an oval, front-end intake with side exhausts. Water cores were mounted vertically on each side of the locomotive with separate lube oil cooling cores mounted behind them. The side radiators were built up from standard, commercially available sections, which were joined with headers (similar arrangements were used by other builders on their contemporary locomotives). Two types of trucks were offered: the Baldwin truck as an option, or a refined General Steel Castings Commonwealth two-axle truck as standard. The GSC truck was double-equalized with drop equalizers and its rigid wheelbase was 8′; it was designed for slow speeds and was limited to a 60-mph maximum. Finally, the VOs were wrapped in a stylish new switcher carbody.

Baby blue and gold VO-660 No. 299, Eddystone's first standard VO,* measured an even 45′ long and rode on the standard Commonwealth trucks. The unit introduced all the design improvements Eddystone had molded — save one. Like Reading 36, BLW 299 employed a power plant built with the old 12½″ bore, the last such unit. Brought to life on April 21, 1939, handsome BLW 299 did not stray far from its birthplace, first undergoing testing and then serving as an Eddystone plant switcher.

Who would lay claim to the first VO-1000 was the subject of an unintentional contest between the Missouri Pacific and the Santa Fe. According to the trade press of the time Missouri Pacific ordered the first VO-1000 (MP 9103) in April 1939, and Santa Fe followed in June 1939 with an order for five VO-1000s (AT&SF 2201-2205). Both orders were to be delivered in November 1939. But as illustrated by Santa Fe's purchase of BLW 62000, and its involvement in the design of the Baldwin switcher truck, the road had played a significant role in the evolution of Baldwin's diesel

switcher line. Indeed, there was little doubt that additional Santa Fe orders would follow the purchase of BLW 62000. AT&SF's order, announced in June 1939, served only to publicly formalize that intent. Baldwin assigned Santa Fe's order an earlier sales order number (39502, versus 39508 for the MoPac order). Eddystone began construction of the six units together, and as it turned out Missouri Pacific 9103 was the first VO-1000 shipped (on November 3, 1939), beating the first of the AT&SF units — No. 2203 — out the door by five days. MoPac 9103 was placed in service at St. Louis on November 17, 1939, and Santa Fe 2203 first answered its owner's call in Chicago on November 23, 1939.

MoPac's single unit and Santa Fe's quintet set the pattern for the VO-1000. Each locomotive weighed 240,000 pounds and promised 60,000 pounds of starting tractive effort at 25 percent adhesion. Each was 48′ long (over couplers) and stood 14′-6″ tall. All six employed the optional Baldwin switcher truck.

For Baldwin, 1940 was a significant year. In anticipation of a steady stream of orders, Eddystone began building a limited number of switchers for stock. This meant that units were built to a near-complete stage, then matched with orders and completed when sales agreements were formalized. Since there were few options, this could be done safely and gave Eddystone the ability to deliver quickly. The demand was there; by year's end Eddystone had more than a score of orders. Four railroads — Reading; Milwaukee Road; Central of Georgia; and Elgin, Joliet & Eastern — placed orders for both the VO-660 and VO-1000. Six

Reading 36, delivered in June 1939, was an experimental unit built to evaluate fabricated underframe construction costs. Other significant features included reverse mounting of the power plant and first use of the Baldwin switcher truck.

*Because Reading 36 received the first fabricated-A-frame VO engine installed in a locomotive, Baldwin considered it the first VO-660, despite its peculiarities and the fact that it was actually completed after BLW 299.

Shown above, BLW 299 was the first standard VO switcher. A VO-660, it displays the characteristics of the earliest oval-grille VOs, including lack of side radiator covers, grille with individual vertical bars, and hood-top headlight. Missouri Pacific 9103, at right, became the first VO-1000 to enter service when it was brought to life at St. Louis on November 17, 1939. The built-in classification lights and mid-hood number-boards were nonstandard, and No. 9103 was the only MoPac switcher to ride the Baldwin switcher truck.

Missouri Pacific

AT&SF 2203, shown at left, went into service in November 1939. Santa Fe is believed to have been the instigator of the Baldwin switcher truck, and the road acquired six VO-1000s equipped with the truck before foresaking the design in favor of the conventional Commonwealth switcher truck.

Standard Steel 12 shows off the layout of the oval-grille VO-660. From front to rear, the radiator compartment, 6-cylinder VO engine, main generator, and 3-cylinder air compressor.

Baldwin VO-1000 demonstrators 307 and 332 were sold as Spokane, Portland & Seattle 30-31. Before being shipped to the SP&S on November 14, 1940, the pair posed at Eddystone.

30

roads — Northern Pacific; MoPac; Terminal Railroad Association of St. Louis; Minneapolis, Northfield & Southern; Seaboard Air Line; and New York Central — plus two industrial firms — Standard Steel Works and American Steel & Wire — placed orders for the VO-660. Five roads opted exclusively for the VO-1000 — Oliver Iron Mining; Minneapolis & St. Louis; Spokane, Portland & Seattle; Union Railway; and Patapsco & Back Rivers — and AT&SF returned with a repeat VO-1000 order.

Industrial customer Standard Steel Works (the member of the BLW corporate family that cast the Baldwin switcher truck) took delivery of the first VO-660 shipped in 1940. Ironically, because the unit (No. 12) had been built for stock, it was equipped not with the truck that its new owner built, but with the GSC Commonwealth truck. The next VO-660 — and the first received by a common carrier — was EJ&E 270, which departed Eddystone on May 6, 1940.

Eddystone was also alive with VO-1000s: One unit originally built for stock went to the Minneapolis & St. Louis as D-340 in April (it had been ordered in March). Then Eddystone pulled out two more built-for-stock 1000-h.p. switchers and prepared them as company demonstrators. Painted baby blue with gold lettering (a la Baldwin 299), the two VO-1000s were given numbers 307 and 332. Baldwin 307 demonstrated on the Pennsylvania and 332 worked on the Reading. When their sales tours were completed, they were used to fill Spokane, Portland & Seattle's order for two units, becoming SP&S 30-31. During a part of its service as a demonstrator BLW 307 had worn Baldwin trucks, but these were removed and replaced with GSC trucks before delivery to the SP&S. When Baldwin's salesman sold the two VO-1000s to the SP&S he had assumed that new units would be provided, and SP&S was not informed about the units' "past." When paint began peeling off SP&S 30-31 after a few months of service, revealing baby blue underneath, there were, to say the least, unpleasant conversations between Portland and Philadelphia.

Baldwin's standard switcher design became the basis for the uncommon when Eddystone built three remarkable VO-1000s for the Oliver Iron Mining Co. Ordered in January 1940 and delivered in July and August of that year, these units were to work in the harsh conditions of Oliver's Hull-Rust ore pit in northern Minnesota, where they would have to meet two unusual requirements. First, the units had to have adequate tractive effort and horsepower to lug 12 loaded 50-ton side-dump ore cars up a 1.5 percent grade at 8 mph. Second, they had to have sufficient compressed-air capacity to operate the side-dump ore cars and unload their trains. Oliver was concerned that the standard Westinghouse Type-W air compressor used in the VOs couldn't handle the latter task, and Eddystone's answer was to lengthen the basic VO-1000 design to accommodate a Gardner-Denver auxiliary air compressor driven by its own wa-

ter-cooled 6-cylinder diesel engine. Each Oliver unit had a welded steel frame (castings would have been far too expensive on a three-unit special order), and between the 8-cylinder power plant and the electrical cabinet (which butted against the cab), workmen inserted the special air compressor and its auxiliary diesel.

The Oliver units included other options as well. To protect it from errant chunks of ore from loaders in the pit the main radiator was shielded by a welded steel grille. For operating flexibility, dual controls were installed in the cab. With the severe cold of Minnesota winters in mind, hot water coils were placed in the fuel tanks near the outlet to the pump line to preheat fuel for the diesels. To prevent the radiators freezing when the units sat idle, water could be drained into storage tanks where it would be warmed by an oil-fired heater. Assigned Nos. 907-909 by OIM, the VO-1000s went to work in the pits on three 8-hour shifts, seven days a week, and earned an overall availability rating of 85 percent.

By the end of 1940 Eddystone had shipped 15 VO-660s and 22 VO-1000s, and more switchers that had been ordered in 1940 would be delivered early in 1941. One such unit — Santa Fe VO-1000 2206 — earned the probable distinction of being the first locomotive for which a diesel trade-in was received. Baldwin agreed to accept Santa Fe 2200 — old BLW 62000 — as credit against No. 2206, which was built to the same specifications as AT&SF 2201-2205. The return of Baldwin's first endcab switcher was not

John F. Kirkland collection

Early in VO-1000 production, Oliver Iron Mining Co. ordered three special switchers for use at its Hull-Rust ore pit. The internal arrangement of these unusual locomotives is shown above during construction. The auxiliary 6-cylinder diesel power plant and Gardner-Denver WBH air compressor are mounted between the main generator and electrical cabinet, just ahead of the cab. The extra equipment was used to operate air-powered side-dump ore cars. OIM 907-909 (No. 908 is shown below) employed nonstandard welded frames.

Warren Calloway collection

Built for stock in early 1940 and delivered in October 1940, Central of Georgia 5 was the only oval-grille VO-660 to ride the Baldwin switcher truck. Shown above nearly 25 years later, CofG 5 rested in New Bern, N. C., in May 1965. Beginning with units shipped in April 1940 Baldwin modified the front of the VO switchers slightly. The size of the air intake grille was decreased and the headlight was lowered. Reading VO-1000 81, working in Philadelphia shortly after its service debut in September 1940, reveals these changes below.

an indictment of its mechanical abilities; instead, being one of a kind the unit did not fit into AT&SF's roster, especially in terms of spare parts. When 2200 returned to Eddystone, the tall, boxy unit was assigned Baldwin "road number" 1, painted baby blue and gold like younger sister BLW 299, and became a plant switcher.

The popularity of the VO-660 and VO-1000 continued to grow in 1941. Eddystone received orders for 42 VO-660s from 19 companies. The VO-1000 fared even better: 52 units ordered by 19 firms. Deliveries of these switchers would run throughout 1941 and 1942. The VO-660 received its biggest boost in 1941 when the Denver & Rio Grande Western ordered nine units; Reading and Central Railroad of New Jersey followed with purchases of four each. New Orleans Public Belt, buyer of Baldwin's 8DE 900/1s of 1937, returned with an order for three VO-660s; these three would become the only VOs with m.u. controls installed by Eddystone. Early in VO production Baldwin began using an air throttle to control engine speed. Combined with the Westinghouse electrical controls this system was referred to as the Baldwin "electro-pneumatic" system, and along with the non-transition electrical system introduced ear-

Martin Zak collection

Reacquired from the AT&SF in October 1940, the only 8OE 660/1 became BLW 1 and worked as a plant switcher at Eddystone. During the 1940s the unit was repowered with a fabricated-A-frame 6-cylinder VO and equipped with Westinghouse electrical equipment.

lier, became a Baldwin standard through the years. It worked well and could effectively m.u. with like-equipped units, but was not compatible with the all-electrical controls used by Electro-Motive and Alco-GE (Baldwin later offered a compatible system as an option).

The most significant VO-1000 order in 1941, 10 units, came from Southern Pacific, which would become a major buyer of Baldwin diesel switchers. Oliver Iron Mining returned with an order for six VO-1000s, but this time OIM opted for standard units with the only option a husky, mechanically driven air compressor. Seven of Baldwin's switcher customers in 1941 — Northern Pacific; SP; P&BR; Nashville, Chattanooga & St. Louis; Southern; TRRA; and Day & Zimmerman, Inc. (on behalf of the U. S. government's Iowa Ordnance Plant) — opted for both the VO-660 and VO-1000.

Effective in early 1941 Baldwin made the first significant mechanical change to the VO switchers. The original radiator system was replaced by a large, front-mounted unit with shutters for airflow control (early VOs used a combination of internal shutters and insulated radiator covers which had to be applied or removed by hand). The new shutters and fan were regulated from the cab (the shutters were air operated and the fan had an air-operated clutch). The new system took in air from the front of the diesel and exhausted it through the top of the carbody, and separate radiators were again used for lube oil and water.

Baldwin changed the cooling system for several reasons. The early hand-assembled radiators were expensive to install, and railroads using the VOs found that the radiators leaked. After the VOs had made a few bone-jarring couplings in yard duty, the header connections often loosened. By 1941, Baldwin was able to purchase a complete radiator assembly specifically designed for the VO switchers, which decreased construction costs and improved performance. The new design also included spring mounting to eliminate impact damage. As a result of the radiator redesign the length of the switchers was increased by 10″ — to 45′-10″ for the VO-660 and 48′-10″ for the VO-1000. Santa Fe VO-1000 2206 was the last of the old design shipped; Seaboard Air Line VO-660 1202, shipped on February 10, 1941, unveiled the new configuration.

THE WAR YEARS: AN ARTIFICIAL MARKET

The U. S. entry into World War Two changed the circumstances under which Baldwin competed for switcher sales. When the War Production Board placed controls on locomotive construction on April 4, 1942, the switcher market became artificial. While the WPB allowed Baldwin to continue switcher production, only 12 of the 66 VO power plants per month that Eddystone could construct were tagged for use in locomotives. Deliveries of new locomotives to the railroads were approved by the WPB based on recommendations received from the Office of Defense Transportation. Alco-GE also produced 660-h.p. and 1000-h.p. switchers, and because the WPB had the power to divert orders from one builder to another, a road that ordered VO-660s from Baldwin might receive Alco S1s instead (or vice versa).

In 1942 Baldwin delivered 42 VO-660s and 49 VO-1000s. The most important event of the year was the first diesel order from the Pennsylvania Railroad. Baldwin had no more precious customer than the Pennsylvania, a Philadelphia neighbor; together, Baldwin and the Pennsy had cast memorable steam and electric motive power, among them the K4 and GG1. PRR's 1942 diesel orders were for 15 units: 9 VO-660s and 6 VO-1000s. All of the 660-h.p. switchers, ordered prior to WPB controls, were delivered in 1942 (PRR 5907 was the first), but the VO-1000s were delayed until 1943.

A footnote to 1942 was the final use of the Baldwin switcher truck on a new unit. The truck had proven to offer no advantages over the standard Commonwealth design, and was more costly to produce. Westinghouse VO-660 No. 10, shipped in June 1942, was the final new unit to feature the truck, and it did so merely because materials were short and the trucks that had been used for a short time under Baldwin VO-1000 demonstrator 307 were available. Only 11 VOs (three VO-660s and eight VO-1000s) ever rode the uncommon trucks, and only 10 left Eddystone with them.

For the VO-660 and VO-1000, WWII and its restrictions presented a bittersweet situation. The WPB regulations that prevented Electro-Motive from building diesel switchers presented Baldwin with a great opportunity to build a strong service reputation in the field, but at the same time the production controls imposed on Eddystone put limits on the market penetration Baldwin could hope to achieve. The controls had the greatest impact on the VO-660. Before the war the VO-1000 had been a slightly stronger seller than the VO-660, and the preference was reinforced during the

By early 1941 Baldwin was able to purchase a radiator specifically designed for the VO switchers. As Iowa Ordnance VO-660 2-100 (foreground) and Northern Pacific VO-1000 109 (rear) take shape the components of the revised cooling system are apparent. Shown are the shutters, lube oil radiator, engine coolant radiator, and air exhaust tunnel which routed air out the top of the hood. Nashville, Chattanooga & St. Louis 15 is typical of the VO-1000s shipped between June 1941 and December 1942. With the new radiator system, both VO-1000 and VO-660 were lengthened by 10″.

TRAINS: Al Rung

TRRA VO-660 534, already a decade into its career in this May 1952 evening scene at St. Louis, tends MoPac headend equipment. In the scene below, sporting trolley poles to actuate Pacific Electric crossing gate circuits, SP VO-1000 1326 works near Wilmington, California. Built in 1942, the VO sports a four-stack exhaust system applied by SP.

Donald Sims

Westinghouse 10, shown above and shipped in June 1942, was the last VO to ride the Baldwin switcher truck. The pair was left over from VO-1000 demonstrator 307. At right, PRR VO-660 5907, which entered service on January 26, 1942, was the first of 643 Baldwin diesels to serve the Pennsy.

war by the fact that the WPB favored 1000-h.p. switchers when approving orders. During a short period in the middle of the war the WPB would not allow Baldwin (or Alco) to build any 660-h.p. switchers. As a result, during 1943 not a single VO-660 was shipped and in 1944 only three were delivered — to the U. S. Navy. Meanwhile, 125 VO-1000s were delivered in 1943 and 178 in 1944.

On January 5, 1945, WPB restrictions on locomotive production were relaxed, and when victory was at hand in Europe and the Pacific the floodgates holding back unfilled orders began to ease open. Eddystone shipped 45 VO-660s to 12 customers in 1945. Biggest buyers: Chicago & North Western (10, plus 3 for subsidiary Chicago, St. Paul, Minneapolis & Omaha), Youngstown Sheet & Tube (8), and New York Central (7). Baldwin delivered 130 VO-1000s to 19 buyers in 1945. Accounting for most of the units were the U. S. armed services (24), Northern Pacific (16), Cotton Belt (14), Frisco (13), Santa Fe (12), Baltimore & Ohio (10), and C&NW (9, plus two for CStPM&O).

During 1945 Eddystone made several changes to the VO exhaust systems. Since production had begun, VOs had featured a single stack in front of the cab, offset to the left. During the first six months of 1945 this was changed to two stacks, and beginning in mid-1945 the two were in turn replaced with four stacks — equally spaced on the VO-1000 and grouped in pairs on the VO-660. In service it had been found that the single-stack system created excessive heat around the main generator. The two-stack system cured that problem by exhausting hot gases from the engine di-

rectly above the exhaust manifold, but in the two-stack design heat expansion caused cracking of the manifolds; the four-stack change was made to cure the cracking problem. In an unrelated change, VO-660s and VO-1000s also began receiving automatic radiator shutters during this period.

As the marketplace began to return to normal at the end of WWII, Baldwin introduced its new line of diesel locomotives powered by the 600-series engines, and that meant the end of production for the VO switchers. The last VO-660 built was Kansas City Southern 1150, which entered service at Greenville, Texas, on May 8, 1946. Francisco Sugar Co. No. 45 was the last VO-660 placed in service (in Cuba on June 15, 1946). VO-1000 deliveries ended after 14 units had been delivered in 1946. Tennessee Coal Iron & Railroad 800-803 were the final VO-1000s. TCI&RR 803 entered service at Pratt City, Alabama, on July 16, 1946.

Baldwin's first major venture into the diesel market was a success. Regardless of whether they had been helped or harmed by the artificial market conditions of the war, the switchers had transformed the company from a steam builder with but a smattering of diesel experience into a diesel-era contender. From 1937 to 1946, Eddystone had turned out the 4 pioneer switchers, 143 VO-660s (including Reading 36), and 548 VO-1000s, a grand total of 695 units. Among the 45 original VO-660 buyers New York Central and Pennsylvania rostered the most units with 12 each, and Reading followed with 11. The fleets of VO-1000s were more impressive. Among railroads, AT&SF had the most (59), followed by Frisco (38), Burlington (30), NP (28), SP

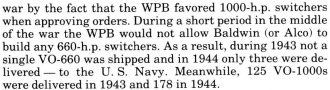

TRAINS: W. A. Akin Jr.

P&WV

L&N 2205 entered service at Louisville on August 9, 1943, and at left 11 years later the VO-1000 clears the ladder at Strawberry Yard in its owner's hometown. The hood-top radiator expansion tank, a feature added to VO-1000s in December 1942, shows clearly. First diesel on the Pittsburgh & West Virginia, VO-1000 30 was put to work at Rook Yard (Pittsburgh) in September 1943. The unit averaged 22 hours duty per day.

TRAINS collection

At top, NYC VO-1000 8606 illustrates several changes made to the VOs during late production. In mid-1944 the styled sheet metal at the base of the cab and battery box was squared off, and the contoured frame ends were also made angular. In early 1945 Baldwin switched to a two-stack exhaust system to reduce heat buildup around the main generator. A two-stack VO-660, yellow-and-green Chicago & North Western 1240 was placed in service in Milwaukee on June 7, 1945, where she was photographed at work above.

About 1945, Reading 36 was repowered with a standard 12¾" x 15½" bore and stroke VO engine. Shown below at Philadelphia, the unit was renumbered Reading 60.

Howard W. Ameling collection

The final VO exhaust system had four stacks, evenly spaced on VO-1000s, grouped in pairs on VO-660s. The last VO-1000s delivered were Tennessee Coal Iron & Railroad Co. 800-803. Shown at top, TCI&RR 800 was placed in service at Pratt City, Alabama, on June 25, 1946. CB&Q 9357, shown above at Cicero, Illinois, on April 19, 1965, was one of 30 VO-1000s which entered service on the Q between November 1943 and December 1944. Typical of VO-1000s built from late 1943 through mid-1944, it has a cast frame with contoured side members, extended stack, and radiator expansion tank.

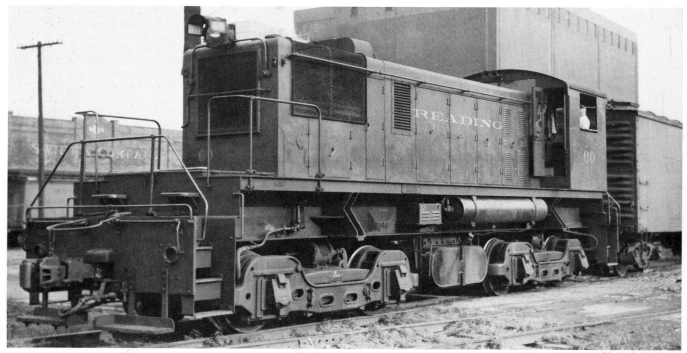

Martin Zak collection

A number of VO switchers were repowered. In December 1958, C&NW VO-660 1243 stood at EMD's La Grange plant with a new EMD-style hood covering a 900-h.p., 8-cylinder 567C engine. The switcher's Baldwin builder's plate is still firmly attached to the frame.

(25), B&O (25), and Cotton Belt (23). Between them, the Army and Navy purchased 66 VO-1000s.

THE VO SWITCHERS IN SERVICE

Baldwin's first endcab switcher — the gallant old one-spot (ex-AT&SF 2200, nee BLW 62000) — worked at Eddystone until around 1953. Prior to 1945 the unit was repowered with a fabricated-A-frame 6-cylinder VO engine and its Allis-Chalmers electrical equipment was replaced with Westinghouse. When its Eddystone days were done, Baldwin 1 was transferred to the Baldwin-Lima-Hamilton plant in Hamilton, Ohio, and eventually the unit went to Boston Metals in Baltimore, Maryland, and was scrapped in 1966. New Orleans Public Belt Nos. 31-33 had extraordinarily successful careers. Their troublesome cast-A-frame VO engines were replaced early with specially built fabricated VOs that incorporated the underslung crankshaft design required for installation in the units. The Belt called Nos. 31 and 32 to duty for the better part of three decades until retirement came in 1966; No. 33 lived on through 1967. Reading No. 36 remained on the company's roster 23 years, until 1962. The unit was rebuilt with a standard 12¾"-bore VO engine and renumbered 60 about 1945.

The VO-660s and VO-1000s built an excellent reputation for Baldwin switchers, and later models would strengthen that reputation. Even on railroads not particularly enamored of Eddystone's road diesels the switchers were looked upon with favor (AT&SF was a prime example). The rugged Westinghouse electrical gear and air throttle system (which featured infinitely variable throttle positions) made them capable yard machines with tremendous pulling power. The VO cylinder heads (which tended to crack) were the only inherent weakness in the VO-660 and VO-1000, and this problem could be cured for the most part with a 600-series modernization kit, which sold for $9000.

The first standard VO switcher — BLW VO-660 299 — worked at Eddystone into the early 1950s, then — with the

Baldwin-Lima-Hamilton merger — was transferred to the ex-Lima plant at Lima, Ohio, remaining there until at least 1966. The two largest users of the VO-660 — NYC and PRR — employed their units for a minimum of 17 years. NYC originally assigned its VO-660s to Buffalo and East Syracuse, New York (one at the depot in Syracuse), and to Niles, Michigan. The Central retired its VO-660s in 1962. Pennsylvania assigned its first Baldwin diesel — VO-660 5907 — to Baltimore, Maryland; eight other VO-660s joined it there. The remaining three PRR VO-660s were originally assigned to Philadelphia (2) and Long Island City, New York (1). Pennsy retired its VO-660s in 1964 and 1965.

As a rule, VO-1000s served longer on Class 1 roads than did VO-660s. The operator with the most VO-1000s, Santa Fe, traded in its earliest 1000-h.p. units (2201-2206) by mid-1962, but newer VO-1000s on the roster were not all retired until June 1971. Through the decades, Santa Fe's VO-1000s were seen across the system, from Chicago to Belen to Bakersfield, and in their last years they were most often found on the AT&SF's lines in Colorado, Texas, and New Mexico.

In the mid-1950s roads that rostered mostly Electro-Motive power began repowering their VO-660s and VO-1000s with Electro-Motive 567-series engines. Among the roads that eventually repowered VO-660s were C&NW, NC&StL, Reading, SAL, and Upper Merion & Plymouth (the latter repowered one VO-660 with an EMD engine, another with an Alco power plant). VO-1000 owners that replaced VO power plants with EMD 567s included Atlantic Coast Line, AT&SF (one unit, No. 2220), C&NW, NC&StL, NP, Reading, SAL, Frisco, P&BR, the U. S. Navy, and U. S. Steel. Santa Fe's rebuilding of No. 2220 went beyond mere repowering. In AT&SF's Cleburne (Texas) shops in 1970, the frame and cab of retired 2220 were used to construct a one-of-a-kind unit — Santa Fe 2450 — with an EMD 567-series 1500-h.p. power plant, GP7-style long hood, and EMD Blomberg road trucks. In 1981, one U. S. Navy VO-

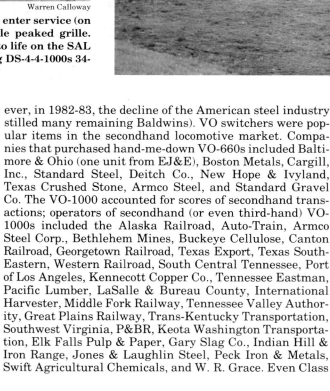

Warren Calloway

American Cyanamid 13, at top, was the first DS-series switcher to enter service (on June 11, 1946), and the only DS-4-4-660 built with the VO-style peaked grille. Seaboard 1417 introduced the DS-4-4-1000 when it was brought to life on the SAL at Jacksonville, Florida, on June 24, 1946. SAL 1417 and Reading DS-4-4-1000s 34-35 also used the peaked radiator styling of the VO models.

1000 was re-engined with a Cummins 600-h.p. diesel.

When purebred VO-660s and VO-1000s disappeared from Class 1 railroading in the early 1970s (examples: Burlington Northern retired ex-NP VO-660 129 in 1971, and sold several remaining VO-1000s in 1972; Western Pacific did not sell its final VO-1000s until 1973, and then two — WP 581 and 583 — went on to serve Auto-Train), repowered Baldwins kept the ghost of Eddystone's VOs alive on America's major railroads into another decade. In 1982, Conrail and Seaboard Coast Line still rostered EMD-repowered VOs. The Conrail units were ex-Reading, the SCL's ex-Atlantic Coast Line VO-1000s, and one ex-SAL VO-660. As late as 1981 Chicago & North Western retained repowered VO-660s and VO-1000s, but by 1982 they were withdrawn. In 1984, VOs — repowered or not — have disappeared from Class 1 railroading.

The early diesel switchers from Eddystone endured longest on short lines, at industrial plants, and in the service of the armed forces — places where they were not so likely to be snuffed out merely because they were orphans in a railroad world now dominated by EMD and GE power (however, in 1982-83, the decline of the American steel industry stilled many remaining Baldwins). VO switchers were popular items in the secondhand locomotive market. Companies that purchased hand-me-down VO-660s included Baltimore & Ohio (one unit from EJ&E), Boston Metals, Cargill, Inc., Standard Steel, Deitch Co., New Hope & Ivyland, Texas Crushed Stone, Armco Steel, and Standard Gravel Co. The VO-1000 accounted for scores of secondhand transactions; operators of secondhand (or even third-hand) VO-1000s included the Alaska Railroad, Auto-Train, Armco Steel Corp., Bethlehem Mines, Buckeye Cellulose, Canton Railroad, Georgetown Railroad, Texas Export, Texas South-Eastern, Western Railroad, South Central Tennessee, Port of Los Angeles, Kennecott Copper Co., Tennessee Eastman, Pacific Lumber, LaSalle & Bureau County, International Harvester, Middle Fork Railway, Tennessee Valley Authority, Great Plains Railway, Trans-Kentucky Transportation, Southwest Virginia, P&BR, Keota Washington Transportation, Elk Falls Pulp & Paper, Gary Slag Co., Indian Hill & Iron Range, Jones & Laughlin Steel, Peck Iron & Metals, Swift Agricultural Chemicals, and W. R. Grace. Even Class

Henry W. Brueckman

Scores of VO switchers moved on to second homes. Pacific Lumber VO-1000s 104 and 105, huddling above at Scotia, California, began their careers in 1945 as U. S. Army V-1800 and U. S. Navy 5. The eight-stack exhaust systems are the handiwork of their new owner — Baldwin called this practice "hot-rodding." Below, Baldwin 299, painted baby blue with gold lettering, served as an Eddystone plant switcher. By 1950, when No. 299 coupled onto a lineup of nine new switchers bound for MoPac and American Cyanamid Co., the venerable VO had an extended exhaust stack, radiator expansion tank, and external radiator shutters.

At left, a dark thunderstorm looms over the Texas horizon as black-and-yellow Georgetown Railroad VO-1000 switcher No. 1003 hurries toward Rabbit Hill, and home, in the fall of 1966. Originally Cotton Belt 1002, this particular Eddystone product is no longer on the Georgetown roster, but the road remained a Baldwin user in 1984.

Jim Hickey

1 Seaboard Coast Line got into the act, purchasing 11 retired Burlington VO-1000s.

So far, four VO switchers have been preserved: the second standard VO-660 built, Standard Steel Works 12 (later renumbered 6712), at the Railroaders Memorial Museum at Altoona, Pennsylvania; Youngstown Sheet & Tube VO-660 607 at the Illinois Railway Museum at Union, Illinois; Western Maryland VO-1000 132 (later Tennessee Eastman 5 and Southwest Virginia 5) at the Spencer Shop Historic Site (North Carolina); and U. S. Air Force VO-1000 7467 at the Tennessee Valley Railroad Museum.

THE DS-4-4-660 and DS-4-4-1000

Baldwin's 1946 replacements for the VO-660 and VO-1000 — the DS-4-4-660 and DS-4-4-1000 — went into production before the last VO deliveries. Externally the new models differed little from their predecessors. The slightly peaked styling of the VO-series front radiator was dropped in favor of a completely flat front end (because VO components were still on hand, the first DS switchers were built with peaked front ends). Deliveries began in June 1946 with a DS-4-4-660 to American Cyanamid Co., which had been ordered in February 1946 and carried road number 13. It was placed in service at Brewster, Florida, on June 11, 1946. Shipments of DS-4-4-1000s began with Seaboard 1417 and Reading 34-35; these also entered service in June. All four featured the VO-style peaked-front radiator, the last to do so. The first DS-4-4-660 to feature the flat-front radiator was P&BR 306 of October 1946; the first such DS-4-4-1000 was SAL 1418 of July 1946.

Even taking into account that the new switcher models were limited to a half year of production in 1946, they did not rack up extraordinary sales that year. Eddystone delivered 15 DS-4-4-660s (to seven buyers) and 24 DS-4-4-1000s (to five customers). New Orleans Public Belt and tiny Chesapeake Western received the most DS-4-4-660s (three each), and Seaboard the most DS-4-4-1000s (eight). The 1947 results weren't much better. While overall railroad motive power purchases were strong, most orders were for road units to dieselize mainline operations. As a result, only seven DS-4-4-660s were delivered to four buyers in 1947. Shipments of DS-4-4-1000s were not particularly strong, ei-

39

ther; 28 DS-4-4-1000s were issued to nine customers. Baldwin's reliable switcher customer — the Reading —took delivery of eight DS-4-4-1000s.

FROM EIGHT CYLINDERS TO SIX

Although DS-series switcher deliveries were minimal, 1947 was a significant year for the switcher line, as major changes were developed that would be incorporated in units ordered in 1947 and delivered in early 1948. The primary reason for the redesign was discontinuance of the normally aspirated 8-cylinder 608NA engine in favor of the turbocharged 606SC. By using the 606NA and 606SC in the DS-4-4-660 and DS-4-4-1000, both models could employ a standard 46-foot frame. The new "combination frame" featured a cast center section with cross braces and drawbar pockets, plus fabricated steel steps and pilots. The cast portion of the frame was supplied, as usual, by General Steel Castings. Because of its turbocharger the DS-4-4-1000 would feature one exhaust stack, while the exhaust system of the normally aspirated DS-4-4-660 was changed to three evenly spaced stacks.

Deliveries of turbocharged 1000-h.p. switchers began in January 1948 with Erie DS-4-4-1000 602. Erie 603-604 followed in early February. The changeover was not without its difficulties. Because the 606SC engine was also being used in Baldwin's DT-6-6-2000, DR-6-4-2000, and DRS-4-4-1000 locomotives, there was — as expected — high demand for the power plant. The turbocharger supplier, Elliot, could not meet the demand for the 606SC's BF-34 turbocharger, and Baldwin was forced to turn to Elliot's BF-40 turbocharger (as used on Alco diesels) instead. A handful of DS-4-4-1000s produced in 1948 were equipped with the BF-40, but Baldwin was unhappy with the smoky characteristics of the BF-40 and returned to the BF-34 as soon as Elliot could supply them.

Deliveries of DS-4-4-660s with combination frames and three stacks began in March 1948 with a 10-unit order for the Pennsylvania (PRR 5957-5966, placed in service in March through May 1948). Pennsy's purchase of the DS-4-4-660 (the order had been inked in June 1947) was an important one for the 660-h.p. switcher; eventually, Baldwin sold 99 DS-4-4-660s to the PRR. Without the Pennsylvania orders, the DS-4-4-660 production line would have been in danger of extinction; in 1948 and 1949, Baldwin built only 18 other DS-4-4-660s for ten customers. Fortunately, the 6-cylinder turbocharged DS-4-4-1000 did not suffer from the same problem — the "switcher depression" of the previous two years was over, and in 1948 and 1949 Eddystone deliv-

At Carolina Junction, Virginia, Norfolk Southern 661 displays the flat grille typically used on DS-4-4-660s.

ered a grand total of 326 turbocharged DS-4-4-1000s.

A HORSEPOWER BOOST FOR A LAGGING SELLER

By mid-1948 it was no secret that the junior member of the switcher line — the DS-4-4-660 — was selling poorly, and Baldwin dropped the model in favor of the DS-4-4-750. Immediate results were promising: Santa Fe, never a buyer of the VO-660 or DS-4-4-660, signed up for nine DS-4-4-750s in August 1948 (for 1949 delivery). The last DS-4-4-660 delivered was PRR 9049 of May 1949, and deliveries of the DS-4-4-750, outwardly a twin of the final DS-4-4-660s, began in July 1949 with AT&SF 525-533. In 1949, DS-4-4-750 deliveries totaled 21 units to six customers.

1950: THE YEAR OF CHANGE

When Baldwin's 1950 standard line of locomotives (including the S-8 and S-12 switchers) was introduced in June 1950, the transition from the DS-series was not a clean break; there was an overlap period. Eddystone took its first order for the S-12 in June (Lehigh Valley, 14 units), yet accepted orders for 10 DS-4-4-1000s from SAL and 24 DS-4-4-1000s from B&O in July. Lehigh Valley 230, the first S-12, was shipped in September 1950, but SAL 1461, the last DS-4-4-1000, was not shipped until January 1951.

The transition from the DS-4-4-750 to S-8 was similar. In May 1950, on the eve of the debut of the S-8, Eddystone issued a pair of DS-4-4-750 demonstrators. Actually, three

Placed in service in January 1948, Cotton Belt 1024 was one of the last 608NA-powered DS-4-4-1000s. Among the earliest 606SC-powered DS-4-4-1000s was Erie 603. Photographed at Eddystone surrounded by freshly fallen snow, the unit was

then shipped off to be placed in service at Port Jervis, New York, on February 7, 1948. The lengthwise-mounted oval exhaust stack indicates an Alco-type Elliot BF-40 turbocharger was employed on the unit.

Above, AT&SF 525, the first DS-4-4-750, sported unusual extended exhaust stacks. Santa Fe received nine DS-4-4-750s in July 1949, the last Baldwin switchers purchased by the road. The redesign of the switcher line in 1948 gave the DS-4-4-660 three evenly spaced exhaust stacks and a cast frame with bolt-on welded steps and pilots. It shared a frame length of 46 feet with the 606SC-powered DS-4-4-1000. Shown below, C&NW 1260 entered service at Milwaukee, Wisconsin, on March 1, 1949.

Top left, Youngstown Sheet & Tube DS-4-4-750 701 was one of the final group of 750-h.p. switchers shipped. The unit had a fabricated frame and carried dual couplers for mill operations. Above left, black-and-white DS-4-4-750 demonstrators BLW 750-751 posed at Eddystone before departing on a West Coast sales tour in May 1950. The trip was to promote the new S-8 switcher, which became available in June 1950. At left, on Pacific Lumber Co. at Scotia, California, in summer 1950, BLW 751 brings a load of timber up to the log dump.

Amid swirling snow, one of the Pennsylvania Railroad's 137 DS-4-4-1000s approaches Overbrook Interlocking in Philadelphia on March 20, 1958. Below, while its crew is away eating dinner, SAL DS-4-4-1000 1459 takes a break from its duties as a yard trimmer at Hamlet, North Carolina, in May 1962. Seaboard received the final DS-4-4-1000s.

Henry W. Brueckman

Above, California Western DS-4-4-1000 53 at Fort Bragg, California, with CW's pair of RS-12s. At right, Tennessee Valley Authority DS-4-4-660 100 at the National Fertilizer Development Center in Muscle Shoals, Alabama, its home since 1949.

Jerry Mart

750-h.p. switchers were built together; one became Eddystone plant switcher No. 301 while the others donned black paint and white lettering as Baldwin demonstrators 750-751. The units were used to promote the forthcoming S-8 to roads in the far west. They demonstrated on the Southern Pacific system (including Pacific Electric and Northwestern Pacific), Arcata & Mad River, McCloud River, Sierra, and Yreka Western Railroad, and several timber companies, including Medford Corp., and Weyerhaeuser Timber Co. In October 1950 Weyerhaeuser purchased the demonstrators and they entered service as Weyerhaeuser 101-102. Meanwhile, in August Pennsylvania placed the first S-8 order, six units. DS-4-4-750 shipments would cease in February 1951 with Youngstown Sheet & Tube 700-702.

The final DS-series deliveries introduced the new all-welded frame which Eddystone expected to use on the majority of its S-series switchers. This frame first appeared on the DS-4-4-1000s shipped to the Pennsylvania in April 1950 (PRR 5578-5584).

When deliveries of the DS-series switchers ended, Eddystone had built 139 DS-4-4-660s, 53 DS-4-4-750s, 56 8-cylinder DS-4-4-1000s, and 445 6-cylinder DS-4-4-1000s, a grand total of 693 units. The DS-4-4-660 had been sold to 19 customers, with the Pennsy's 99 units overshadowing all others (NOPB owned the second most: six). The DS-4-4-750 had attracted 10 buyers: Again Pennsylvania had purchased the most (24), followed by the Santa Fe with nine. The 8-cyl-

inder DS-4-4-1000 was employed by 12 companies, with Reading's 14 units the largest fleet. The 606SC-powered DS-4-4-1000 was sold to 39 buyers. Biggest operators were Pennsy (137), B&O (49), Santa Fe (41), Reading (30), SAL (27), and Missouri Pacific (25, including those held by subsidiary St. Louis, Brownsville & Mexico). Eddystone had dispatched 11 DS-4-4-1000s north to Canadian Pacific and two south to Mexico (to American Smelting & Refining Co.).

YEARS WITHIN YARD LIMITS

The DS switchers acquitted themselves well. Combining the pulling power of the VO models with improved engine performance, many DS-series switchers recorded lengthy careers. The PRR, with 99 DS-4-4-660s, 24 DS-4-4-750s, and 137 DS-4-4-1000s, had far and away the most extensive roster. In their early days, Pennsy DS-4-4-660s could be found in strength mainly at Philadelphia, but also at Mingo

John F. Enoler Jr.

Above left, from 1940 through 1953 Patapsco & Back Rivers acquired 28 Baldwin switchers. Shipped from Eddystone in September 1951, S-12 347 sports an expanded cooling system, special head lamp, open pilot ends, and no footboards — all specifications of the P&BR. The switcher also has a cast frame, an S-12 option until the spring of 1952. Above, the only S-8 built with a cast underframe, La Salle & Bureau County 8 was shipped in October 1951. Lehigh Valley became the first road to place S-12 switchers in service, in September 1950. LV 234 is shown at left in transit from Eddystone at Bethlehem, Pennsylvania, on September 18, 1950, wearing a banner which proudly proclaims its origin.

Junction, Ohio, and Pittsburgh, Pennsylvania. The DS-4-4-750s frequented Washington, D. C., Philadelphia, Harrisburg, and York, Pennsylvania, and many DS-4-4-1000s were to be found at Philadelphia and Harrisburg, Pennsylvania, Canton and Youngstown, Ohio, and Chicago. More than 80 of PRR's DS-4-4-660s survived to be assigned Penn Central numbers after the PRR-NYC merger in January 1968. By mid-1973, the ranks had thinned to seven units, and the last three were retired in August 1975. Twenty-two of the original 24 DS-4-4-750s units were rostered by the Penn Central, although all were retired by 1973, and 133 of PRR's original 137 DS-4-4-1000s were on the books when Penn Central was formed. The ranks were thinned to 14 prior to Penn Central's inclusion in Conrail in April 1976. During the Penn Central years, the road assigned most of its Baldwin switchers to Camden, New Jersey. Finally, the remaining DS-4-4-1000s fell in the shadow of Conrail, but a lone DS-4-4-1000 from another road — Ironton Railroad 751 — earned a brief stint on the Conrail roster as unit No. 8351. It went to the Altoona (Pennsylvania) scrap line on July 20, 1977.

Another major DS user, B&O, originally employed 25 of its 49 units in Pittsburgh, spreading the rest among Philadelphia and Connellsville, Pennsylvania, Benwood, West Virginia, and Cumberland, Maryland. B&O did not retire its last DS-4-4-1000 until 1971. B&O had also leased 10 DS-4-4-1000s to CNJ in 1968 and in 1970 these switchers were sold to the CNJ, but all were out of service by the end of 1970. Santa Fe, owner of nine DS-4-4-750s and 41 DS-4-4-1000s, assigned them throughout the system. AT&SF retired its last DS-4-4-750 in March 1971 and its final DS-4-4-1000 in July 1972.

A number of DS switchers suffered the embarrassment of finding EMD engines under their hoods. One exception: No DS-4-4-750s have been repowered with non-Baldwin engines. Chicago & North Western repowered two of its three

DS-4-4-660s as well as a pair of DS-4-4-1000s belonging to subsidiary CStPM&O. Katy, P&BR, and U. S. Steel also placed EMD power plants under DS-4-4-1000 hoods. (In the case of U. S. Steel, the repowering was performed by locomotive remanufacturer Morrison-Knudsen.) Katy kept the DS-4-4-1000 alive on Class 1 railroads in 1984, with seven EMD-repowered units in service.

Like the VOs before them, the DS-series proved excellent sellers on the secondhand market. Allied Chemical, Nicholson Terminal & Dock Co., Delta Alaska Terminals, and the Seattle & North Coast were among users of secondhand DS-4-4-660s, and Pickens Railroad, Texas Crushed Stone, Texas South-Eastern, and Erman-Howell Co. added handme-down DS-4-4-750s to their rosters. Secondhand DS-4-4-1000s carried many new owners' names, including Buckeye Cellulose, California Western, New Hope & Ivyland, Escanaba & Lake Superior, Indiana & Ohio, Jones & Laughlin Steel, U. S. Steel, Nucor Steel, Municipal Dock Railway, Jacksonville Port Authority, DeKalb County Coop, Consolidation Coal Co., Benson-Quinn Terminals, and North Carolina State Ports Authority. Seaboard Coast Line bought DS-4-4-1000s from the Kentucky & Indiana Terminal (which had purchased two units [53-54] new in 1948).

In 1984, a few purebred DS switchers still served their original buyers. DS-4-4-660s purchased new by Tennessee Valley Authority (No. 100) and Escanaba & Lake Superior (No. 101) were still extant. Among DS-4-4-750s, Weyerhaeuser Nos. 101-102 (the ex-demonstrators) were extant but stored, and as for DS-4-4-1000s, Oakland Terminal No. 101 still was extant. Aside from the repowered Katy units, the last DS-series switchers rostered by a major common carrier were Canadian Pacific DS-4-4-1000s 7070 and 7072. The units were not scrapped until late 1982.

Thus far, only one DS-series switcher, AT&SF DS-4-4-1000 2260, has been preserved. The unit is being held by Santa Fe for historical purposes.

Seaboard S-12 1464 in company with RS-12 1467 glides over the hump at Hamlet, North Carolina, in May 1962. SAL 1464 had come to Hamlet when new a decade earlier.

Ten S-12s shipped in July 1952 represented the Southern's largest single purchase of Baldwin diesel locomotives. It was also Southern's final purchase. After departing Eddystone Southern 2292 entered service at Greenville, South Carolina.

Rock Island 802-806 of September 1952 were the last S-8s delivered to a Class 1 road. At left, RI 802 shows off the welded switcher frame, with only the bottom of the pilot bolted on. Above, although dynamic brakes became an option on all switcher models with the 1950 standard line, Medford Corporation S-8 No. 8 was the lone Baldwin switcher so equipped.

THE FINAL PRODUCTION YEARS: THE S-8 AND S-12 CARRY ON

In 1950 the new S-8 and S-12 put Baldwin in a strong competitive position. The S-8's 800 h.p. equaled that of EMD's 8-cylinder SW8 (first built in September 1950) and exceeded Alco's 6-cylinder, 660-h.p. S3 (introduced in March 1950). The S-12's 1200 h.p. matched EMD's 12-cylinder SW9 (introduced in February 1951) and Fairbanks-Morse's 6-cylinder H12-44 (first produced in May 1950), and overshadowed Alco's 1000-h.p., 6-cylinder S4 (of August 1950).

To further enhance sales of the S-8 and S-12 Baldwin offered a long list of options, including dynamic brakes, cabless boosters (offered on the DS-series but never ordered), m.u. capability, hump control, and roller bearing trucks. Buyers could choose the combination cast-and-fabricated frame used on most DS switchers or the all-welded frame introduced at the end of DS production. (Baldwin offered cast frames long after most builders ceased doing so, largely because the GSC plant was adjacent to Eddystone, minimizing transportation costs and delays.)

The S-series switchers continued the sales pattern which had emerged with the VO models — the more powerful unit

Southern Pacific S-12s 1539-1550, shipped from Eddystone in September and October 1953, were the last Baldwin diesels delivered to the SP. S-12 1541 displays the optional m.u. equipment and signal lights applied to these units.

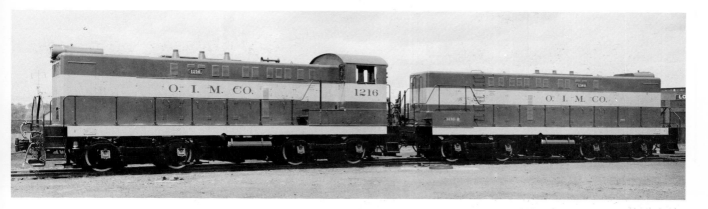

of the pair was the best seller. Eddystone shipped 24 S-12s to three customers in 1950 and 123 to 21 customers in 1951. In contrast, no S-8s were delivered in 1950 and only 30 were shipped to nine customers in 1951. The largest S-12 deliveries in 1951 went to Southern Pacific (22), Pennsylvania (21), and Missouri Pacific (20). Oliver Iron Mining took the most S-8s (14) in 1951.

Oliver Iron Mining had a way of making things interesting in the erecting hall, and its S-8 order proved no exception. The 14 units had been ordered in two groups — eight in November 1950 and six in June 1951 — and were shipped from July through November 1951. There were seven cow-and-calf sets (one unit of each set with cab, one a cabless booster). Oliver was Baldwin's only customer for cow-and-calf switchers (and also the only buyer of similar Alco cow-and-calf sets).

The diesel market flexed its muscles in 1951 (4413 domestic units ordered from all builders), and production of S-series switchers reached its zenith in 1952. The S-12 led the way with 181 units shipped to 23 buyers, and the S-8 followed with 24 turned over to nine customers. Pennsylvania again proved its importance to the Baldwin switcher line by accepting 61 S-12s in 1952.

Of the nine S-8 recipients in 1952, only two — Escanaba & Lake Superior (one unit, No. 102) and Rock Island (five units) — were U. S. common carriers. The RI units (802-806), ordered in December 1951 and shipped in September 1952, were the last S-8s built for a Class 1 road. Whatever the S-8 may have suffered in lack of sales successes it made up for in variety. In 1952, Eddystone delivered two more S-8 cow-and-calf sets to Oliver Iron Mining (1214A/B-1215A/B), and sent a pair of standard units to Cuba — to the United Railway of Havana (8001-8002). For the Medford Corporation of Medford, Oregon (where DS-4-4-750 demos 750-751 had called), Eddystone constructed an S-8 with the dynamic braking option, the only Baldwin switcher so equipped. Medford requested the option to reduce wear on brake shoes and wheels and to lessen the likelihood of fires resulting from wheel/brake shoe sparks during heavy braking. The dynamic brake resistor grids were in a boxy housing in front of the cab.

THE SWITCHER IS NOT SPARED

When the precipitous decline in new locomotive orders hit in 1952 the switcher market was not spared. In 1951 orders placed with all builders had included 683 units of 1200 h.p. and 236 diesels of 800 h.p., but in 1952 those figures were cut by more than half — to 248 and 72, respectively. Because Baldwin depended so heavily on switcher sales, the decline was especially disheartening at Eddystone (through the end of 1952, 61 percent of Baldwin's total diesel deliveries were switchers). Shipments of S-12s in 1953 fell to 83 units (for 16 customers), and S-8 deliveries dropped to only seven units (for three industrial customers: Columbia Geneva Steel, Sharon Steel, and Youngstown Sheet & Tube).

In one attempt to arrest its switcher sales decline Bald-

Had the S-8 cow-and-calf set shown above been delivered, it would have brought Oliver Iron Mining Co. ownership of Baldwin units to 41. The pair was completed in April 1953 on the basis of a verbal order which, when formally issued, went instead to EMD. OIM 1216A was modified and shipped as Armco Steel 1201, shown below, in January 1954. Rebuilt with a cab, OIM 1216B was the last S-8 shipped when it left Eddystone as USP&F 37 in December 1954.

Henry W. Brueckman

At Chinese, California, Sierra S-12s 42 and 40 have 15 cars and a caboose in tow westbound. The pair came to the Sierra from Eddystone in 1955.

win dressed S-12s 1200-1201 in demonstrator colors and dispatched them for a sales tour on the Duluth, Missabe & Iron Range. No S-12 order was forthcoming from DM&IR, but in July 1953 the demonstrators were sold to Rock Island and entered service at Blue Island, Illinois, as RI 758-759.

GE-equipped Rayonier S-12 202 idles near the log dump at Sekiu, Washington. One of Baldwin's last diesels, No. 202 is but four years old in this August 23, 1960, scene.

Certainly the oddest creation to come out of Eddystone in 1953 was McCloud River "S-12" 31. One of two switchers shipped to the McCloud in October 1953, for all intents and purposes No. 31 was actually an S-8. It had no turbocharger on its 606 engine, but to make its appearance match its true S-12 sisters it had a false box installed in place of the turbocharger to funnel exhaust out a single stack.

At Eddystone, 1953 was a year of lasts — Southern Pacific S-12 1550, shipped to SP on October 31, 1953, was Espee's last Baldwin diesel. Earlier, in June 1953, came the last diesel switcher order from the Pennsylvania (as part of PRR's final 14-unit order). The result, delivered in February 1954, was a quintet of S-12s — Pennsy 8100-8104. The five units brought PRR's all-time purchases of Baldwin diesel switchers to 373 units, a figure matched by no other railroad.

In addition to PRR's S-12s, only 16 other S-12s were shipped in 1954. Monongahela received eight (bringing its roster to 27 units), Milwaukee four, C&NW three, and TVA one. S-8 shipments came to an end with two units delivered in 1954. Actually, the pair of 800-h.p. switchers had been

constructed as a cow-and-calf set in April 1953 on the basis of an order expected from Oliver Iron Mining. Although the duo was painted in Oliver colors and given road numbers 1216A/B, the set was never delivered; OIM ordered from EMD instead, and the Baldwin units sat, unused, at Eddystone. In January 1954 Baldwin shipped the cab-equipped unit to Armco Steel at Ashland, Kentucky, as No. 1201, and later in the year Eddystone applied a cab to the calf unit and it departed for Birmingham, Alabama, in December 1954 as United States Pipe & Foundry 37.

With the phase-out of diesel-electric production under-way in 1955, only a handful of S-12s filtered out of Eddystone that year. A trio of S-12s departed to Erie Mining Co., a pair headed for New Orleans Public Belt, two were shipped to the Sierra Railroad, and one S-12 took up duties for Armco Steel, a grand total of eight units.

In January 1956, with little activity at Eddystone, Baldwin sold its plant switcher — DS-4-4-750 No. 301 — to Weyerhaeuser Timber Co., where it maintained the same road number. Before delivery, Eddystone replaced the 750-h.p. 606NA engine with an 800-h.p. 606.

Martin Zak, Extra 2200 South collection

In April 1956 Eddystone shipped PRSL S-12s 6028-6033, the first S-12s built with GE 752-series traction motors and GT-591 main generators.

H. N. Proctor, Extra 2200 South collection

The last diesels of Baldwin's standard switcher line ordered and built were Columbia Geneva Steel S-12s 33-35. The trio was shipped from Eddystone on August 6, 1956. Red-and-white No. 33 stood at Geneva, Utah (near Provo), on June 24, 1964.

William J. Husa Jr.

During this period the supply of Westinghouse electrical gear for the switcher line became depleted, forcing Eddystone to begin using General Electric main generators and traction motors. Between the time in 1953 that Westinghouse began contemplating its discontinuance of railroad electrical equipment and the time B-L-H decided to go out of the diesel-electric business, a new, 6"-longer frame was designed to accommodate the GE gear. The frame design was also modified so that end steps and pilots could be built separately and bolted on rather than welded.

Use of the new frame and GE electrical gear on S-12s began with the six Pennsylvania-Reading Seashore Lines S-12s (6028-6033) shipped in April 1956. In July 1956, Baldwin shipped two more GE-equipped S-12s to Rayonier Lumber Co. as Nos. 201-202. Finally, in August 1956, Eddystone shipped Columbia Geneva Steel's S-12s 33-35. All were GE equipped. Delivery of these S-12s filled the final orders Eddystone had accepted for diesel-electric locomotives. The end was at hand, and with departure of Erie Mining Co. S-12 403 after its use in testing the New Haven RP-210s, the book was closed.

With the erecting halls shut down, the final tally of S-series switchers could be made. There had been 63 S-8 switchers sold to 16 customers in a production run of three years, nine months. The S-8 was unique among Baldwin models in that more than two-thirds of its sales — 45 units — were to industrial customers. Oliver Iron Mining's 18 S-8s easily outdistanced all other buyers (Sharon Steel Co. of Sharon, Pennsylvania, was next with eight). In the six years and one month of S-12 deliveries, 452 units had been issued to 48 original customers. Pennsylvania took honors with 87 units, followed by SP (59 including Texas & New Orleans units), Missouri Pacific (40 including subsidiaries), Monongahela (27), Milwaukee Road (21), Chicago & North Western (16), and Katy (15). Diesel switchers — all models — accounted for 1903 of the 3209 diesels Baldwin built.

NOT READY TO DIE

Because so many S-8s were sold to industrial users many of them had long lives. In fact, more than half of the S-8s constructed recorded 25 years of service. Oliver Iron Mining's S-8 cow-and-calf sets worked in the Minnesota ore

August Staebler Jr.

After beginning its career as somber dressed Erie 621 in May 1952, this S-12 took the red, purple, and white colors of Auto-Train for its own 20 years later. Under a sunny Florida sky, A-T 621 worked at Sanford on July 30, 1972.

Paul Hunnell, courtesy Extra 2200 South

Above, Erie Mining S-12 403 was the last diesel of common carrier size to depart Eddystone. Renumbered 7243, the unit is shown at Hoyt Lakes, Minnesota, on May 22, 1973. At right, Amador Central S-12 No. 9, built in 1951 as Sharon Steel No. 10, is working westbound near Martell, California.

Henry W. Brueckman

region until 1980, then were transferred to various U. S. Steel plants, primarily the Fairless, Pennsylvania, Works (OIM is now part of the Minnesota Taconite Division of U. S. Steel); a few ex-OIM S-8s survived in 1984, but none was in service. Sharon Steel still reportedly owned all eight of its S-8s in 1984, and the last S-8 shipped — U. S. Pipe & Foundry No. 37 — still was owned by that company (now named Jim Walter Resources) in Birmingham, Alabama; however, the unit was stored.

S-8s sold to common carriers were, for the most part, far less fortunate. Rock Island, after employing its five S-8s around Blue Island, Illinois, retired the units in 1965-66. PRR, which originally assigned its six S-8s to Canton, Ohio (4), and Lancaster, Pennsylvania (2), put its 800-h.p. Baldwins to rest in 1966, and New Orleans Public Belt retired its two units around 1968 (however, No. 51 lived on working for nearby Avondale Shipyards).

In contrast, Pennsylvania-Reading Seashore Lines' lone S-8 (6006) survived to be assigned Conrail No. 8553 in 1976. S-8s purchased by short lines also fared well: Escanaba & Lake Superior 102 and LaSalle & Bureau County 8 both survived in 1984. Weyerhaeuser 103 and 105 also remained with their original owner (but were for sale). Dynamic-brake-equipped Medford 8 survived, but on the Magma Arizona Railroad. No S-8s have yet been preserved.

Scores of S-12s enjoyed impressive longevity. The great PRR S-12 fleet, originally spread throughout the eastern end of the system, survived intact through the final, struggling Pennsy years and joined the Penn Central roster in 1968. Pennsy's merger partner, NYC, contributed its entire original contingent of S-12s — 21 units — to the PC roster. By mid-1973 Penn Central had thinned the ranks of its S-12s to 30 units and assigned the diesels to Camden, Baltimore, and Wilmington. Two units, PC 8308 and 8334 (ex-NYC 9310 built in 1951 and ex-PRR 8775 built in 1952) made the Conrail roster in 1976 (where they were joined by 10 ex-PRSL S-12s). None survived long into the Conrail era.

Among other major S-12 operators, Southern Pacific worked most of its units through their twentieth birthdays. SP began retiring its S-12s in 1973, and the units had disappeared by early 1974. In contrast was the plight of the S-12s (and other Baldwins) on the Missouri Pacific. In 1962, MoPac began a wholesale purge of four-cycle power (standardizing on EMD two-cycle locomotives), and MP's Baldwins soon appeared in dead lines.

The S-12 did not escape EMD repowering. C&NW, Katy (one unit), U. S. Steel, and the U. S. Navy exchanged the 606A engines in various S-12s for EMD 567-series power plants. Of these operators, only the C&NW no longer retained repowered S-12s by 1984. Meanwhile, U. S. Steel

50

In 1984, Baldwin's only dynamic brake-equipped switcher survived as Magma Arizona No. 8. Bound for the SP interchange at Magma on November 2, 1968, the ex-Medford Corporation unit totes a string of ore cars near Florence Junction, Arizona.

and the Navy still operated 606A-powered S-12s in addition to repowered units.

Of the 48 original buyers of S-12s, Erie Mining, TVA, the Navy, U. S. Steel, Sierra, and the Air Force still owned Baldwin-powered units in 1984, and Katy still rostered its repowered S-12, No. 34. Many other S-12s moved on to new homes through the years. Operators of secondhand S-12 s included Auto-Train, Allied Chemicals, Amador Central, Blairsville & Indiana, Bethlehem Mines, California Western, Cargill, U. S. Steel, Nucor Steel, Magma Arizona, New Hope & Ivyland, Kennecott Copper, North Carolina State Ports Authority, Rayonier, Erie Mining, Sierra, Metropolitan Stevedore Co., Southwest Lumber Mills, Gettysburg Railroad, Georgetown Railroad, White Pine Copper Co.,

Avondale Shipyards, Ketchican Pulp, and American Smelting & Refining Co. In the case of American Smelting & Refining, the hand-me-down S-12 (AS&R 1) was a notable unit — ex-Rock Island 758, nee Baldwin S-12 demonstrator 1200. In 1984, the unit remained in service. A lone S-12, U. S. Navy 65-00372, is preserved at the Kansas City Railway Museum.

Overall, in 1984 approximately 170 Baldwin switchers of all models (VO-, DS-, and S-series units) remained extant, and among these units were the two Baldwin switchers which made history with their departure from Eddystone: Columbia Geneva Steel 35, the last S-12 built (based at U. S. Steel's Geneva, Utah Works), and Erie Mining S-12 403 (renumbered 7243), the last S-12 delivered.

FROM A GIANT TO A LIGHTWEIGHT

Streamlined passenger-service diesels

WHEN, IN 1939, Eddystone first set its sights on building diesel locomotives for road service, passenger units were a logical place to start. Electro-Motive's E units had proven the diesel capable of locking couplers with heavyweight consists, whether the cars numbered five or twenty. No longer were diesels equated only with fixed-consist, lightweight, articulated passenger trains — such as Burlington's *Zephyrs* and Union Pacific's M-10000-series — that had dominated the mid-1930s. The EMC E unit, and the Alco DL109 which would appear in January 1940, represented the building-block approach to motive power — when more power was needed, more of the 2000-h.p. units could be coupled to the point of a train. While this method is standard today, it flew in the face of late steam-era practice, when ever-more-powerful locomotives were developed to reduce the need for double-heading. With 1939 patent requests for six-engined, 4000-h.p. 1-D + D-1 and 2-C + C-2 diesels (issued in February and November 1939, respectively), Baldwin was preparing diesels big enough to match the largest contemporary steam passenger locomotives on a one-for-one basis. In this quest, the diesels on the drawing boards grew even larger than the 4000-h.p. designs of 1939, and the final result was the massive 6000-h.p. 2-D + D-2 unit — Baldwin No. 6000 — approved for construction.

AN ILL-FATED GIANT

It was in 1940 that word first began filtering out of Eddystone about a great 6000-h.p. creature, but it was not until January 30, 1941, that Baldwin applied for a patent. The 6000-h.p. diesel was based on modular construction, meaning that eight De La Vergne 408 750-h.p. V-8 engines would be used, all mounted crosswise in the carbody. Each engine would have its own Westinghouse main generator and its own overhead cooling and exhaust system, forming an independent power package, or module, that could be installed — or removed and replaced — with no effect on the rest of the locomotive. This modular concept was developed

Each integral power package for BLW 6000 consisted of a 408 V-8 engine, Westinghouse main generator, engine exhaust and cooling systems, and engine room controls.

by Max Essl, a Swiss-born engineer who had joined Eddystone's diesel group.

Use of the 2-D + D-2 wheel arrangement was predicated on Baldwin's experience with similar running gear under straight electrics (the 1-D-1 gear of the Great Northern's Z-1s built in 1926 and the 2-C + C-2 gear of the Pennsylvania's GG1s among them). The main purpose in applying such enormous running gear to a diesel was to give the locomotive excellent tracking ability in high-speed passenger service, but there was a bonus: Baldwin also saw potential in the design for freight service, where the numerous driving wheels would provide tremendous traction. Accordingly, Baldwin planned for optional traction motors in the lead and trailing trucks (all wheels were 40″ diameter). The result would have been a locomotive with 12 powered axles in an unprecedented B-D + D-B wheel arrangement. Baldwin's classification system, a combination of wheel arrangement and power plant package, gave the big diesel its designation: 4-8-8-4 750/8 DE. The road number — BLW 6000 — reflected the unit's horsepower.

Construction began in the summer of 1941. By July the unit's huge truck frames had appeared in the erecting shop, and its mammoth welded underframe — which would double as a fuel tank — began to take form in the tender shop. In August and September work on the undercarriage and frame continued, and eight Westinghouse 370-series traction motors were added to the truck frames. By the end of October the underframe was installed on the completed truck assemblies, which included front pilot and both front and rear drawbars, but on December 7, 1941, America was jolted into World War Two.

In the whirlwind of war that was 1942 construction slowed to a crawl, and not until January 1943 was BLW 6000's hulking carbody added to its running gear. The 4-8-8-4 750/8 DE was impressive, measuring 91′-6″ inside coupler faces, and its 25:54 gearing gave it 117-mph potential. A streamlined, if rather brutish, nose and cab keynoted the carbody, which consisted of nine identical sections with a tenth, larger, section at the rear. Sections one through four would house the four forward power plants, section five held the locomotive's belt-driven air compressor and traction-motor cooling blower, and sections six through nine would contain the rear four engines. Section ten held the steam generator and its water supply.

Early in 1943 management sent instructions to the erecting hall: Have the massive diesel ready, in some form, to make its debut before the board of directors in April. Given wartime limitations, components were on hand for only five of the eight 408 power plants, and only two had been completed and tested. For the unveiling the two operable power plants, plus two inoperable ones (for the sake of appearance) were installed in engine positions 3-4-5-6 (the first was installed on March 8, 1943). On March 24 the 6000 moved under its own power for the first time, and the Baldwin board of directors had its opportunity to look it over — painted, but not lettered — on April 11, 1943.

After its rush engagement the huge diesel returned to the shop through May 1943 to undergo more work before serious testing could begin. Lettering was added to the red, cream, and blue flanks, and the two inoperable engines were removed, completed, and replaced (the fifth was held as a spare). The four engines brought the unit's horsepower

Construction of the 4-8-8-4 750/8 DE began in summer 1941. In the tender shop in April 1942 the mammoth carbody was beginning to take form atop the welded frame. Running gear had been applied, then removed as work progressed.

Resplendent in red, cream, and blue, Baldwin 6000 poses at Eddystone before trial runs on the Baltimore & Ohio and the Reading. After its final run on the Reading, 6000 was stored at Eddystone and finally dismantled in mid-1945.

up to 3000, only half its prescribed amount but still one and one-half times the horsepower mustered by a single EMD E unit or Alco DL109.

During its brief operating career BLW 6000 was hosted by only two nearby railroads: B&O and Reading. The 6000's first test outside the fences of Eddystone was on the B&O on June 16, 1943. With one coach bearing Baldwin, Westinghouse Air Brake Co., and B&O officials, BLW 6000 ran from Eddystone to Elsmere Junction, 32 miles, then returned home. The run was made primarily to demonstrate the high-speed tracking of the 2-D+D-2 running gear, and the return run provided ample proof of those abilities, with the 6000 riding well as it touched 85 mph. Only a minor engine problem on the outbound leg marred the trip.

The next tests were to assess the capabilities of the unit under load. Several runs were made on the Reading's Chester Branch from Eddystone to Gray's Ferry in South Philadelphia with strings of loaded gravel or coal hoppers. (Baldwin often used this line as an outside proving ground since the test track at Eddystone was only three-quarters of a mile long.) While the unit was plagued by electrical problems on these tests, the runs did allow some fine tuning.

Finally, the big diesel was prepared for a major test — hauling nine empty passenger cars from Reading Terminal in Philadelphia to Jersey City, New Jersey, via the Reading and Central Railroad of New Jersey. But on this test serious electrical problems caused the generators to overload and the engines to overheat. Two of the four engines had to be

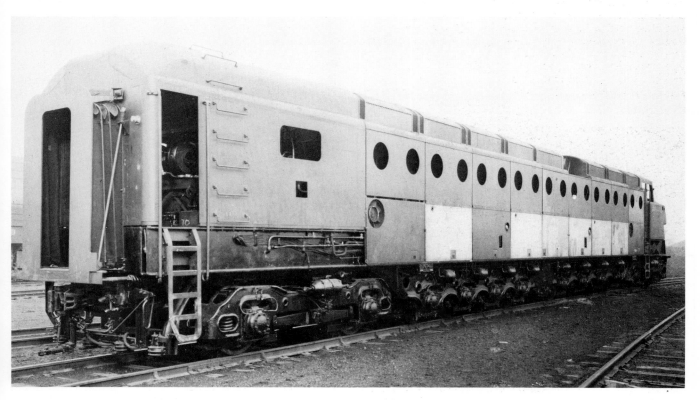

In January 1943 Baldwin 6000 nears completion. The rear of the giant unit matched the styling of the Pullmans it was designed to pull, including a diaphragm.

Baldwin 0-6-6-0 1000/2 DEs 2000 and 2001 combine into 160′ of stylish motive power in front of the brick ediface of Eddystone. The date: May 1945. Note the differences in the exterior radiator shutters of No. 2000 and the interior-mounted shutters on No. 2001.

Above, no steam today. Baldwin 2001, the second 0-6-6-0 1000/2 DE demonstrator, eases into the station at Asbury Park, New Jersey, on the New York & Long Branch, with a CNJ train. The unit was completed in March 1945. Below, on February 11, 1945 — two days before it departed on a tour of the Southeast — Baldwin 2000 stood ready at Eddystone. Despite its graceful lines the locomotive weighed 381,000 pounds.

Ready to join ex-Baldwin demonstrators 2000-2001 in Mexico, NdeM 0-6-6-0 1000/2 DE No. 6002 shines at Eddystone in the summer of 1946. NdeM 6002, which entered service in August 1946, was the last VO-powered diesel Baldwin built.

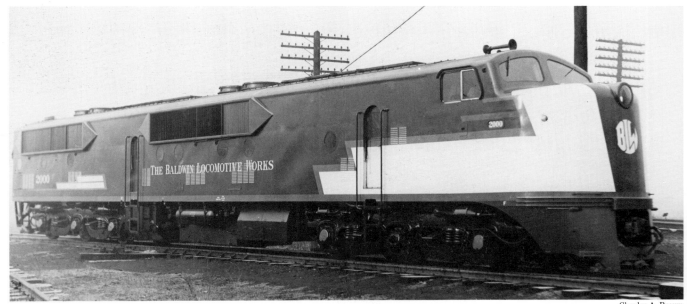

shut down, and after being sidetracked at West Trenton the 6000 limped home on its remaining 1500 horsepower.

Whatever confidence — and interest — management still had in the 4-8-8-4 750/8 DE project ended with the troubles on the Reading, and gone with the 6000 was the company's dream of a 6000-h.p. diesel locomotive. Given the war situation, Baldwin could ill afford further unproductive experimentation. The 408 engine program was dropped — although mechanically sound, the engine was assessed as too costly for competitive production, and there was also concern about its growth potential.* In November 1943 BLW 6000 was stored, never to operate again.

THE EDDYSTONE E UNIT

With the demise of BLW 6000 the spotlight turned to Eddystone's 0-6-6-0 1000/2 DE — the 2000-h.p. A1A-A1A diesel originally devised for sale to customers not interested in a 6000-h.p. locomotive. Unlike the burly 6000, the A1A-A1A unit was graceful and attractive. The prototype unit — BLW 2000 — measured 80' inside coupler knuckles, nearly 9' longer than the Electro-Motive competition and more than 5' longer than Alco's DL109. A tall, rounded nose topped by a flat, two-piece windshield was at the front of the carbody. The portholed carbody shell was laid over a truss-type superstructure welded to the frame.

Inside, two 8-cylinder VO power plants — essentially, engines borrowed from the VO-1000 switcher line — were installed with their generator ends toward the cab. The 15'-6" wheelbase General Steel Castings A1A trucks utilized swing bolsters and single drop-equalizers and were suitable for speeds up to 90 mph. With 40" wheels, gearing to reach that speed was set at 21:58. Westinghouse supplied 480-B main generators and 370-B traction motors, and the unit was equipped with two 1200-gallon tanks, one to feed water to its Vapor Car Heating Co. steam generator, the other die-

* The 408 engine was expanded to a V-12 model — the 412 — for possible sale to the U. S. Navy, but this program was also eventually abandoned.

Built on the running gear of the huge, unsuccessful BLW 6000, Seaboard 4500 was the first DR-12-8-3000. While the artist's conception drawn before construction, below, gave the giant a flatter, taller nose and carbody, when the unit appeared it revealed the true lines of the distinctive Baldwin babyface styling.

sel oil to the VO power plants. Cooling system air intakes with thermostatically controlled shutters were mounted externally on the sides of the carbody. When BLW 2000 was completed, dressed in red, cream, and blue livery, and readied for operation, it weighed in at 381,000 pounds. Starting tractive effort was 76,200 pounds (at 30 percent adhesion); the continuous tractive effort rating was 28,500 pounds (at 21.5 mph).

BLW 2000 was the first new 2000-h.p. passenger diesel designed during the war to be built. (EMD completed the first E7 in February 1945, newcomer Fairbanks-Morse sponsored its first Erie-built in December 1945, and Alco introduced its PA1 in September 1946.) Denied earlier entrance into the road diesel market by wartime restrictions,

Charles A. Brown

At Eddystone on March 30, 1947, Pennsylvania DR-12-8-3000 No. 5823 stands sans pinstripes; in 18 days the unit would enter service on the Pennsy. Five years later, centipede 5823 slips downgrade around Horse Shoe Curve, seemingly enjoying its brief career in passenger service.

Baldwin wasted little time in getting its first 0-6-6-0 1000/2 DE on the road. On January 6, 1945, BLW 2000 highballed, turning in a good performance on a test run on the Reading between Port Richmond and Darby Creek, Pennsylvania. Additional runs were made on the Reading through mid-January, and then — on January 17 — the 2000 began a series of tests on the B&O, including Baltimore-Washington, D. C., Baltimore-Philadelphia, and Philadelphia-Bay View, Maryland, runs.

On February 13, 1945, BLW 2000 headed south. Operating on the Richmond, Fredericksburg & Potomac, the unit hauled Train No. 11 from Washington to Richmond, then, on February 14, coupled onto the second section of Atlantic Coast Line Train No. 75 and made a 16-hour, 34-minute run to Jacksonville, Florida, topping 80 mph (near Florence, South Carolina). From February 16 through February 21, BLW 2000 worked on the ACL out of Jacksonville to Waycross, Georgia, and then on to Savannah, Georgia, where it was turned over to the Central of Georgia. During its stay on the ACL the 2000 had put on a good show, suffering no failures, delivering its trains on time, and locking couplers with the likes of the *South Wind* and *Dixie Flagler*. On the CofG, the unit made a Savannah-Atlanta, Georgia, round trip, then was handed over to the Seaboard Air Line.

On the Seaboard, the 2000 first worked Train No. 3 on February 26. The seven-car train left Savannah 53 minutes behind schedule because of late connections from the north, yet BLW 2000 ushered it into Jacksonville only 19 minutes off the card, making up 34 minutes (and burning 240 gallons of fuel). The unit followed that run with round-trip Jacksonville-Hamlet, North Carolina, duty in the final week of February, then was turned back to the ACL in Jacksonville. Baldwin officials hoped for a repeat of the good showing on ACL earlier in the month.

At 2:22 a.m. on March 3, 1945, BLW 2000 stood coupled to the eight-car consist of the crack *South Wind* at Jacksonville Terminal. The unit was to haul the train to Louisville (via the ACL and L&N), but this was not to be No. 2000's night. Problems in taking on water caused a 12-minute delay in Jacksonville, and as the *South Wind* neared Birmingham electrical problems caused a 51-minute stop. Finally, No. 2000 ran out of fuel and was pulled ingloriously into Birmingham by a steam locomotive. BLW 2000 eventually rolled into Louisville, Kentucky, at 8:45 p.m. — more than 18 hours after it had departed Jacksonville.

Despite its poor showing on March 3, the next day the L&N put the unit back on the southbound *South Wind* and it ran to Montgomery, Alabama, without incident. The unit was then held at Montgomery for the northbound *South Wind* to Louisville (the train operated triweekly) on March 6. Trouble again plagued the northbound train (although

this time through no fault of the locomotive), and the run had to be cut short at Nashville, Tennessee, because floodwaters had closed the line south of Louisville. BLW 2000 returned light to Birmingham, where it was turned over to the Illinois Central. Throughout early March the unit worked on the Illinois Central, primarily hauling trains between Chicago and St. Louis with mixed results. Several trips were interrupted by mechanical problems.

BLW 2000's tour on the IC concluded with a one-day display at Central Station in Chicago, then the unit was turned over to the Chicago & Eastern Illinois, which operated it on two Chicago-St. Louis round trips. The unit was then handed over to the Burlington and ran light to Denver. Baldwin had hoped that the CB&Q would test the 2000 on a train, but the Q's front offices apparently decided that EMD diesels — and none other — would power its *Zephyrs*.

In late April 1945 BLW 2000 locked couplers at Denver with Rio Grande varnish and worked over the D&RGW's main line to Salt Lake City. In the high altitudes of the Rockies the normally aspirated VO power plants did not perform well and had to be derated, and upon returning to Denver, the unit had to be shopped to repair overheated exhaust manifolds.

Following a second light move on the Burlington, this time from Denver to Omaha, the Missouri Pacific was next. Like the D&RGW experience, the stay proved to be a forgettable one. Working on the *Missouri River Eagle* between

Bob Lorenz

Omaha and St. Louis, the unit was plagued by minor electrical problems. Worse, in a head-to-head comparison with the EMD E units most often assigned to the runs BLW 2000 was deemed slightly slower (operating at 5 to 10 mph less than an E unit could accomplish under similar circumstances), and slightly more fuel hungry as well. The Westinghouse 480-B main generators tended to become electrically saturated after prolonged full-power operation, and as a result the unit could not maintain the speeds recorded by Missouri Pacific's Es.

After its MoPac tour No. 2000 was called back to Eddystone. While 2000 had been on the road, Baldwin was building a sister cab unit — BLW 2001 (a B unit was designed but never built). The new diesel was nearly identical to No. 2000, the one major exception being the mounting of its radiator shutters. The external shutters had posed clearance problems on the B&O and Reading, so 2001's shutters were mounted inside the carbody.

BLW 2001 began testing in March 1945. The unit first made a move on the Reading, then was transferred to the Central Railroad of New Jersey for extensive testing and demonstration. It returned to Eddystone in mid-May, where it was set up for m.u. operation with No. 2000. After being moved dead to Maybrook, New York, in early June 1945, the pair tested on the New Haven. There the 4000-h.p. locomotive made runs that included freight hauls between Maybrook and Cedar Hill Yard, and Boston-New Haven

passenger sprints with the *Murray Hill* and the *Colonial*. While some runs were made without incident, many of the New Haven trips were plagued by engine problems and various minor, but irritating, mechanical failures.

Upon completion of the NYNH&H trials in mid-June, the units were transferred to the Boston & Maine at Boston, where they worked passenger (to Portland and Bangor, Maine, via Maine Central), and freight (to Mechanicville, New York, and White River Junction, Vermont). After another New Haven freight run from Boston to Maybrook the units were handed over to the Erie. Following a light move to the Secaucus, New Jersey, engine terminal, they handled an Erie passenger train to Marion, Ohio, and return. On the return trip, a steam locomotive had to be added because one of the steam generators failed.

The B&O was the next host to the demonstrators. The pair ran off a Washington-Chicago round trip, then operated Washington-St. Louis one way. There, the units were turned over to the Gulf, Mobile & Ohio. The GM&O worked them on two St. Louis-Mobile, Alabama, round trips on fast freights and liked what it saw — by GM&O's calculations, each of the units was actually producing 2400 h.p. during the freight trials. From St. Louis, Nos. 2000-2001 ran on the Frisco to Dallas, then over the Texas & Pacific to El Paso. There, the units were transferred to the Southern Pacific and placed in the SP enginehouse to be tuned up and cleaned.

The term of BLW 2000-2001 as company salesmen for-

D. W. Salter

Leading Extra 4503 East toward Howells Yard, Atlanta, Georgia, on June 27, 1947, Seaboard DR-12-8-3000 4503 carries white flags. The big Baldwin centipede had been in service for less than two months when this scene was recorded.

Kalmbach Publishing Co.: Wallace W. Abbey

Forty-eight wheels clatter over the crossing at 21st Street, Chicago, Illinois, as Pennsy DR-12-8-3000 5819 and mate head the *Union* toward Cincinnati, Ohio, October 2, 1950.

mally ended on August 6, 1945, when the units crossed the border from El Paso to Ciudad Juarez, Mexico, to become the property of the National Railways of Mexico. NdeM had purchased the pair — which became NdeM 6000-6001 — to power Train 7/8 on its 521-mile run between Ciudad Juarez and Torreon, Mexico, and had also ordered a third — NdeM

6002. By this time the 0-6-6-0 1000/2 DE was not considered a production model; indeed, even while BLW 2000 was constructed in 1944 plans for the 600-series engine and its associated line of locomotives were well under way. Instead, the 0-6-6-0 1000/2 DE was meant to represent Baldwin out in the field while the 600-series engine was finalized. Baldwin agreed to construct a third unit for NdeM so that all three passenger locomotives would be mechanically identical. With VO switcher applications ending in mid-1946, NdeM 6002 became Baldwin's final VO-powered locomotive when placed in service on August 30, 1946.

The careers of the three NdeM units were not distinguished. Working Train 7/8, they were the only diesels on the Ciudad Juarez-Torreon line, and after Eddystone servicemen stopped tending them around 1947 they quickly fell into disrepair; by late 1948 they were out of service. In the early 1950s Eddystone proposed to rebuild them with 1200-h.p. 606A engines, but the proposal was never accepted. The last of these pioneering Baldwin passenger diesels was scrapped in 1957.

A GIANT REBORN — THE DR-12-8-3000

There was joy at Eddystone in June 1945 when Baldwin took its order from Seaboard Air Line for the first DR-12-8-3000. Not only did the order mean construction of the first 600-series-powered diesel, it also meant that the massive BLW 6000 had served a purpose after all. When SAL personnel had viewed BLW 6000 sitting dormant at Eddystone during the war, it was not necessarily the size of the diesel that had impressed them. SAL was a rugged, undulating railroad ill-suited to high-speed passenger train or perishable freight operations, yet SAL found itself in head-to-head competition for such business with Atlantic Coast Line, a railroad better suited to fast running. In the massive 2-D + D-2 diesel Seaboard saw the makings of a locomotive that could make time over a less-than-ideal right of way, forwarding either passengers or Florida citrus products at speed.

Baldwin took a more realistic tack in designing and building the DR-12-8-3000 for SAL than it had with its massive 4-8-8-4 750/8 DE. The 2-D + D-2 wheel arrange-

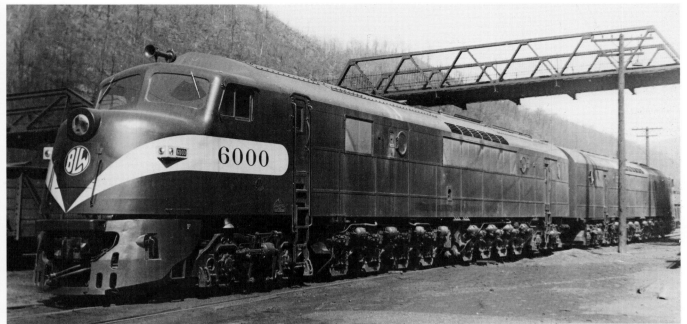

Charles A. Brown

On the Baltimore & Ohio at M&K Junction, West Virginia, blue-and-cream Baldwin DR-12-8-3000 demonstrators 6000A/B pause between assignments. The units were completed in early 1948 based on a Union Pacific order which was canceled before delivery. The duo demonstrated for less than one year, then were stored until scrapped in 1952.

ment of BLW 6000 was retained, of course, but two 608SC engines took the place of the eight 408s proposed for No. 6000. Total horsepower would still be impressive: 3000. The twin 608SCs faced in opposite directions on the main frame of SAL 4500 (unlike those in the 0-6-6-0 1000/2 DE), one generator end toward the cab and one toward the rear. The main generators were Westinghouse Model 489-Bs. In the space between the power plants the DR-12-8-3000 carried a 600-gallon engine cooling system in the top of the carbody, and electrical control cabinets, storage batteries, and traction motor blowers at floor level. The frame carried 3500 gallons of fuel, and a reservoir under the cab floor held 2500 gallons of water for the steam generator, which was located just behind the cab. Control of the locomotive was by electropneumatic throttle (the unit was not set up for m.u.). Baldwin's babyface carbody also originated with SAL 4500. Reportedly, the cab styling of the 0-6-6-0 1000/2 was dropped because Baldwin's sales department felt the company's road diesels should look more like EMD's offerings (the F3 and E7). The cost of fabricating the stylish 0-6-6-0 1000/2 DE nose section may also have been a factor in the change.

Although SAL had ordered the DR-12-8-3000 primarily for its tracking abilities — and although the DR-12-8-3000 provided but half the horsepower of the 4-8-8-4 750/8 DE design — it returned the concept of diesel super power to Eddystone. Completed in December 1945, SAL 4500 weighed more than half a million pounds (577,200 to be exact), and of that weight, 410,000 pounds was on driving wheels. Distributing the weight over many wheels held axle loadings to a maximum of 51,250 pounds.

In spite of the same high-speed 25:54 gearing that BLW 6000 had employed, SAL 4500 was capable of 45,300 pounds of continuous tractive effort (at 20.5 mph). The giant diesel, soon nicknamed "Centipede" for obvious reasons, was — hands down — the most powerful single-unit diesel-electric to be produced in the immediate postwar period. In passenger service a pair of DR-12-8-3000s could match the horsepower of three units from any competing manufacturer. Baldwin would also promote the DR-12-8-3000 as a freight locomotive: One DR-12-8-3000 could match two EMD F3s or

Alco FA1s. Not until the 1960s would a single-unit diesel locomotive surpass the pulling power of the DR-12-8-3000.

SAL 4500 was formally turned over to the Seaboard on December 2, 1945, when Baldwin President Ralph Kelly presented the giant to L. R. Powell Jr., the road's receiver. Catherine Coleman, a registered nurse employed on SAL's *Silver Meteor*, christened the big Baldwin, "The Railmaster" with a bottle of orange juice. Painted in the road's passenger colors, the unit was earmarked for passenger work and Florida-Richmond perishable runs. On December 13, 1945, the locomotive was placed in service at Richmond. It then ran to Jacksonville, where it went to work in passenger service to Tampa/St. Petersburg.

Baldwin seemed to have reason to rejoice with its DR-12-8-3000. Soon after SAL's order for No. 4500 NdeM had ordered 14 units. Like SAL, NdeM needed a locomotive that could operate at speed over routes that were less than ideal

Bessemer & Lake Erie

Originally conceived as a passenger or dual-service locomotive, the DR-12-8-3000 came to be considered a freight hauler. (Baldwin demonstrators 6000A/B even lacked steam generators.) On the Bessemer & Lake Erie at Harrisville, Pennsylvania, the pair applied their 6000 h.p. to a string of hoppers.

Everett L. DeGolyer Jr.

In the scene above, NdeM DR-12-8-3000 No. 6411 works as a helper, pulling Alcos 7419 and 7428 and their train up the Saltillo-Carneros, Coahuila, grade on April 15, 1963. Below left, the last DR-12-8-3000 constructed, NdeM 6413, poses at Eddystone. Inside were two 608SC power plants capable of 3000 h.p. The locomotive entered service on the NdeM on July 20, 1948. Below right, NdeM DR-12-8-3000s returned to Eddystone for rebuilding in 1953 and 1954. Here Baldwin workmen strip one unit's carbody while NdeM 6400, the road's first DR-12-8-3000, awaits its turn.

for high-speed operation, and intended to use the DR-12-8-3000 in passenger service between Mexico City and Nuevo Laredo, Guadalajara, and Torreon, Mexico. Then, in February 1946 the Pennsylvania ordered two DR-12-8-3000s, and followed with an order in October 1946 for 22 more. Pennsy's units were to be semipermanently coupled 6000-h.p. pairs that would handle flagship passenger trains, including the *Broadway Limited*. Meanwhile, SAL returned in July 1946 to order 13 additional units, and the DR-12-8-3000 looked like a winner. But the hard facts were that the model would suffer growing pains and construction delays, and shipments would be slow.

Eddystone made changes to the DR-12-8-3000 based on experience with SAL 4500. One of the most serious problems on the first unit was in its full-height air intakes. All too often they pulled moisture into the electrical system, resulting in immediate failure. The solution was a reduced intake area on the upper portion of the carbody for future DR-12-8-3000s. The 10'-wheelbase lead and trailing trucks of

SAL 4500 were abandoned in favor of new trucks with a 7'-2" wheelbase. Meanwhile, labor and material shortages of the postwar period slowed construction.

Deliveries of DR-12-8-3000s resumed when SAL 4501 was placed in service at Atlanta, Georgia, on March 15, 1947. The remainder of SAL's 13-unit order (4502-4513) was delivered through January 1948, and the great beasts were parceled out to Atlanta and Jacksonville. Although equipped with steam generators, the units were all painted in the road's freight livery and were used almost exclusively in freight service.

In April 1947 Baldwin began to fill Pennsylvania's order. PRR 5823 was the first to enter service (on April 17, 1947), and the rest of the 24 units were brought into revenue service by February 28, 1948. Two sets were assigned to Columbus, Ohio, to work the St. Louis main line, and the rest were stationed at Harrisburg, Pennsylvania. Originally numbered in pairs as 5823A1/A2 to 5834A1/A2, the locomotives were almost immediately renumbered individually,

the units with the "A2" suffix becoming 5811-5822.

National Railways of Mexico had to wait longest for its DR-12-8-3000s; NdeM 6400 was delivered on April 15, 1947, but the second unit — NdeM 6401 — did not arrive until January 1948 and the order was not completed, with NdeM 6413, until July 20, 1948.

While building DR-12-8-3000s for SAL, PRR, and NdeM, Baldwin found a fourth buyer — Union Pacific. UP ordered a pair of DR-12-8-3000s — to be numbered UP 998-999 — in 1947, but the order was canceled before delivery. With a pair of homeless DR-12-8-3000s in the shop, Eddystone completed the units as blue-and-cream Baldwin demonstrators 6000A/B in March 1948. The pair worked on the B&O, Bessemer & Lake Erie, and Chicago & North Western (out of Escanaba, Michigan). After demonstrating for less than one year — and attracting no new buyers — the units were stored. The pair was not scrapped until late 1952, and it is likely that they were kept intact for use in a Baldwin plan to build a steam-turbine-electric for the Santa Fe. That plan was dropped in 1952.

Delivered in July 1948, NdeM 6413, the fifty-fourth DR-12-8-3000, proved to be the last. None of the original buyers reordered, and no new buyers appeared. Surprisingly, the Trona Railway in California seriously considered buying the DR-12-8-3000, but the road wisely chose the more suitable DT-6-6-2000 transfer unit instead (see page 74).

Despite minor external differences, the DR-12-8-3000s that followed SAL 4500 were similar mechanically. All were equipped for m.u. operation when built, and all except Baldwin 6000A/B were built with steam generators. Differences in operating requirements led to a variety of gear ratios; Pennsylvania's units were originally geared for 100 mph, SAL 4501-4513 for 93 mph, and NdeM's for 63 mph. Unit weight also varied, with SAL 4501-4513 being the heaviest (at 585,130 pounds, in service). Units for all three customers were equipped with Westinghouse 370-F traction motors, but the main generators on the PRR and SAL units were Westinghouse Model 471-As, while the NdeM locomotives had Model 489-B generators (as had been used in SAL 4500). Problems were also universal. The units suffered the turbocharger and piston failures that afflicted most early 608SC-powered locomotives, and with twin engines the problem was doubled. The DR-12-8-3000 also had more than its share of electrical problems and oil leaks (which often combined for engine room fires). The Seaboard, in particular, was known to be displeased with the manner in which its DR-12-8-3000s were wired.

THE CENTIPEDES ON THE ROAD

Despite its shortcomings the DR-12-8-3000 provided each of its operators years of service. Seaboard's mammoths worked mainline freights out of Jacksonville and Atlanta north to Richmond early in their careers, but soon were transferred to general freight service in Georgia and northern Florida. The units also regularly worked into Alabama (to both Birmingham and Montgomery). To m.u. EMD and Alco diesels with its DR-12-8-3000s SAL rebuilt the big Baldwins with electric throttles at its Jacksonville shops. Seaboard began retiring the units in 1957, with SAL 4502-4503, 4507, 4511, and 4513 the early victims. The remaining SAL units (including 4500) were not retired until 1961.

On the Pennsy the era of DR-12-8-3000s hauling the road's most prestigious passenger trains was brief, lasting only into the early 1950s, and the centipedes then performed in roles far removed from the point of the *Broadway* or *Spirit of St. Louis*. After being pulled off varnish the centipedes were derated to 2500 h.p. per unit in an attempt to improve the reliability of the 608SC engines. The Baldwins were also regeared for freight service, and finally put into Altoona (Pennsylvania) east slope helper service. PRR's DR-12-8-3000s earned most of their fame pushing tonnage up Horse Shoe Curve to the Allegheny summit at Gallitzin, Pennsylvania, but the units were stored during a

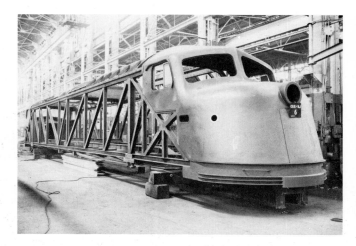

On August 28, 1946, two babyface cabs are in place and truss work is nearing completion as Eddystone constructs Central Railroad of New Jersey's premier DRX-6-4-2000, No. 2000.

With all the pomp of a steam-era dedication ceremony, Baldwin and Central Railroad of New Jersey officials gather in front of DRX-6-4-2000 No. 2000 on November 6, 1946.

Charles A. Brown

Central Railroad of New Jersey (Wharton & Northern) 2002 — last of the road's initial three-unit DRX-6-4-2000 purchase — poses at Eddystone, ready for delivery, on January 24, 1947. The tangerine-and-blue Baldwin would enter service at Jersey City on February 14, 1947.

business slowdown in 1958 and subsequently lost the helper jobs to Alco DL702s. The centipedes spent their final days on freights between Altoona and Enola, Pennsylvania; two sets also worked ore trains from Philadelphia to Paoli, Pennsylvania. Pennsy retired its last DR-12-8-3000s in 1962.

In Mexico the story of the DR-12-8-3000 at first played similar to that of the PRR units: Only for a brief period during their early years did the big Baldwins, all originally based at San Luis Potosi, work passenger trains. Given un-

The first conventional DR-6-4-2000s built were Gulf, Mobile & Ohio 280-281. Below, Baldwin powers the *Gulf Coast Rebel* as GM&O 280-281 roll out of Meridian, Mississippi, bound for Mobile, Alabama, at 7:00 a.m. on September 16, 1952. Although not traded in until 1962, the pair would spend most of its remaining years in storage.

certain maintenance, a number of the units followed their 0-6-6-0 1000/2 DE sisters into storage in the early 1950s. A pair of the units, Nos. 6408-6409, were stricken from the roster in 1954, but the others proved longer-lived. From late 1953 until early 1954, most of the remaining NdeM DR-12-8-3000s were returned to Eddystone for rebuilding. The units were completely stripped, modified, and reassembled, m.u. systems and steam generators were removed, and the 608SC engines were brought up to 608A specifications and rated at 1600 h.p., upgrading the locomotives to 3200 h.p. It is believed that one wrecked unit was rebuilt using components, including portions of the carbody, from one of the BLW 6000A/B demonstrators. After their return to Mexico NdeM used its DR-12-8-3000s in freight duty and pusher service and did not begin retiring the remaining 12 units until 1961. Three — 6401-6402 and 6405 — remained in service into 1971, but with the retirement of NdeM 6402 on August 14, 1971, the curtain finally fell on the last act of the centipede story.

THE DR-6-4-2000 JOINS THE LINE

Only one month after SAL ordered the first DR-12-8-3000 Baldwin took its first DR-6-4-2000 order. While the demonstration tours of the 0-6-6-0 1000/2 DEs had brought mixed results, two railroads were sold on the merits of Baldwin A1A-A1A passenger power: Central Railroad of New Jersey and the Gulf, Mobile & Ohio. CNJ, through subsidiary Wharton & Northern, was the first DR-6-4-2000 buyer, or-

The premier set of sharknose DR-6-4-2000s, PRR 5770A-5770B-5771A, on display at Eddystone. On June 17, 1948, the trio was placed in service at Harrisburg, Pennsylvania. The plaster model shown below previewed the sharknose styling.

dering three (at $180,025 per copy) in July 1945. GM&O followed in October 1945 with an order for two.

The new DR-6-4-2000s would have only a limited resemblance to the 0-6-6-0 1000/2DEs that had promoted them. Inside, 608NA power plants would replace the VOs, and Westinghouse 480-D main generators would be used in place of the 480-Bs in BLW 2000-2001. Outside, the babyface styling introduced on SAL 4500 would be employed, and underneath — in the A1A trucks — Westinghouse 370-F traction motors got the nod over the 370-Ds in the demonstrators.

The CNJ locomotives would incorporate another unique difference: two cabs. CNJ opted for the extra expense of a second cab to avoid turning the locomotives at the ends of their runs. The dual-cab design required a revised internal layout; the power plants were arranged so that the generators faced each other, and the middle of the locomotive con-

Martin Zak collection

Racing south through Middletown, New Jersey, on May 19, 1952, Central Railroad of New Jersey 2005 typifies CNJ's second group of DRX-6-4-2000s (received in 1948). The size of the air intakes was reduced from that of the original DRX-6-4-2000s. Portholes — eight to a side — were done away with, and the position of the cab door was changed.

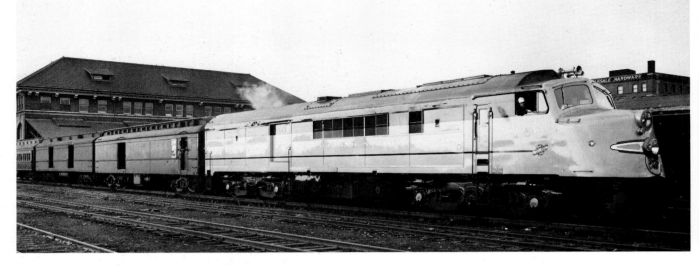

Nestled inside C&NW DR-6-2-1000 No. 5000A was a single 606SC power plant. In concept, the unit mirrored earlier efforts by Electro-Motive for Rock Island and MoPac.

tained the steam generator, air compressor, and overhead cooling systems. Because of this configuration, the CNJ diesels were classified as DRX-6-4-2000s. Production of the GM&O units followed what Eddystone considered its standard DR-6-4-2000 design: one cab, and power plants positioned with generator ends facing toward it (like the 0-6-6-0 1000/2 DEs).

Construction of the first DR-6-4-2000s was plagued by the same production delays Baldwin suffered in 1945-46 with other diesels, and not until late 1946 did the CNJ and GM&O units take final form. About this time — October 1946 — the Chicago & North Western placed an order for half of a DR-6-4-2000. Half? Yes — the locomotive was to be based on the DR-6-4-2000, but with only one engine occupying the front of the carbody and the rear of the unit made into a baggage compartment. Only the front truck would be powered, creating an A1A-3 wheel arrangement. The unusual design mirrored earlier efforts by EMC on behalf of the Rock Island (AB-model Nos. 750-751 of 1940) and Missouri Pacific (MP 7100 of 1940) to create an economical, low-horsepower diesel. Baldwin's designation for this odd unit was DR-6-2-1000.

Central Railroad of New Jersey (W&N) DRX-6-4-2000 No. 2000 was unveiled in a ceremony at Eddystone on November 6, 1946. The 375,000-pound diesel was tangerine and blue, highlighted by red trim. CNJ 2000 entered service at Jersey City, New Jersey, on November 19, 1946, and while awaiting the arrival of its two sisters made an exhibi-

tion tour of the system. CNJ 2001 and 2002 arrived in December 1946 and February 1947. In service, the three locomotives powered 20 weekday trains out of Jersey City on the CNJ's mainline and the New York & Long Branch, replacing seven steam locomotives. The units averaged 333 miles a day on mostly short runs, and their layovers between trains averaged less than an hour.

GM&O's DR-6-4-2000s — 280-281 — were placed in service at Jackson, Tennessee, on January 4 and February 12, 1947, respectively. Belying their Alton-inspired red and maroon, the pair went to work on the southern portion of the GM&O, working the *Gulf Coast Rebel* (St. Louis-Mobile, Alabama). GM&O purchased the units because it had been impressed with the pulling power of the 0-6-6-0 1000/2 DEs, and the road felt that a single DR-6-4-2000 could handle a train which would demand a pair of Alco DL109s. Baldwin's St. Louis sales office could be credited with a job well done in the sale of GM&O 280-281.

From mid-1945 — when Baldwin took the CNJ and GM&O orders — through the end of 1946 the only additional DR-6-4-2000-model order was C&NW's, for the lone DR-6-2-1000 variation. While the DR-12-8-3000 had probably siphoned off some sales, the DR-6-4-2000 could only be termed a disappointment. Then, in 1947, the situation improved. In January Pennsy placed an order for 18 DR-6-4-2000s (six A-B-A sets), and in July 1947 PRR issued a supplemental order for nine more (three A-B-A sets). In September 1947, Baldwin and Central Railroad of New Jer-

Bob Lorenz

Competitors met at Bay Head Junction, New Jersey, when PRR Baldwin DR-6-4-2000 5783A and Alco PA1 5752A stood side by side. Final stomping ground of Pennsy's K4s 4-6-2s, the Long Branch hosted a variety of minority-builder diesels.

Martin Zak

Four Pennsy DR-6-4-2000 cabs and four boosters were regeared for freight service in 1952-53. PRR 5786A, in freight garb, pauses at Enola, Pennsylvania, October 20, 1957.

sey (again through Wharton & Northern) solidified a repeat order for three more dual-cab DRX-6-4-2000s.

As a result of passenger-locomotive orders in 1947, by mid-1948 the shops held a curious assortment of diesels. PRR's DR-6-4-2000s were taking shape, and their shape was curious indeed. When PRR and Baldwin men had huddled together to hammer out the details of the order, Pennsy's favorite industrial stylist, Raymond Loewy, was put to work to improve the unit's looks. Loewy, whose other Pennsy creations included the GG1 and the Baldwin-built T1 Duplex 4-4-4-4 of 1942, created the famous sharknose design by adapting the T1 styling to the diesel. The sharknose quickly ended Baldwin's attempt to build road diesels that looked like EMDs.

In addition to the styling changes the mechanical layout of the locomotive was also substantially revised. The 608NA was replaced by the 606SC, and — as had been done in the CNJ dual-cab units, but not in the "standard" GM&O DR-6-4-2000s — the power plants were installed in the carbody with the generator ends facing each other. The generators were also new, the Westinghouse 471-A (traction motors remained the 370-F). The entire center portion of the PRR DR-6-4-2000s contained cooling systems (overhead) and electrical equipment (at floor level). With the PRR order also came the first DR-6-4-2000 cabless boosters. The B units were shorter than the cab-equipped units (78'-2½" versus 80') and lighter (374,000 pounds versus 385,000).

PRR's tuscan-clad sharknose DR-6-4-2000s (5770A-5787A, 5770B-5786B) were completed and placed in service from June to December 1948. Meanwhile, Baldwin was also constructing the second group of three DRX-6-4-2000s for CNJ (W&N). These were built to the same specifications as the original CNJ trio — with 608NA engines and babyface carbodies — and the only significant variation was the use of smaller air intakes on the carbody flanks. CNJ (W&N) 2003-2005 were placed in service in August and September 1948. Finally, C&NW's odd little DR-6-2-1000, with one of the longer gestation periods of any diesel, was completed (with an old-style babyface carbody but a 606SC engine) and sent west to Sioux City, Iowa. As C&NW 5000A, it entered service there on November 12, 1948, two years and one month after it had been ordered.

While Eddystone built this potpourri of passenger diesels (the last of the DR-12-8-3000s were also in the shops during this period), no new orders for the DR-6-4-2000 were obtained — or ever would be. CNJ switched to road-switchers (purchased from Baldwin, Fairbanks-Morse, Alco, and EMD) for its passenger trains, GM&O returned to the Alco fold (with the PA1), and PRR and C&NW looked to EMD. Consequently, when sharknosed Pennsy A-B-A set 5786A-5786B-5787A was placed in service at Harrisburg, Pennsylvania, on December 15, 1948, production of the DR-6-4-2000 was complete.

Penn Central

Fresh from the paint shop at Eddystone, handsome New York Central DR-6-4-1500 No. 3200 stands ready for its service debut, which occurred on November 22, 1947.

MIXED RETURNS

CNJ's DRX-6-4-2000s worked out of Jersey City for approximately a decade, trading their tangerine-and-blue livery for deep sea green and yellow. Tending busy commuter and passenger schedules, most of the units neared or exceeded the one-million-mile mark during their careers. CNJ double-cabs also worked Reading Co. trains on the Bethlehem Jct. (Pennsylvania)-Philadelphia line. The CNJ withdrew its DRX-6-4-2000s from service around 1957, but usable components were transferred to other CNJ Baldwins

Warren Calloway: Jay Potter collection

Closing in on the end of its career, SAL 2702 idles with 2700 at Tampa, Florida, on September 14, 1963. A new paint scheme, modified nose door, new headlight, and front-end m.u. connections have altered the looks of the Baldwin.

Warren Calloway collection

In 1948, the year it was first placed in service, Seaboard DR-6-4-1500 No. 2702 stands at St. Petersburg, Florida.

Working Seaboard Air Line Train 257 from Tampa to Venice, Florida, SAL DR-6-4-1500 No. 2700 gallops across the mile-wide Manatee River near Bradenton, Florida, in March 1955. Florida runs like this one were the standard fare for SAL's DR-6-4-1500s.

Jim Scribbins

and DRX-6-4-2000 No. 2004 remained on the system as a steam-generator unit until 1968. GM&O's DR-6-4-2000s did not live such fruitful lives. Although they did not meet the torch (as trade-ins to EMD) until 1962, the duo had been stored since at least the mid-1950s at GM&O's Iselin Shops at Jackson, Tennessee. When GM&O discontinued passenger service south of St. Louis on October 14, 1958, any hope the diesels had for a return to service was dashed. As it turned out, they were the only Baldwins ever owned by GM&O. C&NW 5000A had been ordered for a planned Sioux City-Omaha, Nebraska, train, but the service was never begun and 5000A was employed instead on secondary trains out of Sioux City. Later, 5000A was a regular on C&NW's West Chicago-Freeport (Illinois) branch service, and finally was used for various secondary services in Illinois and Wisconsin until retirement in 1958.

Undoubtedly the most successful DR-6-4-2000s (and probably the most successful Baldwin passenger diesels) were PRR's 27 units. All originally based at Harrisburg, Pennsy's tuscan Baldwins were not often able to displace EMD E units on PRR's finest, such as the *Broadway Limited*, but the lanky Eddystone products did appear throughout the system on name trains. After mainline duties early in their careers, they became regulars on the joint CNJ/PRR New York & Long Branch. In 1952-53 a quartet of cabs (5784A-5787A) and boosters (5780B, 5782B, 5784B, and 5786B) was regeared from 22:57 to 15:63 for freight service and assigned to Crestline, Ohio. These units were derated to 1600 h.p. and given Pennsy's Brunswick Green freight

livery. PRR retired the freight units in 1962, and its final tuscan red DR-6-4-2000 was retired in 1965.

COVERING THE MARKET: THE DR-6-4-1500

In 1946 Eddystone's salesmen stood with plans in hand for a third passenger diesel to join the DR-12-8-3000 and DR-6-4-2000. Perceiving a market for an economical, light-duty passenger locomotive, Baldwin offered a one-engine, 1500-h.p. unit, the DR-6-4-1500. Baldwin was alone in offering such a unit, although steam-generator-equipped EMD F3s would prove formidable competition.

The basic appeal of the DR-6-4-1500 was that it could approach the purchase price and operating costs of a 1500-h.p. freight unit (such as the F3), but its A1A trucks made it more suitable for light-rail branch lines. Instead of the 15'-6"-wheelbase trucks used on the DR-6-4-2000, the new unit rode on the Commonwealth A1A truck (also built by General Steel Castings), a swing-bolster design with full equalization between axles achieved through a system of fulcrums and levers housed inside the side members of the truck and over the journal boxes. The 11'-6"-wheelbase Commonwealth truck was not considered a high-speed design, and had first been employed by Baldwin on the French export DRS-6-4-660 road-switchers of 1946 and the DRS-6-4-1500. Above the trucks, a 608SC power plant was tucked into a babyface carbody. In comparison to its freight sister — the four-axle DR-4-4-1500 — Baldwin's vest-pocket passenger diesel was slightly longer: 61' for the DR-6-4-1500 cab unit versus 55'-6" for the DR-4-4-1500 cab; 59'-6"

Posed in its shiny new paint at the Electro-Motive plant in La Grange, Illinois, in March 1955, NYC DR-6-4-1500 No. 3201 does not reveal that an EMD 567-series V-16 has replaced its original Baldwin 608SC. Evidence of an earlier re-trucking to rid the unit of its rough-riding A1A Commonwealth trucks is obvious, though.

for the DR-6-4-1500 booster versus 53'-6" for the DR-4-4-1500 booster. The DR-6-4-1500 was nearly 20' shorter than the 80'-long DR-6-4-2000.

Unfortunately, only two buyers for the DR-6-4-1500 ever came forth. In February 1946, New York Central opted for six units (two A-B-A sets), and in September 1946, Seaboard Air Line ordered three cab units. Production spanned only seven months. On November 22, 1947, NYC placed its first A-B-A set — NYC 3200-3300-3201 — in service, and the following day, Seaboard introduced its first unit — SAL 2700 — at Tampa, Florida. The only significant differences between the SAL and NYC units were in number-board styling and the use of cast pilots with retractable couplers on the NYC cab units. SAL's remaining pair — 2701-2702 — went south to be placed in service at Hamlet, North Carolina, in January 1948, and NYC put its other A-B-A set — 3202-3301-3203 — in service in May 1948.

Considering their limited numbers — just seven cab units and two boosters — the diminutive Baldwins had an interesting history. Seaboard's three DR-6-4-1500s operated mostly on Florida secondary runs (such as the Plant City-Boca Grande and Arcadia-Bradenton trains), and not until 1964 — after 17 years of service — were they sent to EMD as trade-ins on SDP35s.

In contrast to the SAL Baldwins, which, save headlight, nose door, and paint scheme changes remained unmodified throughout their careers, were NYC's units. Within a year of introduction NYC's DR-6-4-1500s were in the Harmon, New York, shops to have their Commonwealth A1A trucks replaced with drop-equalizer A1A trucks (such as those employed on DR-6-4-2000s). To accommodate the extra length of the replacement trucks smaller fuel tanks were installed and revisions were made to the pilots. NYC was dissatisfied with the riding qualities of the original Commonwealth trucks, and it was no wonder: The locomotives were not applied to services for which they had been designed. Al-

though billed as dual-service units on the Central, the DR-6-4-1500s were employed as mainline passenger power (including occasional service on the crack Chicago-Boston *New England States*), and the Commonwealth truck, intended for speeds below 65 mph, was not capable of such duty.

During the mid-1950s the NYC embarked on a small-scale program to repower minority-builder locomotives with EMD 567-series V-16 engines. Included were Lima-Hamilton road-switchers, a number of Fairbanks-Morse C-Line units, and early Baldwin road locomotives. In 1955 the NYC dispatched its DR-6-4-1500s to EMD's plant at La Grange, Illinois, where, in March through May, the 608SC diesels were replaced with EMD V-16s. The Westinghouse electrical gear was retained, but EMD electrical throttles and m.u. equipment replaced the original Baldwin electro-pneumatic equipment. NYC's DR-6-4-1500s were the only Baldwin streamlined passenger units to be repowered with engines of another manufacturer. Assigned out of Collinwood, Ohio, they served most of their remaining days on secondary passenger runs on the east end of the NYC system. In 1951 the booster units were renumbered 3210-3211 and then renumbered again as 3602-3603 in May 1955. The cab units were renumbered 3504-3507 in May 1955. The repowering was not successful, and by 1958 the locomotives were stored. They were stricken from the roster in December 1960.

ILL-FATED LIGHTWEIGHT: THE RP-210

No passenger diesels were included when Baldwin introduced its 1950 standard line, and none was built until construction of B-L-H's three diesel-hydraulic units in 1956. The locomotives were created to power NYC and New Haven lightweight trains and carried the designation RP-210 — and the glorious name "Baldwin Mechydro 1000 horsepower diesel-hydraulic propulsion unit."

The RP-210 was a fascinating package. The Mechydro hy-

Courtesy Morley Kelsey

At Boston's South Station, New Haven RP-210 No. 3001 doesn't look big enough to house two Maybach diesel power plants: an MD-655 1000-h.p. V-12 over its 15'-wheelbase front truck to provide tractive effort, and a 6-cylinder 465-h.p. engine for auxiliary power.

draulic transmission and Maybach four-cycle, turbocharged V-12 MD-655 diesel engine, both imported from Germany,* were mounted directly on the front 15'-wheelbase truck, and the engine and transmission swiveled with the truck on curves. The Maybach engine was a modern, lightweight power plant with a piston displacement of 3930 cubic inches. Its bore and stroke was 7.3" x 7.9", and the engine had a speed range of 600 to 1500 rpm. The attached transmission had four speed ranges, with maximum speeds of

* Although the engines and transmissions for the RP-210s were imported, B-L-H had acquired all necessary manufacturing drawings for future production of these components.

26, 43, 70, and 120 mph. An unpowered, two-axle truck supported the rear of the RP-210, making its wheel arrangement B-2.

The entire output of the Maybach MD-655 engine was earmarked to drive the locomotive, so an auxiliary source was needed to power accessories. For this, Baldwin installed a second Maybach diesel in the center of the locomotive. In NYC's unit — NYC 20 — the auxiliary power plant was a V-8, four-cycle, turbocharged, 570-h.p. engine, and in New Haven's units a similar 6-cylinder, 465-h.p. engine was used. These engines had the same bore and stroke as the Maybach MD-655 and operated at a constant 1200 rpm, turning air compressors and 480-volt a.c. generators to sup-

H. H. Harwood Jr.

Two-month-old NYC RP-210 No. 20 barks into Wellington, Ohio, with the *Ohio Xplorer* in July 1956. Colors — blue and yellow — were a marked departure from NYC tradition.

ply locomotive and train with braking and electrical power.

The New Haven RP-210s — 3000-3001 — were particularly complex creatures. Because they were to power the new Pullman-Standard lightweight *Dan'l Webster* between Boston and New York (and thus use third-rail d.c. power for the trip into New York's Grand Central Terminal), they were equipped with traction motors and related electrical gear, thereby canceling out many of the advantages of using the simple hydraulic drive. Two d.c. traction motors were mounted on the power trucks of the New Haven RP-210s and in turn were connected to the hydraulic transmission, and a third electric motor was installed in the carbody to power auxiliary systems.

When the RP-210s were completed at Eddystone (NYC 20 in May 1956, NYNH&H 3000-3001 in June), they presented a low-slung, husky appearance. NYC 20, dressed in yellow and blue, stood 11' high and 58'-9" long and weighed 87 tons. New Haven's pair was similar in dimensions to NYC 20, but certainly not in livery. NYNH&H 3000-3001 were outfitted with a silver, black, and orange quiltwork scheme that would come to symbolize the years of Patrick McGinnis as New Haven's president.

NYC 20 was first to be delivered. With "Xplorer" emblazoned across its sharknose, NYC 20 and its 392-seat, all-aluminum Pullman-Standard train made their official debut on Track 2 at Cincinnati Union Terminal on May 17, 1956. Through May 21 *The Xplorer* was displayed at Cincinnati, Middletown, Dayton, Springfield, Columbus, and Cleveland, Ohio, and on May 27, 1956, the train began revenue service as the Cleveland-Cincinnati *Ohio Xplorer*. The sleek RP-210 and its consist departed Cleveland at 6:45 a.m. and rolled off a 524-mile round trip before arriving back on the shores of Lake Erie at 7:15 p.m.

By October 1956 NYC 20 had logged 70,005 miles and earned a 92 percent availability rating, but NYNH&H Nos. 3000-3001 had yet to enter service. After prolonged testing of their electrical equipment, New Haven's RP-210s were delivered for test runs. More difficulties ensued: The units had trouble with the third rail of Grand Central Terminal (a problem EMD FL9s later had in 1957) and several electrical fires occurred. Properly controlling the two units on either end of a nine-car train — via 42 electrical connections — proved a problem as well. The units experienced a number of d.c. power system faults, and they would tie up at New Rochelle, New York, during the day, then be operated

into Grand Central for testing after midnight. To overcome momentary losses of power caused by gaps in the third rail small air-actuated pantographs were installed on the roofs.

Following a publicity run from Boston to New York on January 8, 1957, New Haven 3000-3001 and the *Dan'l Webster* finally entered regular service on March 26, 1957. The train worked the New York-Boston route and was also eventually assigned New York-Springfield (Massachusetts) duties. But the operating career of the New Haven lightweight was brief, and on March 21, 1960, the units were officially retired. NYC 20 and the *Xplorer* lasted only a little longer, being retired in May 1960.

The early demise of the RP-210s was a result of the rapid and total collapse of the great lightweight passenger train craze. Once the initial design flaws were overcome, the locomotives themselves operated relatively well. The Maybach engine performed up to expectations and demonstrated excellent fuel economy. On the New Haven, the RP-210s showed their potential for speed, operating on at least one occasion at 110 mph. Probably the RP-210s' worst faults were that they rode extremely hard, which did not endear them to crews, and the Mechydro transmission sometimes overheated at high speeds. The units were also at the mercy of shop force inexperience with hydraulic transmissions and the Maybach power plant, and replacement parts were specialized and sometimes hard to obtain. At Cleveland, NYC personnel were known to call on a local Volkswagen dealer to obtain metric nuts and bolts.

After the RP-210s were retired B-L-H still held a heavy mortgage on the units and the company actively tried to resell them. Prospective buyers were found in Brazil, but when the New Haven units were inspected, they were found damaged by water that had collected and frozen in their oil intercoolers. Eventually, the RP-210s and NYC's lightweight train were obtained by James F. Jones, president of the Pickens Railroad of Pickens, South Carolina. He intended to run excursions, and a limited number were operated. During 1963 *The Xplorer* — with ex-NYC 20 on the point — was used by United Aircraft for tests in development of its Turbotrain. By the latter half of the 1960s, though, the excursion runs of the diesel-hydraulics were over, and in 1969 the sight of once-proud New York Central 20 moldering away on an abandoned spur of the Greenville & Northern at Travelers Rest, South Carolina, made it clear the end was at hand.

George G. Weiss

Its career at an end, once-glorious NYC RP-210 No. 20 was photographed on an abandoned spur at Travelers Rest, South Carolina, in October 1969.

TALES OF THE "GOLDEN GOOSE" AND

Heavy transfer units

IN THE STEAM ERA, transfer service — moving freight cars from one yard to another — was traditionally a refuge for elderly locomotives. Venerable but useful 2-8-0s and Mikes and 2-10-2s, their mainline days done, might be found clanking out their last miles on transfer runs. When, in the mid-1930s, diesel-electric switchers began to prove their economic worth in yard service, it followed that diesels should be well suited to transfer service. Yard work and transfers, after all, were similar; both involved handling long strings of cars, often in dirty, rugged conditions with lots of stops and starts thrown in. But any railroad anxious to push diesels into heavy transfer service in the 1930s was faced with a problem: No suitable new diesel units existed, there were no old, hand-me-down diesels ready to be relegated to transfers, and yard switchers of the day lacked the required muscle.

Enter Illinois Central. Faced with substantial transfer activity between downtown Chicago and Markham Yard (at Homewood, Illinois), in 1936 the IC purchased (from two builders) three diesels designed specifically for transfer duty. From the drafting tables of Electro-Motive and the shops of St. Louis Car Co. came a huge centercab diesel, the T-model. Dressed in basic black, the locomotive was powered by a pair of Winton 201-A 900-h.p. V-12 engines. Power was transferred to the railhead through eight traction motors in four four-wheel switcher trucks, a B-B + B-B wheel arrangement. From General Electric's Erie (Pennsylvania) facility came two six-axle (C-C) boxcab units. One carried a pair of 900-h.p. Ingersoll-Rand 6-cylinder engines, the other held a single 2000-h.p. 10-cylinder Busch-Sulzer diesel. None of these three units merited a repeat order, so in 1940 IC changed tactics, purchasing three model TR loco-

Baldwin Locomotive Works

Charles A. Brown

Left, the old and new guard pass between Joliet and Waukegan, Illinois, shortly after the May 1946 arrival of EJ&E 100. During its first 15 months of service, the prototype DT-6-6-2000 accumulated 73,497 miles on the J.

HE "BLUEBIRD"

motives from EMC. The TRs were, for all intents and purposes, pairs of semipermanently coupled NW2 switchers. One unit of each pair had a cab, the other did not, and so the cow and calf was born. In 1941 IC and Electro-Motive developed a more unorthodox cow-and-calf lash-up. This was the TR1, and underneath the long, switcher-style hood of each unit was a 1350-h.p. 567-series V-16 — the same power plant employed in the FT road diesels. The TR1 rode on another element borrowed from the FT — EMD's Blomberg road truck. The onset of World War Two suspended production of diesel transfer units, but in November 1945 IC and Electro-Motive were back at it, this time with the TR2, a throwback to the model TR cow-and-calf concept. Nonetheless, the TR2 satisfied the requirements of not only the IC, but of six other railroads, and a total of 36 TR2s was built through 1949.

THE BIRTH OF ELGIN, JOLIET & EASTERN 100

As the war ended, the Elgin, Joliet & Eastern searched for a diesel capable of replacing steam in heavy transfer (and road) service. The EJ&E had been an early convert to diesel switchers — it had purchased its first (an EMC SW) in 1936 — and by the end of 1944 the road owned 80 diesel switchers purchased from Electro-Motive, Alco, and Baldwin (Eddystone had supplied three VO-660s and 10 VO-1000s). The next step for the EJ&E was to replace its road power, aging 2-8-2s. The road was not, however, interested in cow-and-calf units, and when EJ&E and Baldwin personnel met the result was the design for EJ&E 100, the first DT-6-6-2000. EJ&E made its commitment firm with a one-unit order in April 1945.

What evolved from EJ&E's requirements was a single unit with six powered axles and twin power plants capable of producing 2000 h.p. The cab was in the center of the carbody, providing bidirectional ability. Baldwin, seeing a niche in the marketplace left vacant by the other builders, was enthusiastic about the huge transfer unit.

Eddystone first constructed a welded steel frame, then positioned two 608NA engines with their Westinghouse 480-C main generators pointed toward the ends of it. The cooling system for each power plant was placed beyond the generators, with radiators set in the the upper portion of the carbody and 36″ exhaust fans situated atop the hood. When Eddystone constructed its 30 0-6-6-0 1000/1 DE streamlined diesels for Russia in 1945, the company had used General Steel Castings' Commonwealth C-type truck, and this same style was used on the DT-6-6-2000. The 13′-wheelbase truck was a rigid-bolster, fully equalized design. Though not a high-speed truck (it was recommended for speeds up to 60 mph), in low-speed service it offered excellent riding and tracking characteristics. Westinghouse 370-F traction motors were fitted to each axle and geared to 42″ wheels.

The first DT-6-6-2000 was a truly massive machine for its day. It weighed 363,300 pounds in working order, measured 70′-6″ long (inside coupler knuckles), and carried 1200 gallons of fuel oil and 30 cubic feet of sand. Using a gear ratio of 15:63, EJ&E 100 was capable of the 60-mph limit allowed by its trucks, yet it offered 108,000 pounds of starting tractive effort (at 30 percent adhesion) and 64,200 pounds of continuous tractive effort at 9.4 mph. The unit was equipped with dual controls and a feature which automatically reduced engine output when a wheel slip occurred. EJ&E 100's cost to its owner: $173,000.

Hulking No. 100 was placed in service at Joliet, Illinois, on May 13, 1946, and immediately began testing. On early

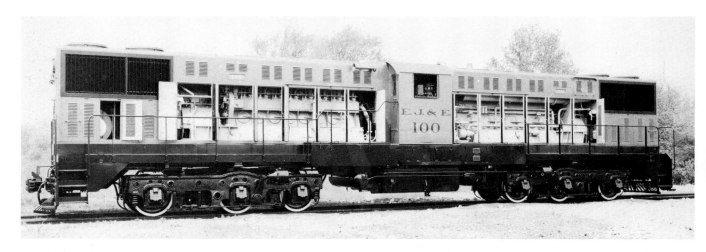

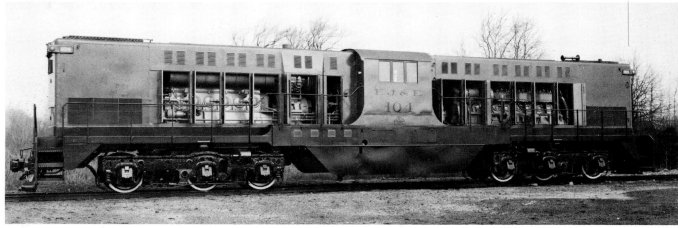

With hood doors open, the differences between the prototype DT-6-6-2000 (EJ&E 100) and a production unit (EJ&E 104) become apparent. Number 100 has twin 608NA power plants with main generators facing away from the cab, and at the ends of the locomotive are individual radiators with side-mounted automatic shutters and overhead cooling fans. The 606SC engines in No. 104 have generators facing the cab, and the cooling system air intakes are just above frame level. EJ&E 104 also features a beveled-nose carbody, and is 3′-6″ longer but approximately 9000 pounds lighter than No. 100.

During the 1940s Cotton Belt purchased 28 switchers and one leviathan road diesel — DT-6-6-2000 No. 260 — from Baldwin. A denizen of east Texas for almost its entire career, it spent its last days wearing SP-inspired gray and scarlet.

EJ&E DT-6-6-2000 115 applies its 2000 horsepower to moving hoppers bound for Gary, Indiana, out of the J's yard at East Joliet. Number 115 began its career at Joliet on June 7, 1948.

Richard K. Smith

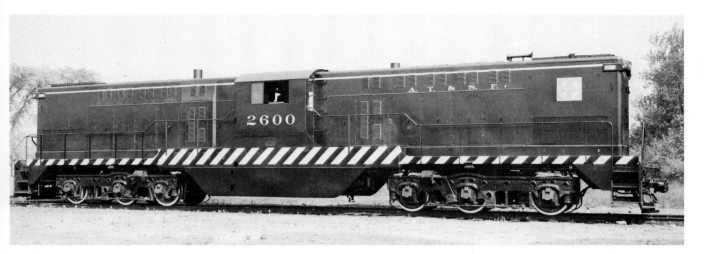

Santa Fe 2600 entered service at Ash Fork, Arizona, in June 1948 as a helper on Johnson Hill. It also served on Cajon Pass. Based on its experience with 2600, AT&SF specified a light-duty dynamic brake on three of the five DT-6-6-2000s delivered in 1949. AT&SF 2605 is one such unit; dynamic brake equipment was installed in one end of the unit only.

runs, the orange diesel — nicknamed the "Golden Goose" by EJ&E men — handled 2932 tons on the J's 1 percent grade between Waukegan, Illinois, and Joliet, and took 6000 tons up the .37 percent rise between Hartsdale and Gary, Indiana. On July 10, 1946, EJ&E 100 showed off for company brass by hauling a consist of 63 freight cars (4284 tons), two cabooses (36 tons), and three Rock Island coaches (210 tons) for railway and Baldwin officers and guests from Gary to Joliet. By August, No. 100 had settled into day-to-day freight service. Each morning around 8 the big diesel departed Gary's Kirk Yard and worked to Joliet, then, after a crew change, rolled on to the northwestern terminus of the road at Waukegan. Night would find 100 back in Gary, ready for another round trip the next day. Through the end of August 1946 EJ&E 100 rolled up 17,010 miles and lugged 45.3 million gross ton miles of freight. Fuel costs per locomotive mile averaged 19.7 cents.

While the J continued to analyze the performance of its prototype unit through 1946, Baldwin was giving the model a strong marketing push and other railroads were taking notice. The big centercab was the most powerful bi-directional freight diesel then available, and Baldwin pitched the DT-6-6-2000 not only as a transfer unit, but as a heavy mainline drag locomotive, a helper, and a hump engine as well.

In January 1947 Baldwin signed a second buyer for its transfer unit: the St. Louis Southwestern (Cotton Belt). At a cost of $199,894 the Cotton Belt ordered one unit for use on its Waco Subdivision. In May the Santa Fe followed suit with a one-unit order, and in August came the final approval from the EJ&E: an order for 25 sisters for No. 100. Baldwin's stake in the transfer unit design was beginning to look good.

606SCS REPLACE THE 608NA

For the production-model DT-6-6-2000 Eddystone made major design changes from the prototype. Foremost was the change in power plant — from the 608NA to the turbocharged 606SC. With paired 606SC engines the unit could retain its 2000-h.p. rating but accomplish it with four fewer cylinders. The engines were turned around, with generator ends facing the cab so that wiring from generator to cab did not have to be run around or under the engine. This also meant that the water pumps could be located closer to the cooling systems, which also came in for changes. Where EJ&E 100 had featured side radiators on both ends and

both sides, all with individual shutter systems and overhead fans, production DT-6-6-2000s would employ a cooling system with side-mounted air intakes and one shutter system overhead on each end. This change and the use of the 606SC also made it possible to reposition the traction motor blowers. On EJ&E 100, they were located directly under the cooling systems at the ends of the locomotive; in the new design, traction motor blowers were moved back slightly and were positioned directly over the trucks. The blowers pulled air from the same intake as the engine cooling system. Compared to EJ&E 100, the production model DT-6-6-2000 was 3'-6" longer (the length was added in the center, between the truck bolsters), yet with the lighter 606SCs on board, total unit weight decreased about 9000 pounds. A more stylish, beveled-nose carbody was incorporated, and end walkways were added.

Production-model DT-6-6-2000s began rolling out of Eddystone in early 1948. The first of EJ&E's 25-unit order — EJ&E 101 — was placed in service at Joliet on March 3, 1948. Work continued on the J's order throughout the summer, and the final unit, EJ&E 125, entered service

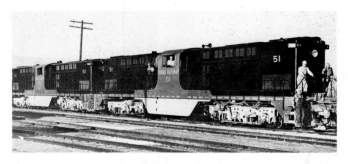

Trona 50-51 were the only DT-6-6-2000s built with m.u. control. Other options on the units included dual controls, dual headlamps, and an automatic speed-control system.

In December 1948, Eddystone issued DT-6-6-2000 demonstrator No. 2000. Attired in an attractive two-tone blue and gray, the diesel became known as the "Bluebird."

on September 13, 1948. Meanwhile, in May 1948, Cotton Belt's DT-6-6-2000 — No. 260 — was placed in service at Pine Bluff, Arkansas, then headed for its assignment in Texas. On June 3, 1948, AT&SF's first DT-6-6-2000 — No. 2600 — was placed in service at Ash Fork, Arizona. Dressed in Santa Fe's "zebra stripe" dress, the big unit was employed on Johnson Hill as a helper (it would also serve at Cajon Pass).

Baldwin salesmen secured additional transfer unit orders in 1948. The Minneapolis, Northfield & Southern ordered five DT-6-6-2000s in January 1948, and one month later the Trona Railway ordered two. The 31-mile Trona had considered several Baldwin models (including the giant DR-12-8-3000) to work its potash and borax trains, but settled on a pair of transfer diesels with an assortment of optional equipment (Trona officials had been among the guests on

EJ&E 100's July 1946 demonstration run). Trona's DT-6-6-2000s were ordered with air-throttle m.u., dual headlamps, and automatic speed control. The speed control sounded a whistle warning when the units exceeded a prescribed speed, then — if speed continued to increase — automatically applied the units' brakes.

One unsuccessful 1948 sales venture occurred when new EJ&E 108 was dispatched to one of the J's sister U. S. Steel roads, the Duluth, Missabe & Iron Range. EJ&E 108 tested on the DM&IR, but even the big centercab could not equal — on a one-for-one basis — the pulling power of DM&IR's articulated steam locomotives, and no order from the ore carrier followed. Better news came from the Santa Fe. Sold on No. 2600's performance, AT&SF issued an order in November 1948 for five additional units (2601-2605). Of these, three (2603-2605) earmarked for pusher service

W. P. Ellis: H. H. Harwood collection

Working as a helper, Baldwin's second DT-6-6-2000 demonstrator — BLW 2001 — assists CNJ F3s at White Haven, Pennsylvania, in July 1950. This unit later became EJ&E 126.

A. C. Kalmbach

Duluth, South Shore & Atlantic 300 was the first of four DT-6-6-2000s rostered by the DSS&A. Effective with DSS&A 300-302, delivered in October 1949, Eddystone moved the radiator air intakes from just above frame level to a position midway up the carbody. Number 300 and her sisters worked road freights east of Marquette, Michigan. At left one of the DSS&A transfer units gets a helping hand from one of the steam locomotives it would soon replace (L-class No. 1051). The train is climbing the eastbound grade out of Marquette near Au Train. After steam disappeared from the DSS&A, normal operations called for a single DT-6-6-2000 to handle freights east of Marquette, while paired Baldwin AS-616s or DRS-6-6-1500s worked west.

around Seligman and Ash Fork, Arizona, were ordered with dual controls and a light-duty dynamic brake. The regenerative braking would allow the locomotives to return light downgrade at higher speeds than could be safely accomplished with only service brakes. The other two units (2601-2602) were equipped with hump control, a system to limit power to the traction motors at low speeds while allowing the power plants to run at maximum rpm. These would be placed in service at Santa Fe's sprawling Argentine Yard at Kansas City, Kansas.

Heartened by the early success of its burly transfer model, Baldwin dispatched a demonstrator on a West Coast sales tour. In December 1948 a handsome gray and two-tone blue DT-6-6-2000 carrying road number 2000 made its debut. Unofficially nicknamed "Bluebird," the unit worked in the West — including tours on Southern Pacific and the Carbon County Railway — throughout the winter and spring of 1949.

Despite BLW 2000's work on the demonstration trail, 1949 was a mixed season for the DT-6-6-2000. Units were being shipped — MN&S's five-unit order was completed in January, Trona's pair went into service in April, and the five Santa Fe units went west from July through November — but new orders were scarce. Quite simply, the demand for locomotives of the size, complexity, and cost of the DT-6-6-2000 was limited. In 1949 only three DT-6-6-2000s were ordered. That order came in May 1949 from the Duluth, South Shore & Atlantic, a 550-mile road spanning upper Michigan and Wisconsin. The road was dieselizing its freight operations and also ordered three Baldwin DRS-6-6-1500 road-switchers (DSS&A already had Alco RS1s purchased in 1945). In brilliant yellow, green, and red livery, DSS&A DT-6-6-2000s 300-302 were placed in service at Superior, Wisconsin, in late October 1949. These units introduced a modification: The cooling system air intakes were moved from just above frame level to midway up the side of the carbody.

Insult was added to the meager 1949 orders when Eddystone missed selling transfer units to its best diesel customer, the Pennsylvania. In November 1949 Pennsy issued an order to Lima-Hamilton for 11 2500-h.p. centercab transfer units, locomotives similar to the DT-6-6-2000. Loss of the sale could be attributed to Baldwin's locomotive falling short of the Pennsylvania's horsepower requirements — PRR was on record as wanting approximately 2500 h.p. from each unit.

THE FINAL DAYS OF THE DT-6-6-2000 AT EDDYSTONE

In January 1950 DT-6-6-2000 demonstrator 2000 was sold to the Santa Fe, arriving on the AT&SF in March and entering service as No. 2606. Despite the end of the career of the "Bluebird," Baldwin was not yet finished, thank you, with demonstrating its transfer diesel. Back on June 6, 1948, the company had issued an order to construct seven DT-6-6-2000s. Three became DSS&A 300-302 in October 1949, two were canceled in the face of the coming production of the 1950 line, and two were completed for stock around February 1950. With two DT-6-6-2000s on hand, but no buyers, Baldwin — as it so often did — issued a demonstrator of an old design to help promote a new model, in this case the successor RT-624. Dressed in a somber one-color scheme and given BLW road number 2001, the unit worked eastern roads in the early summer of 1950, including a stint on the Central Railroad of New Jersey in July. That same month, DSS&A purchased the other homeless DT-6-6-2000 and placed it in service as No. 303 at Superior, Wisconsin, on August 23, 1950.

As it turned out, DT-6-6-2000 deliveries ended with the customer that had started it all: the Elgin, Joliet & Eastern. Demonstrator 2001, its sales stint complete, was sold to the J and became No. 126. Placed in service at Joliet on November 1, 1950, it would be the last transfer diesel sold to the J.

The final production count for the DT-6-6-2000 was 46 units, surely a disappointment to Baldwin. Between the time EJ&E 100 had been conceived and the end of DT-6-6-2000 production the standard road-switcher had become a powerful market force. By early 1950 Alco, F-M, and EMD road-switchers, plus Baldwin's own DRS-series road-switchers, could be purchased and operated far less expensively

Electro-Motive repowered 14 EJ&E DT-6-6-2000s using 567C V-12 power plants. EJ&E 903, posed against the snow at La Grange, Illinois, in February 1956, is ex-EJ&E 103.

than the DT-6-6-2000. Only in very special circumstances could the transfer unit's 400- to 500-h.p. advantage over standard road-switchers be economically applied.

THE SERVICE YEARS — MIXED RESULTS

The DT-6-6-2000 proved itself capable in service, although a handful of units ended their careers prematurely — and others survived in a form that hardly would have been recognized at Eddystone. On the EJ&E the big Baldwins provided mainline power, worked transfers, and handled heavy switching jobs for three decades. Many of the J units, however, went through a startling metamorphosis. In the EJ&E's demanding duty, the original Baldwin 606SC power plants were prone to failures that resulted in excessive down time and maintenance costs. As a cure the road dispatched three units — 103, 112, and 115 — to EMD in 1956. At La Grange they received EMD 567C V-12 engines (the original 606SC power plants were later used in EJ&E's Baldwin switchers). New hoods, lower and wider than the original Baldwin style, gave the transfer units a facelift, and new road numbers — in the 900 series — were applied. M.u. equipment was also added.

The V-12 567C engine was normally rated at 1200 h.p., but those installed in the EJ&E Baldwins could not be used at maximum capacity. The engine produced its rated horsepower at around 800 rpm, but in the DT-6-6-2000s the engines were mated to the original Westinghouse main generators, which were designed to turn at a maximum 625 rpm. Turning the generators faster than that resulted in "lots of fireworks" inside the hoods, so the EMD engines had to be slowed. This was not without its problems: At constant low rpm the engines suffered from poor lubrication and overheating. Eventually speed settings to suit both the power plants and generators were found and the repowerings were considered a tolerable success. Between 1956 and 1958 14 EJ&E DT-6-6-2000s were repowered at La Grange.

At the same time the EJ&E set out to cure the engine problems of others of its DT-6-6-2000s. Beginning with Nos. 107 and 108 the road's Joliet shops installed new 606A engines (the type used in the RT-624). Of the 12 units not repowered at EMD, 10 received 606A engines between 1956

and 1958, and each was given a new 700-series road number. The two DT-6-6-2000s not repowered were the oldest, one-of-a-kind No. 100, and EJ&E 118. Retaining its original form until its demise, J 100 spent its latter days confined to yard duty and was scrapped in November 1961; No. 118 was retired in 1967. EJ&E began cutting up its 606A-powered DT-6-6-2000s in 1966 and laid the last one — 722 (ex-122) — to rest in 1971. The EMD-repowered transfer units began to be retired in August 1969 with No. 913 (ex-113); last to operate was No. 903 (ex-103) in late 1975.

Cotton Belt 260 served remarkably long considering its loner status: It was the only Baldwin road diesel on the St. Louis Southwestern. Eastern Texas was home for the unit, which spent much of its career working Cotton Belt's Waco-Gatesville branch. In its last days SSW 260 wore the Cotton Belt's SP-inspired gray-and-scarlet scheme, and was traded to General Electric as credit on a U25B in 1963.

Santa Fe, which had shown confidence in the DT-6-6-2000 (with three separate, albeit small, orders), lost most of its enthusiasm for the Baldwins within a few years, but they survived into the 1960s. Not long for helper service (relocation of the Santa Fe's main line around Ash Fork ended the need for helpers there), the AT&SF units could be found from Los Angeles to the Pekin branch in Illinois (home of No. 2606). In their final days most of the DT-6-6-2000s worked Argentine Yard, and many ended their lives in storage at Argentine before the last was officially retired in February 1963.

Minneapolis, Northfield & Southern's DT-6-6-2000s replaced Russian Decapods when they arrived in 1949, and proved capable of conquering the grades of the Minnesota River valley that surrounded MN&S's base at Glenwood (Minneapolis), Minnesota. They were dubbed "Blue Dragons" (colors: blue, gray, red) by the men who ran and tended them. The first to be retired — No. 24 — was pulled from service about 1965. Two worked into the 1970s: No. 23 was retired in 1972 and No. 21 toiled on until August 1974. Miraculously, No. 21 survived in storage, and although MN&S is no more (it was merged into the Soo Line in 1982), No. 21 remains, preserved at the Illinois Railway Museum.

In the Searles Valley of California Trona's pair of DT-6-6-

TRAINS: J. David Ingles

In August 1973, after serving more than two decades in the Searles Valley of California, Trona's DT-6-6-2000s were purchased by Peabody Coal Co. At Baldwin, Illinois, a year later, ex-Trona 51 was dressed in Peabody yellow but not lettered.

At right, one of five DT-6-6-2000s placed in service in 1948-49 by the Minneapolis, Northfield & Southern, MN&S 21 lifts 40 cars up the 2 percent grade southbound out of the Minnesota River Valley near Savage in September 1958.

Following the arrival of a dynamic brake-equipped AS-616 (No. 52) in 1954 dynamic brakes were added to Trona's DT-6-6-2000s. The added resistor grids are on each end of No. 50's carbody, above the air intakes. Trailing the transfer unit as it departs Westend, California, bound for the SP interchange at Searles, are Trona 53 (an ex-SP AS-616) and No. 52.

William D. Middleton

Henry W. Brueckman

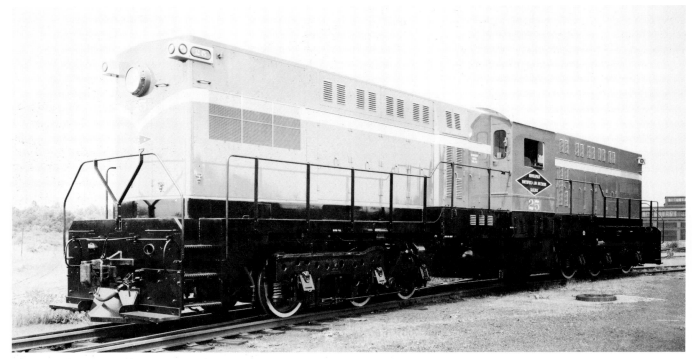

The only RT-624 not to wear Pennsy's Brunswick green, Minneapolis, Northfield & Southern 25 became the last of nine Baldwins on the MN&S when it joined the roster in 1953. The rest of MN&S' Baldwin congregation: one VO-660, one VO-1000, five DT-6-6-2000s, and one DRS-6-6-1500. Pennsylvania 8958-8965 were the only RT-624s built with dynamic brakes. After departing Eddystone, PRR 8958 put the option to good use in helper service based out of Conemaugh, Pennsylvania.

2000s (50-51) created a legacy of service not yet forgotten by employees or train-watchers. Hauling potash and borax trains of up to 2900 tons, the Baldwins bested both the tonnage and their desert environment for 23 years. The Trona supplemented the transfer units with a single Baldwin AS-616 (No. 52) in 1954. The 1600-h.p., C-C road-switcher was equipped with dynamic brakes when new, and to make the centercab units compatible Trona added dynamic braking to them. Later, an ex-SP AS-616 joined the roster, and it was not until 1973 that Trona put its DT-6-6-2000s to rest. Even then their careers were not over: Peabody Coal Company purchased the centercabs in August 1973 and moved them to its southwestern Illinois Baldwin stronghold. Around Lenzburg and Baldwin (yes, Baldwin), Illinois, Nos. 50-51 saw limited use until they were finally sold for scrap in September 1977.

Marquette, Michigan, was the home base of Duluth, South Shore & Atlantic's four DT-6-6-2000s, and from Marquette their primary duty was working road freights east to Sault Ste. Marie and St. Ignace, Michigan. On January 1, 1961, the DSS&A was merged into the Soo Line, and by 1962 DSS&A 300-303 had been renumbered Soo 396-399, respectively. The units remained in their original territory under Soo ownership, although some did call at Soo's

Shoreham (Minneapolis) facility. Number 396 was repainted in the Soo's solid maroon scheme, No. 397 received the road's later flashy red-and-white scheme, and 398-399 retained their original DSS&A colors to the end. EMD Geeps began replacing the big Baldwins on ex-DSS&A runs in 1964, and in 1965 Soo 396 and 398 were scrapped. The other two units were traded in to EMD in 1967.

A BRIEF REPRIEVE: THE RT-624

Despite lagging sales, Baldwin chose to include a transfer unit in its 1950 line of diesels. The 2400-h.p. RT-624 was the new entrant, and Eddystone offered a bundle of options including 24-RL brake equipment, Farr air filter panels, dual controls, dynamic brakes, hump control, m.u., roller bearings, and winterization equipment. Gear ratios of 15:63 and 15:68 were initially offered. The RT-624's length was penciled at 74' even, weight at 354,000 pounds. Westinghouse 480-FZ main generators and 370-DZ traction motors were employed. Starting tractive effort was 106,200 pounds at 30 percent adhesion (compared with 97,500 pounds for the AS-616 road-switcher). Basic price tag (sans options): $206,200 (versus $174,000 for an AS-616).

It is likely that Pennsy's 1949 purchase of the Lima-Hamilton 2500-h.p. transfer units loomed large in Baldwin's decision to offer a new transfer model, and Eddystone lost no time in making up for its missed opportunity. In August 1950 Baldwin landed an order from the PRR for 14 RT-624s (PRR placed an order with Lima-Hamilton for 11 more 2500-h.p. transfer units at the same time). Shipments (PRR 8952-8965) ran from August to November 1951, and the units varied in their optional equipment. All 14 were equipped with roller bearing trucks, and only the first two — 8952-8953 — were not equipped for m.u. These were originally assigned to Conway, Pennsylvania, and Cleveland, Ohio, respectively. PRR 8958-8965 were equipped

with dynamic braking, which necessitated the addition of large resistor grids on each side of the carbody above the cooling system air intakes. These RT-624s were assigned to Conemaugh, Shire Oaks, and Johnstown, Pennsylvania. (Conemaugh units worked as west slope helpers.)

With the completion of its first order, PRR ordered eight more RT-624s (8724-8731) in November 1951. These units would look different, because Baldwin now offered another option, an improved, outside-equalized C-type truck to provide a better ride at speeds over 35 mph (see page 102). Pennsy chose the new truck, a rigid-bolster design produced by General Steel Castings, for its second order. The units were shipped between October 3 and December 23, 1952. Two units, Nos. 8725-8726, went to Elmira, New York, the rest to Philadelphia.

Only delivery of PRR's eight RT-624s kept 1952 from being a disaster for the big transfer model; not a single new order was received that year. True, orders placed for diesel locomotives in the U. S. were down by half from 1951, but the 1952 total — 1829 units — still represented a sturdy market. It looked as if the horsepower boost had provided only a brief reprieve for the transfer unit, and that unsettling fear became fact by 1953. In January, MN&S ordered a lone RT-624 to supplement its DT-6-6-2000 roster, and with its final Baldwin 14-unit order in June 1953, PRR indicated it needed but one more RT-624.

Paramount among the RT-624's problems was Fairbanks-Morse's new H24-66 — the Train Master. At 2400 h.p. the new F-M offering matched the power of the RT-624 and did so with a single power plant. The Train Master could equal the RT-624's tractive effort, outpace it, and at 66′ long was more compact. F-M delivered 29 H24-66s in 1953 and 39 in 1954. With the shipment of MN&S RT-624 No. 25 (equipped with Commonwealth trucks) in July 1953 and Pennsy RT-624 No. 8113 (which closely followed the specifications of PRR's second group of RT-624s) in February 1954, shipments of Baldwin transfer units ended.

NOT EVEN A SCORE OF YEARS

What became of the 24 RT-624s? Minneapolis, Northfield & Southern 25 — just an oddball DT-6-6-2000 to the shop forces at Glenwood — survived only 12 years (until 1965), and was outlived by all but one of the road's DT-6-6-2000s. Pennsy's 23 units were assigned to heavy transfers, main-

J. David Ingles

Soo Line's modern red-and-white image may seem incongruous on a DT-6-6-2000, but here's proof, ex-DSS&A Soo 397 at Marquette, Michigan, in June 1965.

line drag freights, ore runs, and hump duty. Philadelphia was home to many of them; units with the newer outside-equalized trucks were employed regularly as mainline pushers to Paoli, Pennsylvania, and worked other duties (such as the Belvidere, New Jersey, branch out of Trenton) while the original Commonwealth-truck-equipped units often tended the Schuylkill Division to Reading and Pottsville, Pennsylvania. Elsewhere, Pennsy 8959-8960 worked as hump engines at Pitcairn, Pennsylvania, for years, and RT-624s made appearances at Mingo Junction, Ohio (8954-8957 were originally assigned there).

The RT-624s from Pennsy's original order of 14 units were all retired in July 1966, and the eight units from the second order followed in October 1967. PRR's last RT-624 purchased — 8113 — was its last to turn a wheel, too. After working around Philadelphia throughout its career, the unit was renumbered PRR 8966 in 1966, then 08966 in the face of the Penn Central merger in 1968. It was officially retired — at age 15 — by Penn Central in June 1969. Although several ex-Pennsy RT-624s remained in storage for some time at Altoona after retirement, they have been scrapped and the model is now extinct.

Jim Edmonston collection

Production of the RT-624 ended with the shipment of Pennsylvania No. 8113 in February 1954. The RT-624 rode Baldwin's optional GSC outside-equalized C-type truck.

Baldwin was at the forefront in development of diesel heavy road-switchers. Completed in November 1946, BLW DRS-6-4-1500 demonstrator No. 1500 weighed 283,000 pounds.

EDDYSTONE'S TRIPLETS

Heavy road-switchers

FOLLOWING THE 1941 DEBUT of Alco-GE's RS1, the railroad industry began to take notice of the advantages of road-switchers. These utilitarian diesels eliminated the need to turn locomotives at the ends of runs (or to have cab-equipped units at each end of a multiple-unit set), and could work main lines, branches, and even yards. The only real limit to the RS1 was that it was actually a light road-switcher with but modest power (1000 h.p.). After the interruption of World War Two both Alco-GE and Baldwin stood ready to up the ante in the road-switcher race by introducing heavy-duty, 1500-h.p. units.

Baldwin's introduction of heavy road-switchers had its roots in design work conducted in 1944. With the end of the war and development of the 1500-h.p. 608SC engine, those plans were ready to bear fruit. In 1945 W. A. Trayler, master mechanic of the 168-mile Columbus & Greenville Railway in Mississippi, had decided to dieselize, and he believed the best unit for the C&G would be a 1500-h.p. model with six axles to distribute weight, four of which would be powered (the line included spindly trestles and light, 60-pound rail). Because the units would serve as switchers as well as road engines, a bidirectional road-switcher design was called for.

Baldwin's answer to Trayler and the C&G was the DRS-6-4-1500 (A1A-A1A) road-switcher. Trayler was sold (he had also contacted EMD and Alco-GE, but received no firm bid from either), and on September 19, 1945, the C&G ordered five units. The locomotives would be plain-vanilla diesels — no m.u., steam generators, or dynamic brakes. Each would cost $117,500, and Eddystone promised the first

for testing in January 1946 (delays would postpone delivery until late 1946).

In the same month Baldwin received the C&G's order, Eddystone's salesmen also landed another DRS-6-4-1500 order. It was for 24 units, and came from the French Supply Council, which represented the rail systems of French North Africa (Morocco, Algeria, and Tunisia). Together, the C&G and FSC orders gave Baldwin a solid base for beginning heavy road-switcher production.

Baldwin's new DRS-6-4-1500 called for the 608SC engine to be mated to a Westinghouse main generator, which in turn would drive four Westinghouse 370-series traction motors in General Steel Castings' Commonwealth A1A trucks (see page 66 for a description). GSC also supplied the frame, a cast design, with fabricated side members welded in place by Baldwin. The side members were blended into the steps at each end of the locomotive, and the steps and pilots were fabricated assemblies, bolted on. The cab was over the rear truck (the long hood was considered to be "front"), and the electrical cabinet was between the cab and power plant, which had its generator end toward the cab.

On the front of the frame stood a 300-gallon cooling system. Air intakes for the cooling system and traction motor blowers were side-mounted at the front of the long hood, just above frame level. A pair of electrically driven fans on top of the hood exhausted engine cooling air, and automatic shutters controlled cooling system temperature. The short rear hood had several possible uses. One was to house an 800-gallon fuel tank to supplement or replace a 1000-gallon underbelly tank (actually, the 800-gallon tank became

The era of the 1500-h.p. road-switcher dawned on October 8, 1946, when Columbus & Greenville DRS-6-4-1500 No. 601 was placed in service. Baldwin's first domestic road-switcher was the first 1500-h.p. road-switcher by any manufacturer to enter U. S. service.

standard equipment and the 1000-gallon tank optional). Another was to house dynamic braking equipment, with side-mounted resistor grids and top-mounted air exhaust. Yet another short-hood option was a steam generator. In units equipped for steam heating, both the 1000-gallon underbelly tank and the 800-gallon hood tank would be used, one for diesel fuel, the other for water; the customer would choose. The unit could not be equipped with both dynamic brakes and a steam generator.

Eddystone built the first Columbus & Greenville unit — No. 601 — and the first DRS-6-4-1500 for French North Africa — No. 040-DA-1 — together in mid-1946. When completed, C&G 601 weighed 280,000 pounds, with 187,000 pounds on drivers. The locomotive measured 58' long inside coupler knuckles, stood 14' tall, and was 10' wide. It was capable of exerting 42,800 pounds of continuous tractive effort (at 10.5 mph), and with its 15:63 gearing could sprint to 65 mph. Only minor modifications made for foreign conditions — low-clearance cab, left-hand drive, pilot-mounted headlamps, and coupling buffers — set the first export DRS-6-4-1500 apart from its American sister.

C&G 601 departed Eddystone in September 1946, eight months after its promised delivery date. At that, because of labor problems the landmark locomotive rushed out of the shops painted solid green. C&G 601 arrived at Columbus, Mississippi, and was placed in service on October 8, 1946. The purchase contract specified that the first locomotive would have to be accepted by the road before further deliveries were made, and as a result the next unit — No. 602 — did not depart Eddystone until December 10, 1946. C&G 603 followed two days later and all five locomotives were in service by January 22, 1947.

Between the deliveries of C&G 601 and the rest of the C&G order, Eddystone had turned its attention to producing additional FSC units and one more domestic DRS-6-4-1500 — Baldwin demonstrator 1500, completed in November 1946. Similar to C&G 601, there were a few differences: BLW 1500 was equipped with a Westinghouse 489-B main generator (C&G 601 used a 470-series), carried a Clarkson Vapor 1600 lb./hr. steam generator, and, at 283,000 pounds, weighed slightly more. Baldwin billed its new demonstrator

as "A 1500-h.p. locomotive that will haul branch line freight or passenger trains, yet has sufficient power at slow speeds for switching assignments between runs." Outfitted in dark red with silver striping, BLW 1500 departed Eddystone on a demonstration tour in mid-November 1946, and the unit worked on the New Haven and Central Railroad of New Jersey, coupling onto both passenger and freight consists.

Deliveries of the French Supply Council DRS-6-4-1500s began in December 1946. By then, the French organization's orders had increased to 52 units. In addition to the French Supply Council locomotives which differed little from domestic units, a group of unusual DRS-6-4-1500s were also rolling out of Eddystone to fill these FSC orders. The uncommon units had their engine compartments tightly sealed and each unit was fitted with a large Roto-Clone mechanical filter to clean air routed to the power plant, main generator, and traction-motor blowers. These units were ordered primarily to dieselize a 300-mile line south from Oujda, Morocco (on the border with Algeria), through the Sahara desert, and the special equipment was needed to prevent sand from making its way into the engine and electrical gear — with disastrous results. Air for the engine cooling system was still drawn in through front-mounted intakes, which were fitted with fine-screen covers. The Roto-Clone equipment was installed on the carbody sides behind the engine, requiring that the cab be moved to the end of the unit. Eleven Roto-Clone-equipped DRS-6-4-1500s were delivered through late 1947. Meanwhile, delivery of the remainder of the "standard" DRS-6-4-1500s for the French Supply Council ran through March 1948. The Roto-Clone units were based at Oujda and Algiers, Algeria; standard units also worked from Oujda; Constantine, Oran, and Algiers, Algeria; and Tunis, Tunisia.

FROM ONE DESIGN: TRIPLETS

Baldwin had a marketable commodity in its 1500-h.p. road-switcher, particularly so because the unit could be built in three variations. To suit the Columbus & Greenville and French North Africa's railroads the first road-switchers had been equipped with A1A trucks, but the new

Promoted by Baldwin as a multipurpose diesel, red-and-silver DRS-6-4-1500 demonstrator 1500 lived up to its billing on the Central Railroad of New Jersey, handling freight (far right) and passenger duties. The passenger train is departing Elizabethport, New Jersey.

locomotive could also ride B- or C-type trucks. By substituting trucks and ballasting for the intended service, three different DRS-series road-switchers could be offered. This put Baldwin a step ahead of the competition (Alco offered 1500-h.p. B-B and A1A-A1A versions of its RS-series in 1946, but did not build a C-C version until the 1600-h.p. RSD4 of 1951), and once DRS-6-4-1500 production was under way, Baldwin wasted little time in selling the other versions. The first order for the B-B version — the DRS-4-4-1500 — came in March 1946. The model would mark Baldwin's first use of the GSC four-axle Commonwealth truck, a swing-bolster design with double drop-equalizers suited to high-speed operation. The truck had a wheelbase of 10'-8".

Bethlehem Steel's Iron Mines Co. of Venezuela was the first DRS-4-4-1500 customer, ordering three units for use in South America. Western Maryland became the first U. S.

railroad to order the DRS-4-4-1500 when it inked a contract for one unit in July 1946. WM was sampling a variety of diesels (the road also purchased a pair of EMD F3As and one Alco-GE RS2 at about the same time), but Baldwin diesels certainly were no strangers to the "Fast Freight Line." Already at work were four VO-660s and five VO-1000s, and two DS-4-4-1000 switchers were ordered along with the DRS-4-4-1500. Nor did WM's allegiance to Baldwin run only to diesels: Under construction at Eddystone at the time were the road's last steam locomotives — a dozen J1 4-8-4s.

The first significant sales breakthrough for the DRS-4-4-1500 occurred in February 1947 when the Minneapolis, St. Paul & Sault Ste. Marie (the Soo Line), a railroad with only one Baldwin diesel (a VO-1000) on its roster, ordered eight of the road-switchers. The order was all the more promising because it was Soo Line's first bid for diesel road locomo-

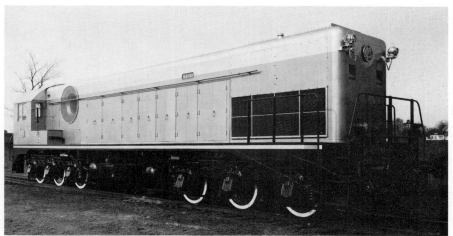

In the early 1960s U. S. builders called sealed carbodies and central air intakes major advances in locomotive design. More than a decade earlier Baldwin built 15 Roto-Clone-equipped DRS-6-4-1500s for desert operation. DA-101 went to Algeria.

tives for itself (the company, controlled by Canadian Pacific, had previously ordered Alco-GE RS1s on behalf of the Duluth, South Shore & Atlantic, another CP subsidiary). In the more cautious mold of the WM, the New York Central ordered a pair of DRS-4-4-1500s in March 1947. With an eye toward putting the Baldwins in secondary passenger service, NYC specified that both units be equipped with SKF roller bearings and steam generators.

While the four-axle unit made its initial strides the six-axle models also drew the attention of railroad chief mechanical officers. As Eddystone pushed out the 52 DRS-6-4-1500s for North Africa, the Norfolk Southern stepped forward in March 1947 with an order for 10 DRS-6-4-1500s. Norfolk Southern was no newcomer to diesel locomotives; Baldwin had delivered the road's first diesels in January 1947 — DS-4-4-660s 661-662 and DS-4-4-1000s 1001-1002 —

and another 660-h.p. switcher (NS 663) was due out soon. The DRS-6-4-1500s would dieselize all through trains on the road's 399-mile main line, thereby putting NS's diminutive Baldwin 2-8-4s out to pasture. Another southern line, the 144-mile Savannah & Atlanta Railway, joined C&G and NS as DRS-6-4-1500 buyers when Eddystone's men returned from Savannah, Georgia, with an order for eight units in May 1947. The S&A units were to be equipped with an unusual GSC Commonwealth A1A truck, a floating-bolster design with rubber members placed between the truck bolster and truck sideframes in place of the conventional swing hanger suspension.

Logically, it should have been far from the world of light-rail roads such as S&A or C&G that Baldwin would sell its first C-C road-switcher, and so it was. In May 1947 the Chicago & North Western put the final DRS-series heavy road-

William D. Middleton

Thousands of miles from its birthplace, a Roto-Clone DRS-6-4-1500 drums into Oujda, Morocco, with the overnight *Morocco-Algeria Express* from Casablanca.

Most French North African DRS-6-4-1500s were very similar to the domestic version. Twin pilot-mounted head lamps, low-clearance cabs, and open-end pilots were the major external differences. Unit DA-5 was constructed in fall 1946.

Raised cab and dynamic brakes characterized Iron Mines Company of Venezuela's trio of DRS-4-4-1500s. Number 1 was completed in June 1947 and placed in service in October.

Western Maryland 170 was the first DRS-4-4-1500 placed in service. The 250,000-pound unit also marked Baldwin's first use of GSC's two-axle Commonwealth road truck.

First of 10 DRS-6-4-1500s on Norfolk Southern was No. 1501, which entered service on October 7, 1947. A fully enclosed, welded pilot replaced the steam locomotive-like slatted pilots used on earlier Baldwin heavy road-switchers.

Baldwin pioneered the concept of modern, six-motor heavy road-switchers. The first DRS-6-6-1500s were Chicago & North Western 1500-1502. After having its portrait taken in the snow at Eddystone, C&NW 1500 entered service on February 18, 1948.

switcher model into the order book with a reservation for three C-C units, designation DRS-6-6-1500.

The first three DRS-4-4-1500s — one for the WM and two for IMofV — were completed in June and July 1947. Western Maryland was the first to take delivery, placing WM 170 in service on July 5, 1947. Dressed in black with gold striping, WM 170 weighed 250,000 pounds (30,000 pounds less than C&G 601) but offered 45,000 pounds of tractive effort at 10 mph (2200 pounds more than C&G 601, because all weight was on drivers). Number 170 was placed in service at Baltimore, but soon after was stationed at Hagerstown, Maryland, for local freight service.

In deference to the conditions in which they would work, the DRS-4-4-1500s built for Iron Mines Co. of Venezuela differed significantly from the WM unit. In the company's ore pits in Venezuela the road-switchers would have to negotiate stiff grades and provide air to unload side-dump ore cars, so they were built with dynamic brakes (the first Baldwin road-switchers so equipped) and oversize air reservoirs. Because the dynamic brake equipment filled the short hood, the air reservoirs were mounted on the frame, underneath the cab. This in turn required that the cab be raised in an unusual, and somewhat unsightly, manner. IMofV 1 and 2 were delivered in October 1947, and a third identical unit — No. 3 — in March 1948.

CAUSE FOR OPTIMISM — THEN CONCERN

In late 1947 the flow of heavy road-switchers out of Eddystone and the new road-switcher orders coming in were cause for optimism. In August, U. S. Steel's Tennessee Coal Iron & Railroad and Kaiser Engineering Co. became the second and third buyers for the DRS-6-6-1500 when TCI&RR placed an order for two units and Kaiser for one.

Kaiser's unit was earmarked for Kaiser Steel's Eagle Mountain Railway, which was under construction in California. The first Norfolk Southern DRS-6-4-1500 — maroon, yellow, and black 1501 — was shipped south to Berkley, Virginia (near Norfolk), and entered service on October 7, 1947. This unit introduced the first, albeit minor, changes in DRS-series design. Gone was the slatted pilot used on C&G's five DRS-6-4-1500s, BLW 1500, WM 170, and the IMofV DRS-4-4-1500s, discontinued in favor of a fully enclosed welded pilot. The size of the cooling system air intakes was reduced slightly as well (and would be again, in early 1948).

Western Maryland issued an order for two more DRS-4-4-1500s in October 1947. For Baldwin, this repeat order was particularly heartening, because it meant WM 170 — in service less than four months — had already met with its owner's approval. At the same time Eddystone took another heavy road-switcher order, this one from Northern Pacific. NP, already operating 31 Baldwin switchers (28 VO-1000s and three VO-660s) ordered one DRS-6-6-1500 and two steam generator-equipped DRS-4-4-1500s. As the year wound down, the orders kept coming: The French Supply Council requested another three DRS-6-4-1500s (upping its total to 55 units), and California's McCloud River Railroad signed its first diesel purchase order — for one DRS-6-6-1500.

At year-end 1947 Eddystone was completing Soo Line's DRS-4-4-1500 order. The first unit, No. 360, revealed another design change. Gone from the frame were the ornate side members; simple, less expensive, straight-cut side members replaced them. Soo 360 was placed in service at Minneapolis, Minnesota, on December 1, 1947.

By December 31, 1947, Baldwin had built and shipped 56 heavy road-switchers, and the company's budding success

Soo Line 360 was the first of eight DRS-4-4-1500s on that road. The unit introduced the use of simple, straight-cut frame side members on Baldwin's heavy road-switchers.

Baldwin's second DRS-6-4-1500 demonstrator, dark green-and-yellow 1501, poses for its portrait in March 1948.

with the type carried into early 1948. January was a time of farewell and a time of welcome at Eddystone when DRS-6-4-1500 demonstrator 1500 ended its company days and was sold to the Union Pacific, becoming UP 1250. The first six-axle road-switcher to wear UP livery, 1250 was shipped to Spokane, Washington, where it began chores for its new owner on January 25, 1948. Meanwhile, Eddystone took the wraps off the DRS-6-6-1500 with completion of C&NW 1500-1502. The new model stood apart from its A1A-A1A sister in several ways. First, it employed the GSC Commonwealth C-type truck, with a 13' wheelbase versus 11'-6" for the A1A. Both the 1000-gallon underbelly fuel tank and the 800-gallon short hood tank were standard equipment (excepting units with dynamic brakes, of course). Standard weight was pegged at 325,000 pounds and starting tractive effort at 81,250 pounds. But the three C&NW units were not quite standard — the fuel tank in the short hood was omitted, and each unit weighed only 287,000 pounds. C&NW 1500 and 1501 entered service at Milwaukee, Wisconsin, on February 18 and February 17, 1948, respectively; No. 1502 was brought to life at Chicago on February 21.

As if to celebrate the C&NW-sponsored premiere of the

DRS-6-6-1500, Baldwin salesmen took two more orders for C-C heavy road-switchers in January 1948. U. S. Steel's Pittsburgh road, the Union Railroad Co., contracted for seven units in a step toward total dieselization, and its neighboring U. S. Steel line, Bessemer & Lake Erie, ordered two. Baldwin workmen, meanwhile, were busy building DRS-6-4-1500s — including one unit of particular interest to the front office. Tacked onto a production run which included French Supply Council units and Norfolk Southern 1502-1510 was DRS-6-4-1500 demonstrator 1501. The unit was operational at Eddystone in early February 1948, and was first used as the guinea pig for a troubleshooting class held for customers' employees. On March 14, 1948, dressed in dark green with yellow trim, it was dispatched on a western sales tour. The first stop was the Southern Pacific (Texas & New Orleans) at El Paso, Texas, on April 10, 1948. The unit worked on the SP, California Western, McCloud River Railroad, and Western Pacific, and ended its tour on Utah's seven-mile Tooele Valley Railway. While it was there, officials of Kennecott Copper Co. inspected and rode the unit — and bought it on the spot. The locomotive was delivered to Kennecott at Magna, Utah (where it be-

No m.u. here! Diminutive McCloud River 15 gets help from DRS-6-4-1500 demonstrator 1501 in 1948. The road had ordered its first diesel, a DRS-6-6-1500, the year before.

Savannah & Atlanta No. 100 was one of eight DRS-6-4-1500s placed in service on the S&A in 1948. The units featured an uncommon variant of General Steel Castings' A1A truck.

All DRS-6-6-1500s rode on Commonwealth 13'-wheelbase C-Type trucks. Northern Pacific 177, delivered in 1948, was the road's first C-C road-switcher, and it remained the only such unit on NP until GE U25Cs arrived in 1964.

came Kennecott Copper No. 901), on October 28, 1948.

In June 1948 Southern Pacific responded to the tour of BLW 1501 with the largest heavy road-switcher order Baldwin had received: three DRS-6-4-1500s and 10 DRS-6-6-1500s for SP proper, plus two DRS-6-6-1500s for subsidiary

T&NO. That same month C&NW contracted for a single DRS-6-4-1500, and in May Missouri Pacific (through subsidiary St. Louis, Brownsville & Mexico) had ordered four DRS-4-4-1500s. But from July on, sales flattened out. The exceptions: Lehigh Valley ordered one 1500-h.p. B-B unit in

John C. Illman

Two steam generator-equipped DRS-4-4-1500s went to Northern Pacific in 1948. NP 500 (ex-175) pauses with Train 422 at Tacoma, Washington, on July 4, 1951.

C. B. Kniskern

First Baldwin road-switcher to wear "Southern Pacific," DRS-6-4-1500 No. 5200 was placed in service at Albany, Oregon, August 22, 1948. Note the train number-boards atop the long hood. At left, year-old C&NW DRS-6-4-1500 No. 1504 stood idle at Kaukauna, Wisconsin, on Sunday, May 29, 1949.

September, BLW 1501 was sold to Kennecott, and Kaiser Engineering purchased a second DRS-6-6-1500 for Eagle Mountain Railway (this order was placed shortly after Kaiser received its first DRS-6-6-1500, No. 1010A, in August). With the poor showing in the final months, sales of heavy road-switchers for 1948 ended at 33 units.

Meanwhile, production churned on: All heavy road-switchers ordered in 1947 were shipped by the end of November 1948. Included were Savannah & Atlanta's eight DRS-6-4-1500s (100-107). With their arrival at Savannah in May and June 1948, the new Eddystone products put some older Baldwins — S&A's little 500-class 2-8-2s — on the endangered species list. Northern Pacific's one DRS-6-

Bessemer & Lake Erie

Bessemer & Lake Erie 401, at K-O Junction (near Osgood, Pennsylvania) with local freight MX-4, was one of seven DRS-6-6-1500s purchased by B&LE. Below, C&O DRS-6-6-1500 No. 5530 joined the roster in November 1949, only two months after Baldwin delivered ten 2-6-6-2s (Eddystone's last steam locomotives for a U. S. common carrier) to the road.

Ordered with m.u. equipment and SKF roller bearings on its trucks, Erie DRS-4-4-1500 No. 1104 was intended for road service working out of Buffalo, New York. The black-and-yellow Baldwin entered Erie service on December 8, 1949.

6-1500 (177) and pair of DRS-4-4-1500s (175-176) were sent west in late summer. NP 177 (soon renumbered 525) took up freight duty at Missoula, Montana, on August 12, 1948, and DRS-4-4-1500s 175-176 (renumbered 500-501 shortly thereafter) were placed in service at Spokane, Washington, on September 22-23, 1948. The four-axle Baldwins held down local passenger jobs and filled in with freight work.

Deliveries in the latter half of 1948 also included a handful of heavy road-switchers ordered earlier that same year. C&NW's DRS-6-4-1500, No. 1504, was placed in service at Chicago on July 15, 1948, and shortly thereafter began branchline duty out of Kaukauna, Wisconsin, to Manitowoc and Merrillan, Wisconsin. SP's first DRS-6-4-1500, No. 5200, started its career at Albany, Oregon, on August 22, 1948, and 5201 joined it there on December 16. SP's third DRS-6-4-1500, No. 5202, was placed in service at Lordsburg, New Mexico, on December 21, 1948.

Equipped with a steam generator and train air signals, Lehigh Valley's lone DRS-4-4-1500, No. 200, was completed in November 1948, but prior to delivery the unit took a quick turn as a Baldwin demonstrator. For one week beginning November 18, 1948, LV 200 was turned over to the Pennsy for trials on the PRR-controlled Long Island. In December the maroon-and-black DRS-4-4-1500 was delivered to the LV at East Penn Junction (Allentown, Pennsylvania), and was placed in service at Sayre. Shortly thereafter, LV 200 was working out of Buffalo, New York, including secondary passenger duties.

At year end, Eddystone's heavy road-switcher deliveries for 1948 stood at 54 units: 34 DRS-6-4-1500s, 12 DRS-4-4-1500s, and 8 DRS-6-6-1500s.

MORE SLUGGISH SALES

While 1949 was a respectable year for America's locomotive builders, Baldwin's heavy road-switcher line did not fare well. During the year not a single domestic DRS-6-4-1500 order was received, and only a two-unit order for Roto-Clone DRS-6-4-1500s from the Moroccan Railway (the railroads of French North Africa placed their own orders by this time) would keep that production line alive. In fact, no

DRS-6-4-1500 would ever again be built for use in its homeland (SP 5202 was the last). The DRS-4-4-1500 garnered but two orders: Erie ordered six units in May, and Pennsylvania-Reading Seashore Lines the same number in November. PRSL specified steam generators and Timken roller bearings, and these locomotives proved to be the last DRS-4-4-1500s ordered.

Something of a late bloomer, the DRS-6-6-1500 attracted orders from seven railroads in 1949. Four new customers joined the waiting line: Duluth, South Shore & Atlantic; Minneapolis, Northfield & Southern; Erie; and Chesapeake & Ohio. All ordered cautiously: C&O and DSS&A three units each, MN&S and Erie one apiece. Three railroads were repeat DRS-6-6-1500 buyers: C&NW and the Union Railroad five each, while Southern Pacific provided cause for celebration with an order for 17 more (15 for SP, 2 for subsidiary T&NO).

Included in this SP order — placed in June 1949, just as SP and T&NO were receiving their first 12 DRS-6-6-1500s — was one unit that would be unique — a cabless booster. SP, like many railroads, was concerned about labor union pressure to place a crew in the cab of each locomotive in a multiple-unit consist. This was not a problem with the first dozen SP/T&NO DRS-6-6-1500s because they were not equipped for m.u., but the SP locomotives in the second order were to be employed in duties requiring paired units, so m.u. capability was a must (the T&NO units in the second order were not ordered with m.u.). As a ploy against being forced to use more than one crew, SP (with encouragement from Baldwin) ordered one cabless booster. (With an eye toward later applying a cab, SP specified that all piping and wiring that would normally lead into the cab be installed.)

By the end of 1949 49 heavy road-switchers had been ordered. While Baldwin had delivered its heavy road-switchers to a respectable number of customers (17 through 1948), most were small-quantity orders, and only SP's commitment approached a big sale. And the competition had stiffened; by mid-1949 EMD was accepting orders for its 1500-h.p. GP7, and production began in October. (The GP7's predecessor, the BL2, had not represented a particu-

Jay Potter collection

Pennsylvania-Reading Seashore Lines 6000-6005 were the last DRS-4-4-1500s built. Photographed at Camden, New Jersey, July 4, 1950, PRSL 6000 was less than three months old.

William D. Middleton

At top, SP DRS-6-6-1500 No. 5218 is dwarfed by the surroundings as it works the Hillsboro-Tillamook, Oregon, branch. Above, only one DRS-6-6-1500 served the Minneapolis, Northfield & Southern. On September 22, 1958, MN&S 15 switches in the yards at Auto Club Junction before heading up the branch to Richfield, Minnesota.

larly significant threat, ringing up only 58 sales in 1948/49.) Fairbanks-Morse, which began building its four-axle, 1500-h.p. H15-44 in 1947, had played an even smaller role in the battle for road-switcher sales than did EMD and its BL2. F-M sifted sales of a mere 30 units from the market in 1947-1949. Before the arrival of the GP7, the Alco-GE RS2 had been the real thorn in Baldwin's side. All told, more than 350 RS2s would be ordered and built (through February 1950) and 70 A1A-A1A RSC2s would be added to that. And while Baldwin's DRS-6-6-1500 stood alone as a C-C diesel, the demand for six-axle power was still formative.

Although not prolific in turning out heavy road-switchers, the erecting hall was nonetheless a colorful place in 1949. Through August, Baldwin's craftsmen tended to the

orders that had been placed in 1948. In addition to the first 12 DRS-6-6-1500s for SP/T&NO, sister units for Bessemer & Lake Erie (2), Union (7), and Kaiser Steel (1) departed in the first eight months of 1949. They were joined by Missouri Pacific's four DRS-4-4-1500s — St. Louis, Brownsville & Mexico Nos. 4112-4115.

SP's first DRS-6-6-1500s (5203-5212) were parceled out to Los Angeles and Arizona (Globe and Tucson), and the T&NO pair (187-188) were assigned to Algiers, Louisiana, for New Orleans-area transfer duty. At least one of SP's Los Angeles-based units, 5212, was lettered for SP-subsidiary Pacific Electric and equipped with a trolley pole to actuate PE's crossing signals. B&LE used its Baldwins (401-402) mostly as heavy switchers and on local freights. Union's DRS-6-6-1500s (originally numbered 608-614, then renumbered 613-619 before delivery) were put to work serving Pittsburgh-area steel mills along the road's main line. A short run — 52 miles — was also the order of business for the Kaiser Steel DRS-6-6-1500s. The pair, 1010A (1948) and 1010B (1949), lugged ore trains from Eagle Mountain Mine to Kaiser's connection with the SP at Ferrum, California. To control long strings of ore jimmies on grades of up to 2.15 percent, both were equipped with dynamic brakes, and their appearance was also marked by the installation of large gyrating safety lights on small platforms immediately above the headlights. MoPac's (StLB&M) DRS-4-4-1500s entered service in late February and early March 1949 and were assigned to the Kingsville and Palestine Divisions.

Eddystone next began to fill 1949 orders. By year end C&NW's five DRS-6-6-1500s (1505-1509), DSS&A's three units (200-202), C&O's trio of C-Cs (5530-5532) and Union's second batch of DRS-6-6-1500s (620-624) had been placed in service. The Moroccan Railway's order for two DRS-6-4-1500s was filled (both units were Roto-Clone-equipped), as was Erie's order for six DRS-4-4-1500s (1100-1105). Baldwin also made partial deliveries on SP's 17-unit DRS-6-6-1500 order (SP 5213-5227; T&NO 189-190). Production of heavy road-switchers for 1949 ended at 57 units (11 DRS-4-4-1500s, 2 DRS-6-4-1500s, and 44 DRS-6-6-1500s).

Customer specifications and two design changes lent individuality to many of the units constructed in 1949. C&NW 1505-1509 featured large gyrating safety lights encased in special shrouds on top of the hoods. The North Western units went to work at Norfolk, Nebraska, in Au-

Operator of the largest fleet of DRS-6-6-1500s, Southern Pacific rostered 25 units, plus four assigned to subsidiary Texas & New Orleans. T&NO 190 began its revenue-earning days at Fort Worth, Texas, on December 7, 1949. SP 5227 was the only cabless DRS-6-6-1500 built. The booster had dynamic brakes and a "swayback mule" frame.

gust 1949. Erie DRS-4-4-1500s 1100-1105 were built with SKF roller bearing truck journals and m.u., and the optional equipment was put to good use in road freight service out of Buffalo, New York. Effective with the Erie DRS-4-4-1500s and Union's second group of DRS-6-6-1500s those two models began sporting air intakes raised to a position halfway up the carbody side.

Effective with T&NO DRS-6-6-1500 189, which entered service in December 1949, the C-C road-switchers were equipped with a welded frame, with end steps and pilots bolted on. This was Eddystone's first use of a welded frame on a road-switcher. Unfortunately, the design details of this new frame had been overseen by engineering personnel transferred to Baldwin from parent Westinghouse. Unfa-

miliar with the idiosyncrasies of diesel locomotive design, the engineers included no inverse camber in the frame (many locomotive frames are built bowed up in the middle so they will flatten out when the heavy internal components are added). When the 52,500-pound 608SC power plant and its 471-series main generator were eased into place, the new frames sagged in the middle. Baldwin employees immediately nicknamed the units built with this frame "swayback mules," but other than in appearance the problem was not serious and production continued.

CURTAIN CALL FOR THE DRS-SERIES

As the new standard line of 606-, 606A-, and 608A-powered locomotives took form on the drawing tables in

The grilles on the rear hood of McCloud River DRS-6-6-1500 No. 29 are for its dynamic brake equipment. The road's second DRS-6-6-1500, No. 29 was placed in service in 1950.

early 1950 the curtain calls for the DRS-series road-switchers began. For all intents and purposes, 1950 belonged to the DRS-6-6-1500. The exceptions: PRSL's six DRS-4-4-1500s ordered in 1949 (6000-6005) were delivered to Camden, New Jersey, in April 1950, and in August the Moroccan Railway ordered another two Roto-Clone DRS-6-4-1500s, this time for delivery in 1951. Meanwhile, the C-C unit continued in its role as late bloomer — and best seller. By January 31, 1950, shipment of the second order for SP/T&NO was complete. T&NO 189-190 were assigned to Fort Worth, Texas, while SP 5213-5227 were distributed among Tucson, Arizona (3), San Diego, California (2), and Portland, Oregon (10). Among the Oregon group was SP 5227, the one-of-a-kind DRS-6-6-1500B. The booster and its standard mates became particularly noted for working the SP's rugged Hillsboro-Tillamook (Oregon) branch.

In March 1950 Minneapolis, Northfield & Southern's one DRS-6-6-1500 (No. 15) was placed in service. The blue-and-gray unit joined five DT-6-6-2000 transfer units working out of Glenwood, Minnesota. Meanwhile, more orders arrived: By April 1950, Erie's commitment to the DRS-6-6-1500 had grown from one unit ordered in 1949 to an even dozen. Erie 1150-1161 were built with m.u. and roller bear-

ing trucks, and nine (1153-1161) were equipped with dynamic brakes. Delivered in April through September 1950, they were assigned to Salamanca, New York. Repeat DRS-6-6-1500 orders also came from McCloud River (one unit) and B&LE (five units). Equipped with dynamic brakes, McCloud River 29 was shipped in July 1950, joining 1948 sister 28 in the tall pine country of northern California. B&LE's five units — 403-407 — were shipped to Greenville, Pennsylvania, in May through July 1950.

As it was for Baldwin's entire diesel line, 1950 was a year of transition for the heavy road-switchers. In addition to the DRS-6-6-1500 orders mentioned previously, Baldwin received one more: SP's third order, for 12 units, in March 1950, all slated for August/September 1950 delivery. This order was never filled with DRS-6-6-1500s — instead, SP would receive the first 608A-powered, 1600-h.p. AS-616s. In July 1950 while C&O, TCI&RR, and DSS&A all ordered AS-616s for late 1950 and early 1951 delivery, the DSS&A also ordered the last DRS-6-6-1500. The unit had been constructed for stock around April 1950 and thus was available immediately, but before delivery to the DSS&A it served a brief stint as BLW demonstrator 1500 (the second) in August 1950 on the Pittsburgh & West Virginia. Then, as

H. H. Harwood Jr.

The second BLW 1500 was built for stock about April 1950, then sold to the DSS&A (as No. 203) in August 1950. Before delivery the unit demonstrated briefly on the Pittsburgh & West Virginia. It was photographed on the P&WV at Rook, Pennsylvania, in August 1950.

Curtis C. Tillotson Jr.

DSS&A 203, the unit was placed in service at Superior, Wisconsin, on August 23, 1950. It was not only the last DRS-6-6-1500 to leave Eddystone, but was also the final domestic DRS-series road-switcher of any kind to do so (on the same date, and under similar circumstances, the DSS&A placed the next-to-last DT-6-6-2000 in service, see page 75).

Export business kept production of one model — the DRS-6-4-1500 — going well into 1952. The two Roto-Clone DRS-6-4-1500s ordered in 1950 by the Moroccan Railway were forwarded to Oujda, Morocco, in July 1951 (bringing the final number of Roto-Clones built to 15), and the following month another order — for three standard DRS-6-4-1500s equipped with steam generators — was received from Morocco. These units (040-DC-331 to 040-DC-333) were dispatched to Oujda in July 1952, nearly two years after AS-series heavy road-switcher deliveries had begun. The units had been ordered as DRS-6-4-1500s so that the Baldwin fleet of the Moroccan Railway would be standardized. But because the 608SC power plant was out of production by 1952, the final three DRS-6-4-1500s were actually powered by 608A power plants, which were derated to 1500 h.p. The units also used the welded frame. The trio earned a footnote as the only DRS-6-4-1500s equipped with roller bearings.

When the last DRS-series locomotive had departed, the sales success of Baldwin's first heavy road-switchers could be measured. Eddystone had built 91 DRS-6-4-1500s (62 for export), 35 DRS-4-4-1500s (3 for export), and 83 DRS-6-6-1500s (all for domestic service). The 209-unit total placed Baldwin second as a builder of heavy road-switchers behind Alco-GE through most of the period (until General Motors began its drive to an eventual sale of 2729 GP7s through 1954). Export sales showed potential, and the late sales of the DRS-6-6-1500 seemed to promise a springboard for the new C-C AS-616. Overall, only switcher sales had outperformed the heavy road-switchers.

THE YEARS ON THE ROAD — AND RETIREMENTS

Diesel locomotives have finite life expectancies, and one rule of thumb for first-generation diesels employed in road freight duty called for 15 years of economical service. Vic-

Durham & Southern 365, ex-Norfolk Southern DRS-6-4-1500 1508, heads a quartet of Baldwin diesels rolling 48 cars at 35 mph near Carpenter, North Carolina, May 1, 1971. With two-axle B-type trucks replacing its original A1A trucks, the unit had become, for all intents and purposes, a DRS-4-4-1500.

Donald Sims

Cresting the hump at Pasco, Washington, was a regular event for Northern Pacific DRS-4-4-1500 501 (ex-176).

Gary G. Allen

SP's first Baldwin road-switcher went to the Ferrocarril de Nacozari S.C.T. Still wearing road number 5200, it headed a mixed train on the Nacozari in January 1967.

J. J. Young Jr.

Purchased with a steam generator for local passenger duties, Lehigh Valley DRS-4-4-1500 No. 200 had been demoted to yard work at Sayre, Pennsylvania, by the early 1960s. Although one of a kind on the LV, No. 200 worked until 1971.

Burdell Bulgrin: H. H. Harwood Jr. collection

One of only two DRS-4-4-1500s purchased by the New York Central, No. 7301 (ex-8301) works in Chicago, Illinois, in 1958. Two stacks indicate the presence of an EMD V-16 under the hood, the result of a 1956 repowering.

tims of wrecks and fires excepted, a locomotive retired much before 15 years had almost certainly not overwhelmed its owner with its virtues. Twenty years or more in service was a creditable showing, and 30 years an extraordinary show of longevity.

DRS-series heavy road-switchers fell into all these categories. Happily, the first — Columbus & Greenville 601 — fell into the latter. For more than 35 years C&G 601 labored on the Delta Route, surviving even its owner's brief extinction (C&G was merged into Illinois Central Gulf in 1972 but regained independence in 1975). Columbus & Greenville 601 remained in service into the fall of 1983 and is slated for permanent display by the railroad at Columbus, Mississippi. C&G 602 was wrecked and retired in December 1961, but the other three DRS-6-4-1500s, 603-605, remained extant in early 1984, although all were retired.

Baldwin's second domestic heavy road-switcher, UP DRS-

6-4-1500 1250 (ex-BLW 1500), was less fortunate. After only 14 years on the UP, 1250 sat dead at Omaha, Nebraska, and was officially retired in August 1962. Following retirement, 1250 was nearly united with its only older domestic sister — C&G 601 — when the C&G dispatched officials to Omaha to look it over. But C&G's men liked their Baldwins pure, and they found the UP unit greatly modified (it had been jury-rigged with EMD electrical components and extensively rewired); UP 1250 went to scrap.

During the 1960s most domestic DRS-6-4-1500s left the rosters of their original owners, including all eight units of the Savannah & Atlanta and 10 of the Norfolk Southern. In 1951 the Savannah & Atlanta came under the control of the Central of Georgia and in 1961 joint operation was approved. CofG was acquired by the Southern Railway in 1963, and as part of the Southern empire, S&A's Baldwins were outcasts and were sent to EMD in 1965 as trade-ins for GP35s. A better fate awaited three of Norfolk Southern's units: NS 1504, 1507, and 1508 were sold in 1965 and 1966 to the Durham & Southern in North Carolina. The three became D&S 363-365 and were re-equipped with B-type trucks to put all weight on drivers (making them DRS-4-4-1500s). D&S kept the units until 1973, when they were replaced by GP38-2s. D&S 363-364 were sold to Rail-to-Water Transfer Corp. of Chicago, Illinois, where they remained until early 1984. D&S 365 was sold to the Morehead & Morgan Fork Railroad in eastern Kentucky, and later went to the Hobet Mining Co. of Clifftop, West Virginia, as a cabless, Cummins-diesel-powered mine shifter.

The SP's three DRS-6-4-1500s left the road's roster in 1965. SP 5202 was traded to EMD and scrapped, but SP 5200 and 5201 fared better. In August 1965 the Nacozari Railroad (Ferrocarril de Nacozari S. C. T.), a 77-mile line between Nacozari and Agua Prieta, Mexico, that had been operated by the SP, became independent. Numbers 5200 and 5201 went to the Mexican line, where they retained their original road numbers. In 1968 the line became part of the Pacific Railroad (Ferrocarril del Pacifico) and the Baldwins were sold to Chihuahua Pacific Railway (Ferrocarril de Chihuahua al Pacifico) and assigned CH-P Nos. 401 and 400. Both have been scrapped.

Ex-Baldwin DRS-6-4-1500 demonstrator 1501 remained serviceable on Kennecott Copper into the early 1980s, although the workers who built the unit would never have recognized it. It was wrecked around 1952 and Baldwin supplied a new welded frame and B-type trucks to replace its original A1A trucks (making the unit a DRS-4-4-1500). The steam generator was removed and in the 1970s the unit received a chopped nose. In 1984 the locomotive was extant but stored.

Aside from the peculiar Cummins repowering of ex-D&S 365 (nee NS 1508) only one DRS-6-4-1500 — Chicago & North Western 1504 — was repowered. The unit was dispatched to La Grange, Illinois, where EMD replaced the original 608SC engine with a 1500-h.p. 567C V-16. A Geepstyle long hood was also applied. As a Baldwin/EMD hybrid, C&NW 1504 survived into 1981. In 1984, reports indicated that some of the North African DRS-6-4-1500s were still extant.

The first DRS-4-4-1500, Western Maryland 170, served the road for more than two decades. Along with the rest of WM's Baldwin diesels, for most of its career No. 170 worked out of Hagerstown, Maryland. In January 1969 it was sold for scrap. WM's other two DRS-4-4-1500s — 171-172 — went to EMD in 1969 as trade-ins. WM 170's fate was representative; most DRS-4-4-1500s toiled into the 1960s, but only a few survived longer. Certainly the least fortunate were the four belonging to Missouri Pacific subsidiary St. Louis, Brownsville & Mexico; they were swept away in MoPac's 1962 drive toward an all-EMD roster. The Soo Line, operator of the largest contingent of DRS-4-4-1500s at eight units, employed them mostly in Minnesota and North Dakota, often assigning them to mixed trains west of Thief

Donald Sims

NP's lone DRS-6-6-1500 served for 24 years. Along the way, it was renumbered to 525 (from 177) and repowered with an EMD V-16. The unit became BN 407; it was retired in 1972. Below left, in their later years Erie DRS-6-6-1500s congregated at Buffalo, New York. Ex-Erie 1153 displays the gray, ma-

roon, and yellow livery of successor Erie-Lackawanna. Below right, the EMD repowering of C&NW DRS-6-6-1500s drastically altered their appearance. A tall, Geep-style long hood covers its 567C V-16 as No. 1502 stands in company with an F-M H16-66 at Marinette, Wisconsin, August 2, 1966.

Joe Tutsky: Howard W. Ameling collection

Howard W. Ameling

River Falls, Minnesota. They were also used as switchers in Minnesota's Cuyuna iron ore range. In 1962, Soo 362 was sold to the Durham & Southern (where it became D&S 362), remained on the railroad until 1973, then was sold to Rail-to-Water Transfer Corp., where it remained until early 1984. The rest of the Soo DRS-4-4-1500s were dropped from the roster in the mid-1960s, with No. 360 officially being the last to go. It was traded to GE as credit on U30Cs.

Erie's six DRS-4-4-1500s spent their lives on the east end of the road and endured to wear the colors of Erie Lackawanna after the 1960 merger of Erie with Delaware, Lackawanna & Western, but most were purged from the roster in 1966; EL 1105 was rebuilt into slug B-66 at the road's Hornell, New York, shops in 1966. EL 1100 was not scrapped until 1970. Pennsylvania-Reading Seashore Lines' DRS-4-4-1500s — the first diesels on the railroad — were primarily passenger locomotives, hustling commuters and vacationers away from Philadelphia and Camden to Atlantic City and other points in lower New Jersey. Dubbed "Green Hornets" by PRSL men, the units were geared at 15:63 for a 75 mph top speed. PRSL traded three of its six units to EMD as credit on GP38s in 1969. That same year, Baldwins 6001 and 6003 were leased to Penn Central. PRSL operated its last DRS-4-4-1500 — No. 6003 — through late 1971.

Two railroads repowered DRS-4-4-1500s: Northern Pacific and New York Central. NP 500 was scrapped in 1960 due to a wreck, but 501 (ex-176) was repowered in 1966 with an EMD 567C V-16 engine. In its later years, the unit was assigned duty at NP's Pasco, Washington, hump, and it survived to become Burlington Northern 406 before retirement in June 1972. New York Central never found much to like in its pre-1950 Baldwin road diesels, and its pair of DRS-4-4-1500s was no exception. Based early on at Utica, New York, the pair was renumbered 7300-7301 in 1951, and in April and May 1956 NYC's Collinwood (Ohio) shops installed an EMD 567C V-16 power plant in each. At the time the units were less than eight years old. In later years both units were stationed at Englewood, Illinois, and often frequented LaSalle Street Station, Chicago, as coach yard switchers. NYC 7300 was retired and scrapped in 1966; 7301 was again renumbered — to 5991 — before being retired in 1967.

Ironically, the Lehigh Valley, owner of but one DRS-4-4-1500, pulled as much life out of the model as any road. In the early 1960s LV 200 worked briefly at Florence Yard in Bethlehem, Pennsylvania, but thereafter spent its days near LV's main shop at Sayre, Pennsylvania, working heavy switching and the interchange with the Erie Lackawanna at Waverly, New York. LV 200 operated at Sayre

Stan Kistler

On October 21 and 22, 1950, Kaiser Steel's two DRS-6-6-1500s headed an excursion train of the Railway Club of Southern California over the Eagle Mountain Railway. Battling long strings of ore cars was more often the calling of the red, orange, and gray Baldwins.

until 1971 and was traded in to EMD in December 1972.

The DRS-6-6-1500 was, for the most part, employed in the rugged service for which it was designed — slow, heavy hauling. Perhaps nowhere was this more the case than on the three U. S. Steel roads that originally purchased the model — B&LE, TCI&RR, and Union. Bessemer & Lake Erie employed its seven units on local freights and at the Conneaut, Ohio, docks. They were also available for pusher duty out of Conneaut. B&LE sold 401-402 to U. S. Steel sister Elgin, Joliet & Eastern in March 1956 and the units became EJ&E 500-501. The rest survived until 1973, the same year the EJ&E put its secondhand units to rest. TCI&RR employed its two units on "mainline" trains to U. S. Steel's Fairfield Works near Birmingham, Alabama. (In 1953, the TCI&RR's name was changed to Tennessee Coal & Iron Division, then the name of the whole operation was changed to the Fairfield Works in 1963.) In 1967 the units were renumbered 161-162, then were removed from service around 1968. The last U. S. Steel-owned railroad to operate the DRS-6-6-1500 was the Union Railroad. Between October 1959 and March 1965 Union's 12 units were repowered with EMD 567C V-16s and modified with GP18-style long hoods. Beginning in 1968, chopped noses were applied. Union's Baldwins were nicknamed "Buffaloes" for their unorthodox appearance. It was not until ex-DM&IR SD9s arrived in 1979 that the death knell sounded for Union's Baldwins; 616 was the last to operate.

Elsewhere east of the Mississippi, Erie's 12 DRS-6-6-1500s joined the EL roster in 1960, and mostly lugged coal trains and toiled in the yards at Buffalo, New York, until the middle 1960s. Erie Lackawanna 1150 was rebuilt as slug B-65 at Hornell, New York, in July 1965, but was stored at Marion, Ohio, by 1968. The year 1966 marked the end of the line for the rest of the EL units. Chesapeake & Ohio's trio of DRS-6-6-1500s, originally assigned at Russell

(5530) and Stevens, Kentucky (5531), and Walbridge, Ohio (5532), never strayed far from assignments in C&O's traffic-dense Ohio/Kentucky region. Number 5532 was retired in 1963 and traded to EMD, 5531 was retired in 1967, and 5530 (after being renumbered 2200) was retired in August 1969.

In the Upper Midwest, DSS&A employed its four DRS-6-6-1500s as mainline power, working mostly west of Marquette, Michigan. The units also worked Marquette-area switching runs and handled the Houghton branch. While the units were popular with crews, the road found that if the power plants were not torn down approximately once a year for installation of new bearings and, quite often, piston rings, the engines began to suffer from low oil pressure. With DSS&A's marriage into the Soo Line in 1961 the units became Soo 384-387. Save for occasional trips to Minneapolis' Shoreham yard and shops, they remained in DSS&A territory until dropped from the roster between 1964 and 1968; the units last saw service around 1966.

Neighbor Minneapolis, Northfield & Southern kept its lone DRS-6-6-1500, No. 15, in service until a fire caused its retirement in 1974. (It was not scrapped until May 1981.) Similarly long-lived were the C&NW DRS-6-6-1500s. The North Western found the big units useful, but with only 68 Eddystone-built diesels on the roster, stocking Baldwin power plant parts was an unwanted expense. Between 1958 and 1960 C&NW's eight DRS-6-6-1500s were repowered with EMD 567C V-16 engines at EMD's La Grange plant. The hybrid veterans went on to record lengthy careers. Stationed at Green Bay, Wisconsin, and Marshalltown, Iowa, in their later years, the last one left C&NW's roster in 1981. Northern Pacific also extended the life of its DRS-6-6-1500 by repowering. NP 525 (ex-177) was given an EMD 567C V-16 in 1959, and worked much of its later life — in the company of its repowered DRS-4-4-1500 sister — at the Pasco (Washington) hump. It survived to become Burlington

J. P. Lamb Jr.

SP DRS-6-6-1500s 5222 and 5225 and an unidentified AS-616 apply 4600 horsepower to shove freight cars over the hump at Inglewood Yard, Houston, in July 1964. The two 1500-h.p. units began serving SP at Portland, Oregon, 14 years before.

Richard Steinheimer

SP Baldwins meet in the yard at Hayden Junction, Arizona. DRS-6-6-1500 5212 has 13 empty ore cars bound for the Kennecott Copper pit at Ray, while two more Eddystone products bracket loads bound for Kennecott's concentrator.

Northern No. 407 in 1970, but was retired in 1972.

In the Southwest, Kaiser's DRS-6-6-1500s toiled away lugging ore until replaced by GE U30Cs in 1968. Early in their lives the pair led what may have been the only DRS-6-6-1500-powered passenger excursion run ever: On October 21 and 22, 1950, the duo headed a Railway Club of Southern California train over the Eagle Mountain Railway. During their long tenure on the Eagle Mountain the units exchanged their original red, orange, and gray livery for a C&O-look-alike blue-and-yellow paint scheme and new road numbers — 1025-1026. In 1972, both units were sold to Peabody Coal Company (via Railway Supply Co., Inc.) and they began hauling coal trains near Lenzburg, Illinois. Number 1025 finished its career with Peabody, while 1026 was sold again in 1978 — to Koppel Bulk Terminal in Long Beach, California, where it was retired in 1980.

The greatest DRS-6-6-1500 operator was Southern Pacific. The 29 big Baldwins of SP and T&NO found regular work in Oregon, California, Arizona, Texas, and Louisiana. Three, 5203, 5210, and 5212, were assigned to the Pacific Electric for part of their careers. When new, two — 5216-5217 — were based at San Diego, California, and worked San Diego-Yuma, Arizona, via SP-controlled San Diego & Arizona Eastern, where each unit was capable of lugging 975 tons up the 2.2 percent ruling grade of Carriso Gorge. Because of their great lugging ability SP often assigned single Baldwins throughout the system to trains that required two units of other manufacture. While this was a plus-mark for the big engines it often overloaded them, causing breakdowns. Because only one unit was assigned, the offending Baldwin then received a black mark on its record for crippling a train on the road, an example of Baldwin diesels actually being able to pull too much tonnage for their own good. The SP lost its first DRS-6-6-1500 when 5221 was wrecked at Albany, Oregon, in April 1959 and scrapped in October of that year. Wholesale retirements began around 1963; the last SP units were retired in 1970, those of subsidiary T&NO were retired in 1965 and 1966. The lone DRS-6-6-1500B — SP 5227 — was renumbered twice, to 5500 in 1951, then to 4900 in 1955, and was retired in 1969.

A handful of SP DRS-6-6-1500s survived after their SP days were done. SP 5204 and 5207 were sold to the McCloud River in 1964, where they joined McCloud's original pair (28-29). SP 5204 was used for parts only, but 5207 became McCloud 35. There it remained until 1969, when it was sold to U. S. Steel and stationed at the Geneva (Utah) Works. There, the unit became No. 39 and received a chopped nose. It survived into the early 1980s. McCloud's original two DRS-6-6-1500s were replaced in 1969 by SD38s, but No. 29 went on to the Magma Arizona Railroad and it remained in service in 1984. SP 5208 was donated in 1969 to the Pacific Coast Chapter, Railroad & Locomotive Historical Society, and will eventually be displayed at the California State Railroad Museum in Sacramento as a fitting tribute to Baldwin's original line of heavy road-switchers.

R. T. Sharp

After retirement on the McCloud River in 1969, DRS-6-6-1500 No. 29 got a new lease on life on the Magma Arizona. Climbing out of Superior, Arizona, bound for Magma on December 17, 1970, the unit wears road number 10 for its new operator.

NEW TRIPLETS

The 1950 standard line heavy road-switchers

BALDWIN'S STANDARD LINE introduced in 1950 included three heavy road-switchers powered by the 608A turbocharged 1600-h.p. engine. Replacing the A1A-A1A DRS-6-4-1500 was the AS-416; the B-B DRS-4-4-1500 was dropped in favor of the AS-16; and the C-C DRS-6-6-1500 was replaced by the AS-616. Use of Westinghouse 370-series traction motors and 471-series main generators was continued. A gear ratio of 15:63 was considered standard for all three models, but optional 15:68 gearing was available on the AS-16 and AS-616, and 17:62 (80 mph) on the AS-16. As had been the case on the DRS-series, 42″ wheels were standard. Major options included dynamic brakes, m.u., steam generator equipment (Vapor Car Heating Co. or Elesco), roller bearings (Hyatt, SKF, Timken, or Fafnir), dual control stands, 24-RL brake control, Gardner-Denver 6-cylinder water-cooled air compressor, Farr air filter panels, flange oilers, signal lights (Mars figure eight or Pyle-National Gyra-light), and hump control. A cabless booster version of the AS-616 was also offered. Externally, the three AS-series road-switchers matched their predecessors, although that would soon change.

The new models and the marketing push they received dramatically sparked sales of heavy road-switchers. Shipments began in September 1950 with SP's dozen DRS-6-6-1500s-turned-AS-616s, and SP immediately ordered 18 more AS-616s (including five cabless units). Seven other roads ordered AS-616s in 1950 — TCI&RR opted for five, C&O for a whopping 26, DSS&A for five, Pennsy for nine, Union for three, Milwaukee for four (two of which were to be cabless boosters), and Pittsburgh & West Virginia for one unit — for a total of 83 AS-616 orders in 1950.

Orders received in 1950 for the AS-16 totaled 32 units. Katy ordered eight, Erie six, Western Maryland four, Reading opted for ten, Soo Line bought two, and Missouri Pacific (via subsidiary International-Great Northern) also ordered two. Even the traditionally slower-selling A1A-A1A model did well: 11 AS-416s were reserved by four buyers. Savannah & Atlanta and Columbus & Greenville each opted for one, Algerian Railway ordered four, and Norfolk Southern ordered five units.

With the close of 1950 the AS-series was showing real promise. The 83 AS-616 units ordered in just 10 months matched the entire production of DRS-6-6-1500s exactly, and sales of AS-16s were within three units of equaling the total DRS-4-4-1500 output. Of course, 1950 was the year when orders placed for diesel locomotives in the U. S. skyrocketed to 4473 units. The market was huge, and there was room for all comers.

Most orders placed in 1950 were for 1951 delivery, but there were exceptions. SP's DRS-6-6-1500s-turned-AS-616s (5228-5239), of course, marked the first AS-series shipments in early September 1950. These dozen units were all built sans m.u. (the reason no boosters were included in the order) and were placed in service in Arizona, California, Oregon, and Nevada. Late in September 1950 the first AS-16s were shipped. Katy's order for eight — placed only four months earlier as part of a push by M-K-T to dieselize all principal passenger and freight operations — was filled in September and October 1950 with units numbered 1571-1578. The first Baldwin road-switchers on the M-K-T (11 DS-4-4-1000 switchers were already on the roster), they went to work out of Parsons, Kansas, working freight runs to St. Louis. The AS-416 also made its debut in 1950 with Savannah & Atlanta 108, shipped on December 6, 1950. Eddystone's 1950 deliveries of AS-series road-switchers were completed with two of the five AS-616s ordered by TCI&RR (1502-1503) and 11 of the 26 AS-616s ordered by C&O (5533-5543).

Several of the AS-series road-switchers delivered in 1950 included unusual features. Katy's eight AS-16s all employed cast frames (a la the DRS-4-4-1500), the only AS-16s so equipped. Subsequent units would use a one-piece welded frame with end steps and pilot faces permanently attached (only the very bottom of the pilot was a removable, bolt-on section). At Savannah & Atlanta's request AS-416 No. 108 was built with the unusual GSC A1A truck used on the road's DRS-6-4-1500s, and the unit also came with a cast frame. All subsequent S&A AS-416s would share these characteristics, but standard AS-416s would have welded frames and the standard A1A truck.

M-K-T AS-16 No. 1578 was shipped to Parsons, Kansas, on October 4, 1950, then went to work lugging tonnage to St. Louis. Katy's original group of eight AS-16s (1571-1578) were the only such units built with cast frames.

Completed in late 1950, Tennessee Coal Iron & Railroad 1502 was among the earliest AS-616s. The big Baldwin lacked m.u.; had the "swayback mule" underframe.

Western Maryland's total commitment to the AS-16 was four units (173-176). AS-16s 175-176 were shipped in June 1951 and assigned to Hagerstown, Maryland. Options included Hyatt roller bearings, underbelly fuel tanks, five-chime horns, and m.u. (rear end only).

The SP and TCI&RR AS-616s utilized the "swayback mule" welded frame dating back to the DRS-6-6-1500, but effective with C&O AS-616 5533, shipped in November 1950, Eddystone began using a redesigned welded frame for the six-motor road-switcher. The frame was an AS-616 exclusive and could be used to ballast the model up to a weight of 377,000 pounds; it featured thick side members, the depth of which varied depending on the desired total unit weight. On most units the side members were deep enough that the frame had to be notched above the trucks to provide clearance for the brake cylinders. As with the welded AS-16 frame, the new AS-616 frame had pilot faces and end steps permanently attached, with only the lower portion of the pilot removable, and the swayback feature of the old frame was done away with. (The new frame became standard, but the swayback frames were used until the supply ran out. As a result, Milwaukee Road, SP, and PRR AS-616s delivered in 1951 came with the older frame.)

1951: THE ZENITH

With most AS-series road-switcher orders from 1950 yet to be filled and new orders rolling in at a record pace, 1951 marked the zenith of heavy road-switcher production at Eddystone. The last units ordered in 1950 to leave were two MoPac (I-GN) AS-16s — 4195-4196 — shipped on November 29, 1951. Among units ordered in 1950 and delivered in 1951, the most unusual (and deluxe) were the four Algerian

Railway AS-416s (040-DF-1 to 040-DF-4) dispatched to Algiers in September. These featured roller-bearing trucks, steam generators, pilot-mounted dual headlamps, left-hand drive, and low-clearance cabs.

There were a few uncommon units among the AS-16s. Of Reading's 10 ordered in 1950 (530-535, 560-563), the latter four carried steam generators for passenger service out of Philadelphia. The six AS-16s Erie had ordered in 1950 were shipped in May through July 1951 (1106-1110, 1140). One — No. 1140 — was equipped with a steam generator and was originally assigned secondary passenger duty at Buffalo, New York. Milwaukee Road's two pairs of cab-and-booster AS-616s ordered in 1950 were shipped to the road in April 1951. Milwaukee 2100A-2100B were placed in service at Minneapolis, 2101A-2101B at Milwaukee. In 1951 SP also received its five cabless AS-616s ordered in 1950. SP boosters 5501-5502 were shipped in April, then were set up at El Paso, Texas, and Willits, California (on SP subsidiary Northwestern Pacific). After departing Eddystone in October, SP AS-616 boosters 5503-5505 entered service at Eugene, Oregon. Earmarked for hump service, these three units were ballasted to 374,000 pounds, and given slow-speed 15:68 gearing and dynamic brakes. SP also took delivery of 13 standard AS-616s (5240-5252) to complete its 18-unit 1950 order. All were equipped with dynamic brakes. Numbers 5250-5252 were to work with the AS-616 boosters at Eugene and like the boosters were heavily

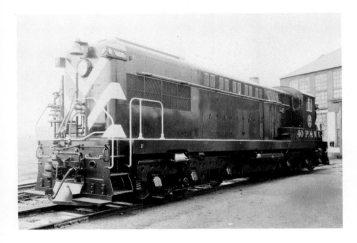

Pittsburgh & West Virginia purchased only one Baldwin heavy road-switcher — AS-616 No. 40. Shipped to P&WV in May 1951, it was sold to the Pennsy (No. 8114) in 1965.

White wheel rims spruce up m.u.-equipped Missouri Pacific (International-Great Northern) AS-16 No. 4195 as it poses for the company photographer at Eddystone in the fall of 1951.

Heavyweights, SP AS-616 5251 was ballasted to 377,000 pounds, booster 5504 to 374,000 pounds. Shipped in October 1951, they were assigned to hump duty at Eugene, Oregon.

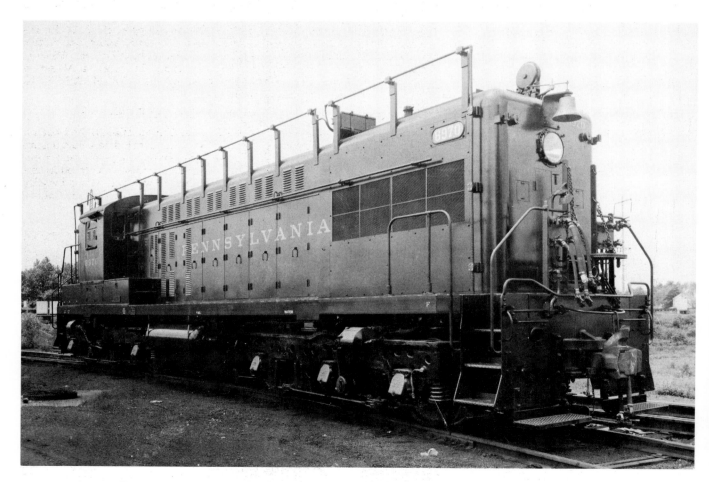

Pennsylvania 8970-8971 were the only AS-616s built with steam generators. Other options included m.u., roller bearing truck journals, and Pennsy's radio phone system. Number 8970 was shipped in June 1951 and entered service at Mingo Junction, Ohio.

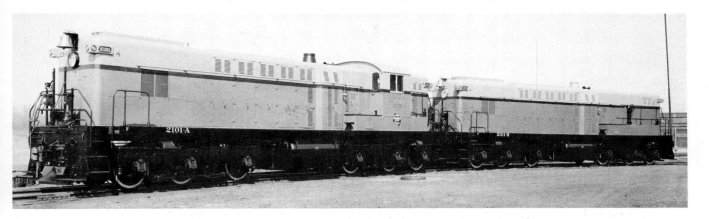

Milwaukee 2101A-2101B was the second of two pairs of cab-and-booster AS-616s shipped to CMStP&P in April 1951. Two years later the road applied cabs to both boosters.

ballasted (to 377,000 pounds each) and geared at 15:68.

PRR AS-616s 8966-8974 were dispatched in May and June 1951. Two — 8970-8971 — carried steam generators (the only AS-616s so equipped), and wore PRR's familiar radio phone antenna system. These two AS-616s, along with PRR 8966, 8969, and 8973-8974, were originally assigned to Mingo Junction, Ohio. PRR 8967-8968 took up residence on the Pennsy's Monongahela Division, and Pennsy 8972 entered service at Scully, Pennsylvania (on the joint PRR/Pittsburgh & Lake Erie road, the Pittsburgh, Chartiers & Youghiogheny Railroad).

Just as 1951 was the zenith of heavy road-switcher production, so it was for sales of the AS line. By year-end, Baldwin had orders for 100 AS-616s, 50 AS-16s, and one AS-416, a total of 151 units. The sales-leading AS-616 drew orders from nine railroads in 1951. Largest buyer was —who else — SP, with an order in March 1951 for 34 AS-616s (all cab-equipped), 26 for itself and eight for T&NO. C&O and DSS&A also returned as repeat AS-616 buyers, ordering 11 and 2 units, respectively. C&NW, Union Pacific, and Kaiser Steel, all operators of one or more DRS-series road-switchers, now contracted for the AS-616; C&NW ordered three, UP six, and Kaiser Steel two. Houston Belt & Terminal, which owned Alco-GE and EMD switchers, ordered its first road-switcher and its first Baldwin diesel, a single AS-616. The AS-616 also made its entry into the foreign market in 1951: The Central of Brazil Railway (Estrada De Ferro Central Do Brazil) ordered 32. Of these, 12 were specified

with wide-gauge (5'-3") trucks, and 20 were ordered with meter-gauge trucks, lightweight frames, and low-clearance cabs. Also, U. S. Steel ordered 12 AS-616s for its Orinoco Mining Co. in Venezuela (this order was later cut to nine).

The AS-16 attracted orders from four railroads in 1951, among them three repeat buyers — Reading for 29, Katy for six, and Erie for 10. The new customer was the B&O, which ordered five AS-16s in June 1951 for use on its coal-laden Monongah Division. Only the AS-416, which, like its DRS-6-4-1500 predecessor, had become a favorite of southern lines with light rail, did poorly. The Savannah & Atlanta was back again in 1951 with another single-unit order, the only AS-416 ordered that year (it would become S&A 109).

Against 1951 orders Eddystone shipped 23 of the 50 AS-16s (2 of 10 ordered by Erie, 15 of 29 for Reading, and Katy's complete order of 6) the same year. Four of UP's six AS-616s were delivered in 1951, bringing the total of AS-series heavy road-switchers shipped in 1951 to 120 (47 AS-16s, 10 AS-416s, and 63 AS-616s).

FROM BOOM TO BUST

The success of the AS-series line in 1950-51 had been a tonic at Eddystone, and Baldwin decided to construct an AS-616 demonstrator. Wearing green and yellow and numbered appropriately B-L-H 1600, the unit was placed in service on March 17, 1952. Its sales tour began with a lengthy stint in the West, including visits to the Carbon County

Jay Potter collection

One of six Union Pacific AS-616s, UP 1263 displays the welded frame with deep, notched side members which first appeared on units shipped in November 1950.

Below, as built in March 1952, B-L-H AS-616 demonstrator 1600 rode GSC's original Commonwealth C-type trucks. Above, in August 1952, before shipment to the DSS&A, the unit was re-equipped with the GSC outside-equalized truck.

Railway, Tooele Valley, and SP system. In August 1952 No. 1600 returned to Eddystone to be fitted with Baldwin's new outside-equalized truck, and was dispatched to the Duluth, South Shore & Atlantic in September. About this same time the DSS&A received AS-616s 209-210 (to fill its 1951 order), both equipped with Baldwin's standard GSC Commonwealth trucks. Together with ex-demonstrator 1600 (purchased by the DSS&A and assigned No. 211), the units would allow B-L-H an opportunity to compare the performance of the two types of trucks under identical service conditions. At speeds over 35 mph the new outside-equalized truck was vastly superior to the old, and, in fact, the new design rode well up to 70 mph. As a result, the new truck became an option on Baldwin heavy road-switchers (and on the RT-624 transfer unit as well).

Premier AS-16 on Baltimore & Ohio, No. 900 departed Eddystone in May 1952 to begin its career at Grafton, West Virginia. The unit displays the original AS-series carbody style, welded frame, m.u., and SKF roller bearings.

The demonstration term of AS-616 1600 was largely for naught. In 1952, with the market for new diesel locomotives more than halved from the previous year, sales of the heavy road-switcher line took a beating. From record sales of 151 such units in 1951 orders plummeted in 1952 to a total of 25! Despite No. 1600's best efforts, the C-C model earned only two orders for a total of seven units. B&LE ordered two, and the Paraña-Santa Catarina Railway (Rêde Viacão Paraña-Santa Catarina) of Brazil placed a bid for five meter-gauge units which — like Central of Brazil's meter-gauge AS-616s — would feature lightweight frames and low-clearance cabs.

The AS-16 proved the sales leader of the heavy road-switcher line in 1952, with sales of a mere 13 units. Reading, Katy, and PRSL opted for four units each, and B&O ordered one (this supplemental order was placed in July, about the time B&O placed in service the five AS-16s from its 1951 order — 900-904). Reading's order, placed in February, was later canceled. The AS-416 accounted for five units on a single order from Norfolk Southern (the road's second AS-416 order). Most railroads that favored Baldwin diesels had already ordered the quantity needed, and the lag in national sales gave other builders (EMD and Alco-GE) the chance to decrease their lead times on orders.

Although the sales offices were quiet, the erecting halls were not; 1951 orders kept Eddystone busy through 1952. All units ordered in 1951 were built and delivered by the end of 1952 with two exceptions: Central of Brazil's 20 meter-gauge AS-616s (special construction and transportation considerations, and customs requirements for the foreign sale delayed delivery until 1953), and five of the nine AS-616s U. S. Steel's Orinoco Mining Co. had ordered in 1951 remained to be delivered. Also included in 1952 shipments were B&LE's two AS-616s (408-409) and Norfolk Southern's five AS-416s (1606-1610) that had been ordered earlier that same year. In total, 106 AS-series heavy road-switchers were shipped in 1952.

AS-series production in 1952 was an assembly line matter, with customer preferences molding differences among units. Example: Savannah & Atlanta AS-416 109 was shipped in July, and as usual for S&A units, employed a cast frame and unusual floating-bolster A1A trucks. While Central of Brazil's meter-gauge AS-616s were yet to be delivered, the South American road's dozen wide-gauge units (3371-3382) were built and began crossing the Caribbean in the summer of 1952. These uncommon 5'-3" gauge units had outside-equalized trucks and dynamic brakes. They entered service at Barra do Pirai (northwest of Rio de Janeiro). Orinoco Mining's four AS-616s that were delivered were placed in service at Puerto Ordaz, near Santo Tomé de Guayana on the Orinoco River in northeast Venezuela. The new railroad ran from Puerto Ordaz to Cerro Bolivar, 90 miles. Mainline grades were held to 1 percent, but grades on mine trackage reached 3 percent. The Orinoco AS-616s were equipped with m.u. and dynamic

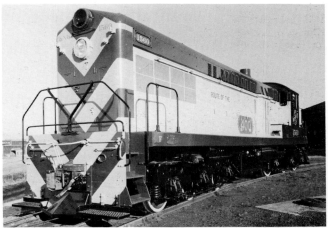

At top, the biggest diesel, hands down, on the Houston Belt & Terminal was AS-616 No. 32, a 1952 Eddystone product. Chicago & North Western 1560-1561 were the lightest domestic AS-616s, weighing in at 287,000 pounds each. Kaiser Steel purchased two AS-616s, Nos. 1012A-1012B. Signal lights and dynamic brakes were options, and the trucks on the Kaiser units featured slightly taller than usual center pins, eliminating the need for notches in frame above the brake cylinders.

brakes (the rest of Orinoco Mining's units followed in 1953).

SP took delivery of the most AS-series road-switchers in 1952, receiving the 34 AS-616s ordered in 1951 (SP 5253-5278 and T&NO 177-184). SP's roster of AS-series heavy road-switchers (including T&NO units) reached 64 units, and although it wasn't known at the time, the road's Baldwin heavy road-switcher purchases were complete. Among the 1952 SP arrivals were four units — 5273-5276 — which featured Pyle-National signal lights built into the top of the hood on both ends; these AS-616s were destined to work on Pacific Electric and the extra signal lights were for grade-

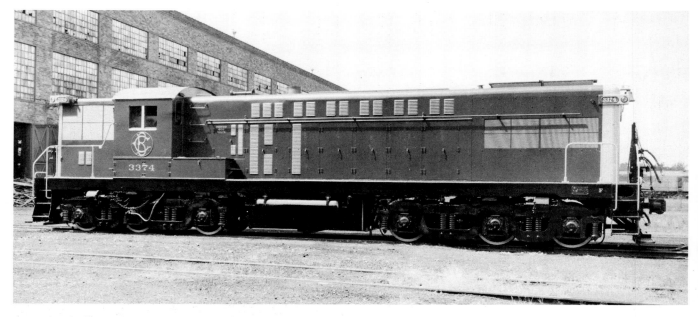

At top, Central of Brazil AS-616 No. 3374 was one of 12 wide-gauge (5'-3") diesels constructed for the road in 1952 that featured dynamic brakes, m.u., and outside-equalized trucks. Above, Orinoco Mining Co. AS-616 No. 1001 posed at Eddystone before shipment to Venezuela.

Southern Pacific operated the largest fleet of AS-616s — 56, plus 8 more on the T&NO. Among the final arrivals in 1952 were four units — 5273-5276 — bound for service on Pacific Electric and equipped with Pyle-National signal lights.

In 1953 B-L-H AS-616 test-bed/demonstrator 1601 introduced revised heavy road-switcher styling and a longer welded frame designed to accommodate GE electrical equipment.

Reading AS-16 No. 587 posed at Eddystone in 1952 before shipment to nearby Reading, Pennsylvania. Reading AS-16s 551-554 and 576-589 were equipped with dynamic brakes.

crossing protection. Although all left Eddystone lettered for SP, at least three (5273-5275) were lettered for Pacific Electric early in their careers, and at least two (5273-5274) were equipped with trolley poles. T&NO's eight new AS-616s were parceled out among Avondale, Louisiana, and San Antonio and Houston, Texas. SP and T&NO AS-616s (and DRS-6-6-1500s and DRS-6-4-1500s) formed an arc of Baldwin territory that stretched all the way from the Pacific Northwest to the Gulf of Mexico.

Belatedly, a few railroads' rosters of Baldwin heavy road-switchers were becoming significant. Besides SP, chief among these were C&O and Reading. C&O's fleet of AS-616s had grown to 37 by the end of 1952 (5533-5569) and Chessie's three DRS-6-6-1500s could be added to that. C&O placed its Baldwin behemoths, which weighed as much as

365,000 pounds each, in the heart of its system. AS-616s were assigned to Stevens, Kentucky (near Cincinnati), and Russell, Kentucky, on the main trunk east to the Alleghenies, and at Columbus and Walbridge, Ohio, on the heavily trafficked route to Lake Erie. From Toledo to Cincinnati to Huntington, West Virginia, C&O's burly AS-616s could be found locking couplers with mainline drags and locals, and tending heavy yard work and transfer jobs. Chessie assigned its Baldwins to some of the toughest work on the railroad, and they were up to the task.

Reading had 39 AS-16s in service by the end of 1952 and, like C&O's AS-616s, they could be found performing a variety of duties. At as much as 265,500 pounds each the AS-16s were the heaviest diesels then on the Reading. That, coupled with their ability to lug long and lug hard, was

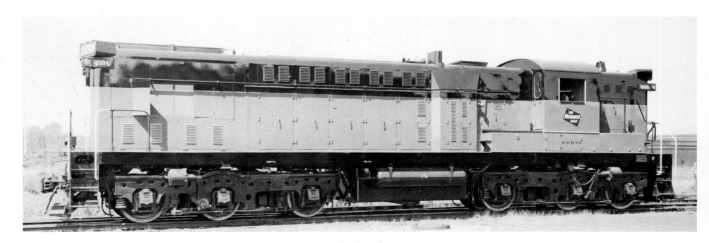

Shipped in August and September 1953, Milwaukee Road 2104-2107 were the last AS-616s built with the original GSC Commonwealth C-type truck.

Reading's final AS-16s — 551-554 — were shipped in October and November 1953. They were the first of the series to employ the revised road-switcher carbody. The upper grille on the long hood indicates No. 552 has dynamic brakes.

C&O's last two AS-616s (5528, 5529) had GSC outside-equalized C-type trucks. At left, the duo leads a mine run out of Russell, Kentucky, in the summer of 1955.

H. H. Harwood Jr. collection

Reading's reason to assign the Baldwins primarily to the coal territory west of the railroad's namesake community in Pennsylvania. The AS-16s could also be found easing along local freights on Reading subsidiary Wilmington & Northern, and, of course, the steam generator-equipped units hurried passengers in and out of Philadelphia.

THE SKY OVER EDDYSTONE GROWS DARKER

Although a few roads were finally accumulating sizable Baldwin fleets, the picture at Eddystone was far from bright. The sales drought which had begun in 1952 eased only slightly in 1953. C&O started the year off well enough with a January order for another pair of AS-616s, but by year-end orders had been received for only 55 more heavy road-switchers. Besides C&O, two other railroads chose to add more AS-616s to existing congregations: Milwaukee Road contracted for four (all cab-equipped this time), and Pennsylvania ordered another pair (as part of its final Baldwin order). The Trona, owner of two Baldwin DT-6-6-2000 transfer units (50-51) since 1949, opted to add a single AS-616 to its roster. But *the* 1953 heavy road-switcher order came from outside the U. S. In September, National Railways of Mexico, which had not taken delivery of a new Baldwin diesel since its last centipede arrived in July 1948, ordered 20 AS-616s. NdeM had sent a delegation to observe AS-616s on SP, and the delegation liked what it saw. A promise of prompt delivery was also certainly a factor.

While AS-616 orders totaled 29 units in 1953, its four-axle sister, the AS-16, accounted for 25. These orders came from four repeat buyers and one new customer. Missouri Pacific (this time through subsidiary St. Louis, Brownsville & Mexico) ordered six AS-16s, B&O one, PRSL six, and Reading ten. The new customer was the Nickel Plate Road, and NKP's purchase of two AS-16s was something of a surprise in motive power circles. One of the last great citadels of steam, NKP had received its last steam locomotive —

Lima 2-8-4 779 — on April 28, 1949. Since 1940, though, NKP had also been buying diesel yard switchers, and by 1950 it had given orders to EMD, Alco-GE, F-M, Lima-Hamilton, and Baldwin. (Baldwin's contribution had been two DS-4-4-1000 switchers built in 1947 for use at Cleveland, Ohio.) In 1951 road diesels started appearing on the Nickel Plate, too — in the form of 13 EMD GP7s. In May 1953, NKP ordered 25 more GP7s — and two AS-16s. In truth, NKP's AS-16 order was primarily the result of personal allegiances forged in the steam era between NKP's mechanical staff and Lima sales personnel, some of whom had joined Baldwin in the Baldwin-Lima-Hamilton merger.

The AS-416 brought up the rear in heavy road-switcher sales in 1953 with one order from ever-faithful Norfolk Southern. NS's order (its third overall): three units, to become NS 1611-1613.

TIME FOR A REDESIGN

As early as 1952 Baldwin had considered redesigning the heavy road-switcher line. Particularly on the AS-616, customer options were numerous and the original carbody simply didn't have space for much optional equipment. Any unit equipped with dynamic brakes had to have an entire short hood custom-built to carry the large side-mounted resistor grids and top-mounted exhaust, and the fact that units equipped with dynamic brakes could not carry a steam generator or the short-hood tank (which had been increased to 900 gallons for the AS series), or both, was a deterrent to sales. Special lights also presented problems; there wasn't room in the upper portion of the long hood for a second large lamp casing, and when a railroad requested safety lights (as SP and C&NW had), expensive carbody work was required to build a special peaked hood end.

In 1953 another problem materialized, this one serious enough to force a redesign, when Westinghouse began to contemplate discontinuance of its heavy electric traction equipment. Baldwin protected itself with a request to

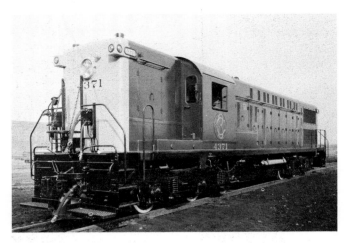

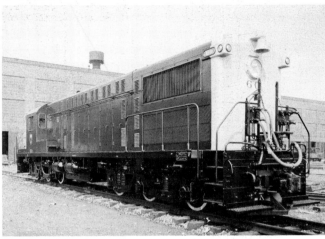

In 1953 and 1954 Eddystone completed 25 meter-gauge, 1600-h.p. road-switchers, 20 for Central of Brazil (such as CofB 4371, top) and 5 for Paraña-Santa Catarina (such as No. 60). The units were designated AS-616Es ("E" stood for export).

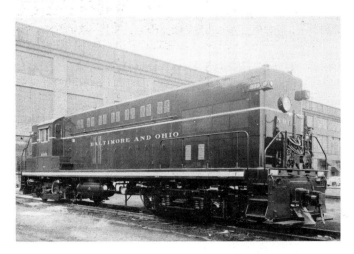

Two features of late AS-16s — tall carbody, and welded frames with bolt-on steps and pilots — were obvious, but the 6″ increase in overall unit length was not so readily apparent. Baltimore & Ohio 899 was shipped in February 1954.

General Electric to design a main generator compatible with the 625-rpm 608-series engine, and GE's answer was the GT-590 main generator, which would feed power to GE 752-series traction motors. Using the GE traction motors would mean installing larger traction motor blowers, and to

accommodate the larger blowers Eddystone had to lengthen the frame of the AS-series heavy road-switchers by 6″.

New welded frames were designed for all three models, with only small variations among them (the AS-616 frame retained its ability to be heavily ballasted). The frames were designed with bolt-on step and pilot assemblies, something of a throwback to the old cast frames. Baldwin engineers also created a new carbody design. The height of both long and short hoods was increased to within 2″ of the cab roof, allowing room for a number of interior changes. Dynamic brakes could be installed in the front of the long hood, with the resistors above the air intake grilles. With the dynamic brakes moved out of the short hood, that space would be free on all units for installation of a steam generator, a 900-gallon fuel tank, or both.

As a test-bed for the new design, Baldwin constructed an AS-616 in early 1953. Except for employing Westinghouse electrical equipment, the unit incorporated all the new features. It rode on the outside-equalized C-type truck. For display at the Atlantic City (New Jersey) Railroad Exhibition in June 1953, the unit was decked out in a demonstrator livery of brown, red, and gold, and numbered B-L-H 1601.

Actual application of the new design to orders was piecemeal, because Baldwin used up old stock before switching entirely to a new design. In a few cases the use of the old design was the result of customer requests. Although the redesign had been precipitated by the need to accommodate GE electrical gear, Baldwin continued using Westinghouse equipment as long as the supply lasted. (Only two heavy road-switchers would be built with GE electrical equipment. Baldwin purchased enough GE gear to equip 22 heavy road-switchers, and when production ceased the leftover GE equipment was sold.)

In 1953 deliveries of heavy road-switchers declined dramatically in the face of the second straight year of poor sales. Only 21 AS-16s went to five customers; Katy received four (1585-1586, 1787-1788, from its 1952 order), PRSL 10 (6007-6016, filling 1952 and 1953 orders), and B&O one (905, its 1952 order), all the old design. Katy 1787-1788 and all 10 of the PRSL units were equipped with steam generators. Katy's were placed in service at Parsons, Kansas, and powered the *Katy Flyer* on the Parsons-St. Louis line. PRSL's units joined their DRS-4-4-1500 siblings at Camden, and B&O 905 went into service at Smithfield, Pennsylvania. Deliveries of AS-16s with the new carbody and frame began with four units for the Reading (551-554) and with Nickel Plate's two units (320-321). The NKP units entered freight service out of Brewster, Ohio, on the Wheeling & Lake Erie. Reading's four AS-16s, equipped with dynamic brakes and electric throttles, were a result of that road's order for 10 placed earlier in the year. Near the delivery date, Reading cut back the order to four, but all 10 were nearing completion when the cancellation came, so Baldwin finished the entire lot, delivered four to the Reading, and held the remaining six in hopes of finding another customer. (The task would be made more difficult because of the units' special equipment, and the wait for a customer would be a long one.)

Deliveries of AS-616s in 1953 ran to 32 units. C&O 5528-5529 were dispatched to Russell, Kentucky, in July, and Milwaukee Road 2104-2107 were shipped to Milwaukee, Wisconsin, in August and September. All used the older-design carbody, but C&O's two differed from their 37 older Chessie sisters in that they rode on outside-equalized trucks and had the 6″-longer frame.

Eddystone's largest delivery of heavy road-switchers in 1953 went to the Central of Brazil, which received the 20 meter-gauge units (4371-4390) ordered in 1951. These units, actually designated AS-616E ("E" for "export"), employed dynamic brakes, m.u., and floating-bolster C-type trucks. The units weighed approximately 211,000 pounds, and featured low-clearance cabs. All 20 were placed in service at Belo Horizonte, north of Rio de Janeiro. Baldwin

also completed Orinoco's nine-unit AS-616 order (deliveries had begun in 1952). A "tenth" AS-616 was soon included in Orinoco's deliveries because one unit — Orinoco 1008 — was severely damaged shortly after its construction. The tenth unit, Orinoco 1010, was actually a rebuild of No. 1008. Because of the near-total reconstruction of the AS-616, it was given a new road number and a new Baldwin construction number and date (but retained its original power plant). No AS-416s were delivered in 1953.

THE DEMISE BEGINS

One look at Baldwin's 1954 order book makes it clear why that was the year the company began planning its exit from the diesel-electric locomotive market. In contrast to the solid sales of the early 1950s, orders for only 14 AS-series road-switchers were taken in 1954. AS-16 orders bracketed the year: Nickel Plate ordered a second pair in January and B&O ordered nine in December (bringing its total to 16 units). Only two other orders arrived. In October, Norfolk Southern once again asked for AS-416s (two this time, to be 1614-1615) and in December the Oregon & Northwestern, a 51-mile logging line, spoke for B-L-H test-bed/demonstrator No. 1601.

AS-series shipments for 1954 were nearly as scarce as orders. Delivery of Parana-Santa Catarina's five-unit order for meter-gauge C-Cs, which dated back to May 1952, was completed in February 1954 (like the CofB meter-gauge units, these were designated AS-616Es). They were placed in service at Botucatu, northwest of São Paulo, Brazil.

Working to fill 1953 orders, the erecting hall churned out Norfolk Southern AS-416s 1611-1613 and dispatched them in January. B&O AS-16 899 was shipped to Baltimore in February, and six AS-16s for MoPac — StLB&M 4326-4331 — were shipped to Houston, Texas, in June and July. Of the 23 AS-616s shipped to fill 1953 orders, PRR received two, Trona one, and NdeM 20 units. Pennsy's pair — 8111-8112 — were shipped on February 15 and 18, respectively; PRR 8112 was the last new diesel Baldwin ever shipped to the road. Trona AS-616 52 was shipped in March to join the road's DT-6-6-2000s at Trona, California, and NdeM's score of Baldwins — 6800-6819 — departed for Monterrey, Mexico, between March and May; NdeM 6819 was the last AS-616 constructed. All AS-616s delivered in 1954 rode the outside-equalized truck. Rounding out 1954 deliveries was Nickel Plate's pair of AS-16s ordered earlier that same year. The NKP units, 322-323, were shipped in mid-June and joined NKP 320-321 working out of Brewster, Ohio.

The total heavy road-switcher delivery count for 1954 was 40 units; all except NS AS-416s 1611-1613 were the new design (except, of course, Westinghouse electrical equipment continued to be used). Norfolk Southern's trio of AS-416s employed the shorter, one-piece welded frame and low carbody hoods, undoubtedly at the customer's request.

1955: THE PRODUCTION FINALE FOR HEAVY ROAD-SWITCHERS

With only an asterisk in the record book, 1955 marked the end of Baldwin's heavy road-switcher era. Sale of test-bed/demonstrator 1601 to the Oregon & Northwestern in December 1954 marked the last order for the company's most popular heavy road-switcher, and when ex-B-L-H 1601 departed Eddystone as O&NW 1 in January 1955 (with m.u. equipment added), it became the last new AS-616 to leave, making the final AS-616 tally 222 units. Production of AS-16s ended with shipment of B&O's nine-unit 1954 order (890-898) in May and June 1955. The units entered service at Grafton and Keyser, West Virginia. The final count of four-axle, 1600-h.p. road-switchers was 127 units.

Two of the southern railroads which had been customers for A1A-A1A road-switchers since the early days of the DRS-6-4-1500 gave the AS-416 its last fling. In March, two Norfolk Southern AS-416s — 1614-1615 — were shipped to fill the road's 1954 order. NS returned in June with a final

Missouri Pacific

Martin Zak

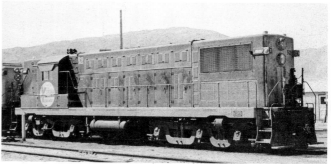

Henry W. Brueckman

Jim Zwernemann

MoPac (StLB&M) AS-16 No. 4327, one of six AS-16s the road received in 1954, was destined to lead a journeyman's life. Renumbered 936, the unit was sold in the 1960s to United States Pipe & Foundry, where it worked as No. 43, then was resold in 1972 to Peabody Coal Co. The last new diesel to depart Eddystone bound for the Pennsylvania Railroad was AS-616 No. 8112, shipped on February 18, 1954; 12 years later the historic unit was photographed at Conway, Pennsylvania, on June 23, 1966. Trona AS-616 No. 52 joined the road's DT-6-6-2000s (50-51) in the harsh California desert in 1954. The upper grille in the long hood is for No. 52's dynamic brakes. National Railways of Mexico 6800-6819 of 1954 was the last group of AS-616s constructed. Number 6804 paused at Nuevo Laredo, Mexico, on August 13, 1963.

order for two units, bringing its purchases to 17. In April 1955, Savannah & Atlanta ordered its third and last AS-416. S&A 110 was shipped to Savannah, Georgia, in August 1955, and Norfolk Southern 1616-1617 departed Eddystone in December 1955. These units, which brought the model's final production count to 25 units, represented opposite extremes in construction. Like all previous Savannah & Atlanta units, S&A 110 was constructed on a cast frame that had otherwise been passé for years, and the unit was built with the old carbody styling and unusual A1A trucks,

John A. Rehor: H. H. Harwood Jr. collection

Nickel Plate's second pair of AS-16s (322-323) arrived on the NKP in 1954. Four years later, the duo stood at Brewster, Ohio, home to all four of the road's AS-16s. The units had electric throttles so they could m.u. with EMD and Alco diesels.

all at S&A's request. NS 1616-1617, on the other hand, were the only AS-416s of the "new design" to be built. In addition, the supply of Westinghouse electrical gear had finally run out, and the two NS units were built with GE components. Most notably, completion of NS 1617 marked the end of all Baldwin heavy road-switcher production.

Only a postscript remained to be added to the story of Baldwin heavy road-switchers. The six AS-16s left from Reading's partially canceled 1953 order still sat at Eddystone — still without a home. In October 1955 the Pennsyl-

vania-Reading Seashore Lines purchased all six (filling out its roster of AS-16s at 16 units). Before turning the AS-16s over to the PRSL, Eddystone removed the dynamic brakes and electric throttles and added standard Baldwin electro-pneumatic throttles. Steam generators were added to two units, PRSL 6026-6027. PRSL 6022-6023 were shipped in December 1955, and the remaining four (6024-6027) departed in February 1956. When PRSL 6026-6027 were shipped on February 29, 1956, the end had come. From the delivery of Columbus & Greenville 601 in 1946 to the deliv-

Donald Sims

In January 1955, ex-B-L-H AS-616 test-bed/demonstrator 1601 was shipped to the Oregon & Northwestern as O&NW No. 1. Hauling log trains became its primary duty.

Jim Wade

ery of PRSL 6027 less than a decade later, Baldwin had sent 583 heavy road-switchers into the world.

THE YEARS AT WORK

On many railroads the AS-series road-switchers followed in the footsteps of their DRS-series kin (18 operators of AS-series units had purchased DRS-series diesels). In no case was this more true than with the AS-416. All three domestic users of the AS-416 — Norfolk Southern, Columbus & Greenville, and Savannah & Atlanta — also operated DRS-6-4-1500s. S&A's three AS-416s were traded to EMD in the mid-1960s as part of the purge of Baldwin power under CofG/Southern Railway control, but Columbus & Greenville's lone AS-416, No. 606, enjoyed the longevity of most of its older sisters. For years C&G 606 was used as a yard switcher at Columbus, Mississippi, but later, during and after the period of Illinois Central Gulf control, it became a road engine. In early 1984, it still worked for C&G.

Most of Norfolk Southern's AS-416s provided nearly two decades of service. The oldest — 1601-1605 — were stricken from the roster in the mid-1960s (replaced by GP18s and GP38s), but Nos. 1606-1613 and 1615-1617 were still at work in 1973. In 1974 Norfolk Southern was merged into the Southern Railway, and only NS 1616 survived thereafter. The unit was sold to Peabody Coal Company. As PCC 1616 it was used as a backup locomotive to the ex-Kaiser DRS-6-6-1500s stationed at Lenzburg, Illinois. Today, ex-NS 1616 — the second-to-last Baldwin heavy road-switcher constructed — survives at the Spencer Shop State Historic Site in North Carolina.

The AS-16 was a creature of the East and Midwest; of the 127 constructed, only 28 regularly operated west of Chicago for their original owners. The "western" AS-16s belonged to Katy, MoPac, and Soo, and the units had vastly different careers. Among MoPac's eight, I-GN 4195-4196 were placed in service at San Antonio, Texas, and StLB&M 4326-4331 began their duties at Houston, Texas. StLB&M 4326-4331 were renumbered 935-940, but all left the MoPac roster in the minority-builder purge of the middle 1960s. However, 935 and 937 went on to the Iron Mines Co. of Venezuela, and 936, 939, and 940 moved on to United States Pipe & Foundry in Birmingham, Alabama, becoming USP&F 43-45. In 1972, the three were again sold, this time to Peabody Coal, which was amassing a sizable Baldwin roster which eventually included four models — DRS-6-6-1500, DT-6-6-2000, AS-16, and AS-416. USP&F 44-45 retained their old

Warren Calloway

Although shipped in August 1955, at the road's request Savannah & Atlanta 110 had a cast frame. It rode the unusual GSC A1A trucks used on all S&A DRS-6-4-1500s and AS-416s. Norfolk Southern 1616-1617, shipped in December 1955, were the last AS-416s, the last Baldwin heavy road-switchers, the only AS-416s with the modernized AS-series tall carbody, and the only 1600-h.p. Baldwins with GE electrical gear.

road numbers on Peabody Coal, and lugged coal from mine to barge loader at the River Queen Mine near Central City, Kentucky. USP&F 43 became Peabody 343 and was stationed at Peabody's Lynnville (Indiana) mine, where it was plagued by mechanical problems and seldom operated. Peabody no longer employs Baldwins.

While MoPac began its move toward an all-EMD roster in the early 1960s, its neighbor — the M-K-T — started even earlier, in a different fashion. Between 1956 and 1960 the original power plants of Katy Alco FAs and RS3s and Baldwin switchers and AS-16s were discarded in favor of EMD 567s. The AS-16s were repowered with 567C V-16s and re-equipped with GP9-style long hoods between February 1958 and March 1960. The units were also renumbered about this time (1787 became 124, 1788 was retired, and 1571-1586 became 126-141). In 1972, 14 of the repowered AS-16s received a surprise extension to their careers when they were purchased by the Chicago & North Western. On the C&NW they were assigned to Green Bay, Wisconsin, and were not retired until 1981. Soo Line's pair of AS-16s, 379-380, spent much of their careers working around Supe-

Nearing the end of their careers, Norfolk Southern AS-416s 1615, 1608, and 1609 ride the timbers at Lillington, North Carolina, on the Fayetteville branch, March 24, 1973.

The only AS-416 on the Columbus & Greenville, No. 606 handled switching duties at Columbus, Mississippi, throughout much of its career. On September 9, 1973, the big Baldwin toiled at just such work.

M-K-T AS-16 No. 1573, Baldwin class of 1950, was repowered by EMD in February 1958. Under the unit's new Geep-style long hood rests a 1500-h.p. V-16 567-series power plant.

Wherever there was heavy hauling to be done, Eddystone's diesels seemed to appear. Soo AS-16 No. 380 assembles loaded ore cars at a mine on the Cuyuna Range in Minnesota.

rior, Wisconsin, and in Minnesota's Cuyuna Range. Soo 379 went to EMD in trade for SD40s delivered in 1969; No. 380 was trade-in credit for Soo's GE U30Cs of 1968.

Perhaps the most hapless AS-16s were the four owned by the Nickel Plate. Out of place on NKP's EMD- and Alco-dominated roster from the day they were delivered, the units were dispatched to Alco (320-321) and EMD (322-323) in 1959 for repowering. At the time, the eldest of the lot was less than six years old. The Schenectady-repowered pair received 16-cylinder 251B engines and RS11-style long hoods, while the La Grange-repowered duo received V-16 567C engines and Geep-style long hoods. As hybrids, NKP's AS-16s enjoyed average lifespans. When Nickel Plate was merged into the Norfolk & Western in 1964, NKP 320-323 became N&W 2320-2323, later 7900-7903. The EMD-repowered locomotives lasted longest, with 7902 being stripped at Roanoke in 1977.

The greatest stand of the AS-16 was in its home state of Pennsylvania and the states immediately surrounding — New York, New Jersey, Maryland, West Virginia, and Ohio. Erie's 16 units were originally assigned to Buffalo and Port Jervis, New York, Croxton and Secaucus, New Jersey, and Meadville, Pennsylvania. During their careers they never ventured far from that home territory; Marion, Ohio, was the west end of their world. Erie (and later Erie Lackawanna) freight-service AS-16s worked drag freights and ore trains, served in yards, and after the EL merger dug in as helpers on the Scranton Division's (ex-DL&W) Pocono grade. Erie 1140, the road's lone steam generator-equipped AS-16, became something of a fixture on mail trains

between Youngstown and Marion, Ohio. Most Erie Lackawanna AS-16s were scrapped in June 1966; all were gone shortly thereafter. Erie 1116 was purchased by Durham & Southern for parts. Erie's neighbor to the south, the Reading, had the most AS-16s, eventually rostering 43 units. The rugged territory west of Reading, Pennsylvania, was the domain of most of Reading's somber units throughout their careers. The road retired its last AS-16s in 1969.

On the other side of Philadelphia from the Reading Co., Pennsylvania-Reading Seashore Lines' 16 AS-16s lived quite different lives. PRSL was geared largely to its seasonal passenger business, and steam generator-equipped 6007-6016 and 6026-6027 tended to that business and also worked freights. Except in emergencies, numbers 6022-6025 were strictly freight locomotives. PRSL 6007, 6009, and 6011 were traded in on EMD GP38s built in 1967, and two more units — 6012 and 6015 — went for GP38s in 1969. In 1969, PRSL 6008 and 6010 were leased to Penn Central. PRSL was included in Conrail in 1976, and three 20-year-old AS-16s — 6016, 6024-6025 — survived to become Conrail 8397-8399. Conrail officially retired the trio in October 1976; PRSL 6024 is known to have been active as late as August 1976.

On the Western Maryland AS-16s 173-176 were assigned to Hagerstown, Maryland, where, for all intents and purposes, they stayed for more than a decade and a half until being traded to EMD in 1969. Not so homebound were the AS-16s of WM rival Baltimore & Ohio. In the company of contemporary RF-16 sharknose freight diesels, B&O's 16 AS-16s primarily worked in West Virginia, eastern Ohio,

Peabody Coal AS-16 No. 44, shipped from Eddystone in 1954 as MoPac (StLB&M) 4330, rests between trains at River Queen Mine, near Central City, Kentucky, in March 1976.

The first of 43 AS-16s on the Reading was No. 530, which departed Eddystone in July 1951. Nearly 15 years later, on May 7, 1966, No. 530 was nearing the end of its career as it led sister 533 westbound through Rutherford, Pennsylvania.

At North Randall, Ohio, in July 1956, the mixed cadence of 608A and Alco 244-series power plants shatters the silence as Erie AS-16 No. 1112 heads coal hoppers bound for Cleveland. Erie's Baldwin road-switchers had electric throttles.

Not yet relettered for their new owner, but working for Penn Central and renumbered 6966-6967, two ex-Pennsy AS-616s work as the Bay View hump engines at Baltimore, Maryland, in January 1969.

H. H. Harwood Jr.

H. H. Harwood Jr.

James F. EuDaly

Over a million pounds of Baldwin diesel power shove on the rear of a westbound coal train assaulting Cheviot Hill near Cincinnati, Ohio, on October 21, 1964.

Martin Zak

Maryland, and Pennsylvania. In the late 1950s and early 1960s, again in the company of the RF-16s, the B&O units worked north out of Pittsburgh to Rochester (on B&O's Buffalo, Rochester, & Pittsburgh), and also on the Lorain (Ohio) branch; in the late 1960s, some found their way to the Cincinnati area. B&O's AS-16s were renumbered twice — first to 6200-6215, then to 2234-2249. Three went to EMD in 1969 (2237, 2242, 2247), another four in 1970 (2240, 2245, 2248-2249), and four more in 1971 (2241, 2243, 2244, 2246). The other five were sold to Peabody Coal in 1969; all continued to carry their final B&O road numbers. The 2234 was stationed at Shawneetown, Illinois, 2235 was used for parts and sat derelict at Peabody's Jasonville (Indiana) shop, 2236 was assigned to Central City, Kentucky, 2238 worked at Bevier, Missouri, and 2239 was employed at Freeburg, Illinois. All were sold for scrap by 1975 except 2235, which was rebuilt by Morrison-Knudsen in 1978 as PCC slug 01 and was used at Marissa, Illinois, with an EMD Geep. Of the 127 AS-16s constructed, none was active in 1984.

Most popular among Baldwin heavy road-switchers, the massive AS-616 left its mark in the U. S., Mexico, and South America. Like its elder sister — the DRS-6-6-1500 — the AS-616 was a pure and simple beast of burden, to be used anywhere long, heavy strings of freight cars needed to be moved. Not surprisingly, many AS-616s found work in the heavily industrialized regions of Ohio and Pennsylvania. C&O's great fleet of 39 AS-616s spent most of their lives pulling or pushing coal trains, and following their years spread out in the Ohio River basin they migrated to Cincinnati, where they worked transfers and pushed trains out of Cincinnati up Cheviot Hill. C&O retired eight units through 1966, and in 1967 the remaining AS-616s began being renumbered into the 2200-series, but shortly afterward wholesale retirements began. All were off the roster by the end of 1971, but not all went immediately to the scrapper. In November 1967 C&O transferred five AS-616s — 2212, 2219, 2225, 2229, and 2231 (ex-5547, 5555, 5562, 5567, and 5569) — to affiliate B&O. B&O retired 2225, 2229, and 2231 in 1969, but 2212 and 2219 survived until 1971; the latter was even relettered B&O and renumbered 2250. C&O AS-616s 2209, 2217, 2220, and 2222 (ex-5542, 5553, 5556, and 5558) were leased during 1971 to the

Bessemer & Lake Erie. Surprisingly, the first C&O AS-616 retired was destined to be the last survivor. In January 1958, Chessie sold 5533 to Pan American Engineering, which in turn sold it to Kaiser Steel. The unit became Kaiser 1020 (later 1029), and worked with Kaiser's six-axle Baldwins at Eagle Mountain Railway in California. In 1971 the big C-C was transferred to Kaiser Bauxite at Discovery Bay in Jamaica, where it carried number 5107.

U. S. Steel's two AS-616 users in Pennsylvania — B&LE and Union — employed them in the same service as their DRS-6-6-1500s. On the B&LE the similarity did not stop there: AS-616s 408-409 went to scrap in 1973, the same year that Bessemer purged its last DRS-6-6-1500s. On the Union, the units were not so fortunate. Troubled by weakness in the welded frames of AS-616s 625-627, Union chose not to repower its newest Baldwins when the DRS-6-6-1500s received EMD power plants. Union's three AS-616s were retired in 1964, a decade and a half before the road's last DRS-6-6-1500. The exact opposite occurred on the third domestic U. S. Steel road to operate the AS-616. TCI&RR (by then the Fairfield Works) retired its DRS-6-6-1500s in the late 1960s but extended the life of its five AS-616s by repowering them with EMD engines. These units — 1502-1506 — were renumbered 163-167; they survived in 1984, some operating for U. S. Steel's Birmingham Southern.

Pennsy's 11 AS-616s, originally split between Ohio and Pennsylvania, migrated to Conway Yard near Pittsburgh in the years that followed. Pennsy brought its fleet to an even dozen in 1965 by purchasing Pittsburgh & West Virginia's sole AS-616, No. 40. It became PRR 8114 and for a time stayed at Altoona, Pennsylvania, where it had been placed in service. In the darkening days of the Pennsylvania Railroad the units traveled to Baltimore and were assigned numbers in the 6900-series. Pennsy began retiring AS-616s in 1966, ex-P&WV 40 was retired in September 1967, and by June 1969 (after creation of Penn Central), the number of AS-616s had decreased to five. All were retired by the end of 1972.

In the upper Midwest the AS-616 was a common sight on three roads — DSS&A, C&NW, and Milwaukee — for years. DSS&A's eight worked with their 1500-h.p. sisters west of Marquette toward Superior. This end of the line was rugged and often required paired units, while the flatter east end of

A. C. Kalmbach

Baldwins meet as AS-616 No. 208 rolls past DRS-6-6-1500 No. 201 on the Duluth, South Shore & Atlantic. DSS&A employed eight AS-616s, four DRS-6-6-1500s.

the railroad was entrusted to single DT-6-6-2000s. DSS&A 211 (ex B-L-H demonstrator 1600) often operated alone on the DSS&A, and regularly worked mine runs. With the Soo Line merger DSS&A 204-211 became Soo 388-395. For the most part, the Baldwins stayed in their old home territory; however, some went to Minneapolis, working out of Shoreham Yard. As was the case with their older C-C sisters, the units were replaced by Soo Geeps by 1966. While Soo accountants were undoubtedly pleased (the units' operating costs were high compared to the EMD replacements), crews missed the Baldwins. Example: On the hill into Houghton, Michigan, the AS-616s could lug 900 tons; the Geeps that replaced them were good for only 600 tons. The last Soo units were traded for SD40s which arrived in 1970.

Two-thirds of Chicago & North Western's roster of three AS-616s suffered the same fate as their DRS-6-6-1500 and DRS-6-4-1500 counterparts — repowering. In July and August 1962, C&NW 1560-1561 were repowered with EMD prime movers. C&NW 1604 was not repowered and was retired in 1964. Even with repowering, the hybrid units were retired in 1977.

Milwaukee's eight AS-616s enjoyed the longest lives of any in the upper Midwest. Early on the road decided that its pair of AS-616 boosters could be better employed as stan-

dard units, so in 1953 Milwaukee equipped both with cabs, renumbering them from 2100B-2101B to 2102-2103. The most common assignment for the AS-616s was transfer work in the hilly territory around the Twin Cities. It was there, and at Aberdeen Yard in Aberdeen, South Dakota, that the Baldwins played out their careers until replaced by EMD MP15ACs in 1976.

In the West, AS-616s flexed their muscles in an unusual variety of duties, working hump yards, flat yards, and transfers, hauling ore and lumber, serving as pushers, and easing up branch lines and short lines. For much of their careers hump and yard service was the job for Union Pacific's AS-616s, and Pocatello, Idaho, and Ogden, Utah, were the places to find them battling long strings of cars. From 1964 to 1968 UP 1262 and 1265 were leased to Ogden Union Railway & Depot. All UP's units were traded to EMD in 1968-69. Another AS-616 well versed in working yard and terminal trackage also ended its career in 1968 —Houston Belt & Terminal 32. The big C-C performed the heaviest road and switching jobs along HB&T's 53 miles of line connecting Houston's Class 1 carriers, and although long gone, was the most powerful (and only six-axle) diesel ever owned by the HB&T.

Through the years units of the great SP/T&NO roster of 64 AS-616s could be found working on the Pacific Electric, pushing trains over Donner Pass, tackling the barren ore country of Arizona or the pine forests of Oregon, grinding away at yards at Eugene, Los Angeles, and Houston, and handling other rugged tasks. SP lost its first AS-616s on July 12, 1959, when 5260-5261 and booster 4904 (the cabless units had been renumbered from 5501-5505 to 4901-4905 in 1955) plunged through an open drawbridge and into the Napa River. All three units were subsequently scrapped. Additional retirements began in 1964 and the last unit — 5233 — was retired in mid-1970. SP's other AS-616 boosters were retired between 1966 and 1970, and T&NO's AS-616s were put out to pasture between 1965 and 1969.

As with its DRS-6-6-1500s, the SP sold a number of AS-616s. The first was 5249, which went to the Trona in 1960. There, as No. 53, it joined Trona's original 1600-h.p. C-C, No. 52, and DT-6-6-2000s 50-51. Trona 52-53 both lived on in 1984.

In 1961 SP sold two AS-616s — 5250-5251 — to Kaiser Bauxite in Jamaica. After being ferried from New Orleans to Port Kaiser, the pair took road numbers 5106-5105. In 1961 SP 5273 was sold to ITT-Rayonier, where it became

NdeM

NdeM created homely No. 6821 using parts from wrecked AS-616s. The result was an A1A-A1A unit with a 608A engine derated to 1000 h.p. by removing the turbocharger.

116

 John C. Illman

Delivered in 1952 as SP 5276 and sold to Rayonier in 1968, AS-616 No. 76 rumbles along at
45 mph with empty log cars near Railroad Camp, Washington, on October 8, 1970.

No. 45. More units followed; 5275 became Rayonier 90 in
1962, 5272 became Rayonier 70 in 1967, and 5276 became
Rayonier 76 in 1968. These diesels were extant on the logging line in 1984. Rayonier 76 became something of a celeb-
rity in 1976 when it was painted red, white, and blue for
America's bicentennial.

SP 5253 was the most traveled of SP's big Baldwins. In
1963 the unit was sold to the McCloud River Railroad, and
after serving that line for five years as No. 34, was again
sold in August 1969, this time to Oregon & Northwestern
(where it became No. 4). There it joined not only O&NW 1
(ex-B-L-H demonstrator 1601), but also SP sisters 5239
(which had become O&NW 2 in 1964) and 5274 (which had
become O&NW 3 in 1968). In 1984, all four AS-616s remained on the O&NW. In 1968, SP 5257 became Roscoe,
Snyder & Pacific 400, but the unit was retired by the Texas
short line only two years later.

Perhaps no AS-616s worked harder than those of Kaiser
Steel. On Kaiser's Eagle Mountain Railway the pair of six-
axle road-switchers lugged heavy ore jimmies to and from
the SP connection at Ferrum, California. Kaiser 1012A-
1012B were renumbered 1027-1028 and one — 1027 —
eventually found its way to Kaiser Bauxite in Jamaica.
There it received road number 5108. Number 1028 was sold
to Rayonier as No. 14.

Across the border in Mexico, NdeM's 20 AS-616s worked
in a variety of freight duties. In 1957, following wrecks,
NdeM 6809 and 6814 were repowered with EMD 1750-h.p.,
567C V-16s and rebuilt with EMD-style long hoods. Wrecks
also claimed several other units in the late 1950s and early
1960s, and two unique locomotives resulted. In 1962 and
1963 NdeM's San Luis Potosi shops used parts from
wrecked and retired AS-616s 6808, 6815, and 6817 to construct rebuilds 6821 and 6820, model designations SLP-1
and SLP-4. Except for a low, chopped nose the SLP-1 maintained much of the appearance of an AS-616, but mechanically it was quite different. The center traction motor of
each truck was removed, making the unit an A1A-A1A, and
the power plant was derated to 1000 h.p. The SLP-4, NdeM
6820, was a creation which looked nothing like an AS-616
save for its trucks. This locomotive featured a full-width
carbody salvaged from a wrecked EMD F, and a homebuilt
and only moderately stylized cab. Inside rode an EMD 567-
series V-16. The NdeM began retiring its other AS-616s in
the mid-1970s; by mid-1981, only one standard AS-616 —
6806 — remained, but it, too, was soon retired. And what of
National Railways of Mexico 6819 — the last AS-616 constructed at Eddystone? It was scrapped in the late 1970s,
thus joining all but a lucky handful of its Baldwin heavy
road-switcher kindred in history.

117

The elegant lines of Baldwin's RF-16 are apparent in this front-on view of New York Central Shark 3812, posed at DeWitt Yard, Syracuse, New York, on March 18, 1952, when the stylish unit was just over two months old.

THE "HAULING FOOL"

Streamlined freight-service diesels

WHEN AMERICA'S RAILROADS began the wholesale replacement of steam power after World War Two, one of the most lucrative portions of the huge diesel locomotive market was certain to be streamlined, four-axle cab and booster units for mainline freight and dual-service operation. By virtue of its introduction of the FT in 1939 and production of 1096 1350-h.p. FTs (through November 1945), Electro-Motive had a firm grip on this market at the war's end, and La Grange further strengthened its position by introducing the 1500-h.p. F3 in July 1945. Alco-GE had considered development of a diesel freight locomotive before the war, but owing first to lack of a suitable power plant and then to wartime restrictions, the company did not put such a diesel on the road until October 1945. Alco-GE then tested its three-unit (A-B-A) locomotive — the "Black Maria," — on several eastern roads near Alco's Schenectady, New York, plant. While the "Black Maria" was never duplicated, it helped lay the groundwork for Alco-GE's entry into the market, and in January 1946 the first 1500-h.p. 244-series-powered FA/FB series locomotive was delivered to the Gulf, Mobile & Ohio.

BALDWIN'S DR-4-4-1500

Baldwin formally joined the competition for streamlined freight diesel sales in September 1945 when the Central Railroad of New Jersey (through subsidiary Central of Pennsylvania) ordered 15 1500-h.p. freight units (five A-B-A sets). Eddystone's answer to CNJ's needs was the 608SC-powered DR-4-4-1500, but postwar labor problems, material shortages, and difficulties in settling on a final design plagued the DR-4-4-1500 program, and it was not until early March 1947 that construction of the first CNJ units began. Despite the delays, Baldwin landed a second order for the DR-4-4-1500, then a third. In March 1947 the New York Central signed on for four DR-4-4-1500 cabs and two boosters, and in May 1947 Missouri Pacific ordered eight cabs and four boosters.

To transfer the 608SC's power to railhead in the DR-4-4-1500, Baldwin employed a Westinghouse 471A main generator and 370-series traction motors (both offered in the DR-12-8-3000). The traction motors rode in General Steel Castings Commonwealth Type B trucks, the same trucks introduced under the DRS-4-4-1500 during this period. The 608SC power plant was oriented on a GSC cast frame so that the main generator and air compressor faced the cab. The main electrical control cabinets were installed at frame level immediately behind the engine, and the radiator cores and exhaust fans were mounted above them. An air tunnel directed cooling air from intakes mounted on the sides of the carbody to the radiator cores. Air reservoirs were also

Prototype for the DR-4-4-1500 was Central Railroad of New Jersey (CRP) A-B-A set 70-K-71. Full-height air intakes, unshrouded dynamic brake grids, flush number-boards, and the tapered cab roof made the set unique.

located in the rear of the units. The CNJ DR-4-4-1500s were equipped with dynamic brakes, and three grilles were placed adjacent to the rooftop fans to provide cooling air for the dynamic brake resistors. Babyface carbody styling — in vogue at Eddystone since its introduction on SAL DR-12-8-3000 No. 4500 — wrapped the package. When the first DR-4-4-1500s rolled out of the erecting bay each unit measured 53'-6" inside coupler knuckles. At that, the Baldwin offering was the longest of the freight cabs, two feet longer than Alco's FA1 and nearly three feet longer than EMD's F3A.

The first three DR-4-4-1500s were delivered to Central Railroad of New Jersey (CRP) in November 1947. The A-B-A set wore CNJ's tangerine-and-blue livery and was assigned a number and letter combination: 70-K-71. The set was placed in service at Jersey City, New Jersey, on November 11, 1947.

When the DR-4-4-1500 prototypes went to work in freight service a debilitating design flaw quickly became apparent. The cooling system air intakes occupied the full height of the carbody at the rear of each unit, and air pulled into the intakes passed through the radiator air tunnel, through the radiator cores, and was exhausted by the roof-mounted fans. It was soon discovered that moisture drawn into the carbody through the large air intakes caused frequent shorts in the electrical cabinets, which were directly below the radiators. (Piping systems not properly segregated from wiring also contributed to electrical failures.) Subsequent CNJ DR-4-4-1500s were constructed with a revised carbody intake pattern which eliminated the full-height grilles, and in a related change, shrouds were placed over the rooftop dynamic brake grilles to prevent water from entering from above. (Through the years CNJ revised the air intakes several more times, indicating that the problem was not solved by the initial changes.)

The premier DR-4-4-1500 A-B-A set worked alone on the CNJ for seven and one-half months, then sister units began to be placed in service. From July to September 1948 eight more cabs (72-79) and four boosters (L, M, R, S) were brought to life at Jersey City. In addition to the air intake revisions, the later cab units displayed minor cosmetic changes. CNJ 70-71 had flush number-boards, but all subsequent units featured protruding, canted number-boards, and while the roofs of CNJ 70 and 71 were built with a gradual slope from the top of the windshield to the roof of the engine compartment, the newer units featured a flatter cab roof with a sharp step behind the air horn up to the height of the engine compartment. With delivery of A-B-A set 78-S-79 to Jersey City on September 26, 1948, the 15-unit order was complete. Meanwhile, an equal number of Electro-Motive F3s had also taken up residence on the Jersey Central Lines, and no further orders for Baldwin freight

cabs would be placed with Eddystone salesmen by the CNJ.

More steps were taken to improve the streamlined freight unit when the NYC and Missouri Pacific DR-4-4-1500s were built in the fall of 1948. Internal equipment was rearranged to cure the air intake and electrical problems experienced with the CNJ units. Externally, the most obvious modification was a 2' increase in the length of the cab units. The added length pushed the cab ahead of the front truck bolster, allowing room for the electrical cabinets to be placed behind the cab bulkhead, safely away from the rear air intakes and contaminants drawn into the rear of the carbody. The storage batteries were moved from a vulnerable position beneath the frame to inside the carbody, just behind the cab, which made room for a larger underbelly fuel tank and allowed placement of the air reservoirs beside the fuel tank instead of in the rear of the carbody. Another change was the employment of welded underframes rather than cast, and use of combination fabricated/cast pilots with

W. R. Osborne: Dolzall collection

Working westbound out of High Bridge, New Jersey, on September 19, 1949, CNJ 70, the first DR-4-4-1500, already displays modifications that include shrouded dynamic brake grids, revised air intakes, and canted number-boards. CNJ 75 (the second unit) has the smaller air intakes used on all DR-4-4-1500 babyface units after the prototype set.

119

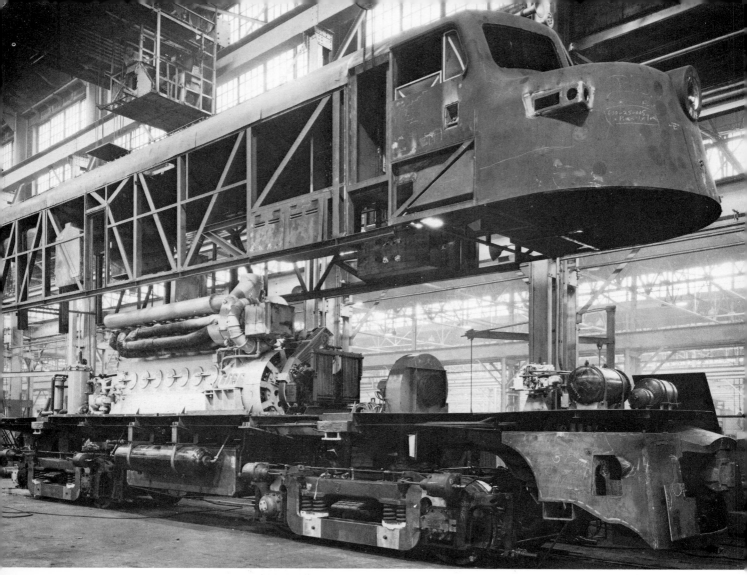

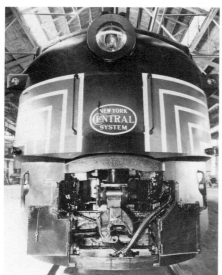

At top, a babyface carbody hovers over trucks, frame, and 608SC power plant as an NYC DR-4-4-1500 takes shape in Eddystone's "tender shop" in 1948. Completion of NYC 3400-3700-3401 (left and above) in late 1948 marked the introduction of a significantly revised freight cab design. The trio entered service on October 26, 1948.

retractable couplers. MoPac's units did not have dynamic brakes and thus lacked the three roof-mounted grilles. A steam generator option was never offered on the DR-4-4-1500, but NYC ordered its units equipped with steam lines and train-order signal equipment so they could be used in tandem with other locomotives (namely, NYC's DR-6-4-1500s) that were equipped for passenger duties.

NYC's DR-4-4-1500s, numbered 3400-3403 (cabs) and

3700-3701 (boosters), were placed in service at Cleveland, Ohio, between October 26 and October 30, 1948. The cabs were dressed in NYC's "lightning stripe" scheme with the light gray band ending just above the rear engine compartment door, but only white lettering brightened the somber boosters. MoPac, on the other hand, specified that its DR-4-4-1500s be dressed in the road's standard blue-and-gray livery (with gold trim and red emblem). MoPac 201A-208A

Shark-nose styling came to the DR-4-4-1500 with Pennsylvania's units of February 1949. The A-B-B-A set led by PRR 9570A became the second quartet of Pennsy DR-4-4-1500s to enter service when they were unleashed at Crestline, Ohio, on March 22, 1949. Red, white, and gray were the colors of BLW 6001, the DR-4-4-1500 demonstrator that toured the U. S. in 1949-50. Delivery to the Elgin, Joliet & Eastern followed the set's tenure as a company salesman.

The last babyface DR-4-4-1500s entered service for the Missouri Pacific in December 1948. MoPac 203 was one of 12 DR-4-4-1500s on the road, all without dynamic brakes.

(cabs) and 201B-204B (boosters) were placed in service at St. Louis, Missouri, in December 1948.

THE DR-4-4-1500 BECOMES A SHARKNOSE

From May 1947 when MoPac ordered its DR-4-4-1500s through the fall of 1948, Eddystone did not land a single order for the unit. But October 1948 brought a breakthrough — a big one — and not surprisingly, the central figure was the Pennsylvania Railroad. Pennsy ordered 26 DR-4-4-1500 cab units and 26 boosters. These units would bear little resemblance to the CNJ's original DR-4-4-1500s, or even to the refined versions built for the NYC and MP. Just as Pennsy's 1947 orders for DR-6-4-2000s had resulted in that model being made over in shark-nose styling, so this order transformed the freight cab. With the shark-nose styling the length of the DR-4-4-1500 was decreased — cab units to 54'-4½", boosters to 52'-7". The cooling system was redesigned as well, with air intakes mounted along the top of the carbody sides (as had been done with the shark-nose DR-6-4-2000). Dressed in Brunswick green and accented with PRR's gold striping, shark-nosed DR-4-4-1500s first

rolled out of Eddystone in the early weeks of 1949. On February 28, 1949, at Crestline, Ohio, Pennsy placed its first A-B-B-A set in service. The units wore numbers 9568A-9569A (cabs) and 9568B-9569B (boosters). Deliveries continued throughout the first half of 1949, and when PRR 9592A-9593A and 9592B-9593B were placed in service at Altoona, Pennsylvania, on July 29, 1949, the 52-unit order was complete. In November 1949 Pennsy issued a follow-up order for eight more cabs and eight more boosters, all of them for 1950 delivery.

While the Pennsy's healthy orders had rescued the DR-4-4-1500 from oblivion and given it a stylish new look, the model was still far from a hot seller. In an attempt to improve sales Baldwin had decided in 1948 to issue a four-unit (A-B-B-A) DR-4-4-1500 demonstrator, and serious preparation for this set of locomotives began when the shark-nose design was finalized with the first PRR order. The shark-nose demonstrator quartet, dressed in gray, red, and white and numbered 6001, was completed in early June 1949 and immediately dispatched on a coast-to-coast sales tour. Included in the 6001's journey were Western Maryland; Cen-

121

Elgin, Joliet & Eastern

The final version of the DR-4-4-1500 appeared in April 1950. Changes included wider frame side sills, screen mesh air intakes, and the cab moved one foot further forward (with a corresponding reduction in the length of the nose). PRR 9700A was the first example of this refined version of the DR-4-4-1500. The unit entered service at Renovo, Pennsylvania.

Baldwin DR-4-4-1500 demonstrator set 6001 settled in on the EJ&E in December 1950, becoming EJ&E 700A-701A (cabs), and 700B-701B (boosters). Half of the quartet, EJ&E 701A-701B, reveals the orange-and-green livery that the Sharks wore during their service on the "Chicago Outer Belt."

H. N. Proctor

The unforgettable shape of Baldwin's shark-nose diesel is recorded on film as Baltimore & Ohio RF-16 No. 859 picks up orders on the fly at WH Tower, Greene Junction, Connellsville, Pennsylvania, on August 14, 1954. Trailing the locomotive are 150 empty hoppers on their way to Morgantown, West Virginia.

Above right, in the fall of 1952 NYC 3803 (ex-3403) is but four years old, but already the unit and two of its kindred have been saddled with the drudgery of working the hump at Selkirk, New York. The DR-4-4-1500s were not popular on the NYC. At right, trailing a short freight consist, weary CNJ DR-4-4-1500s 72, 71, and 77 keep the faith eastbound at Phillipsburg, New Jersey, on April 23, 1966. By this time the units' original tangerine-and-blue color scheme was long forgotten, and the Baldwins toiled away their final days in an appropriately somber drab green.

122

B&O 855-855A were two of 14 RF-16s which introduced the type on the road in November and December 1950. All 14 were placed in service at Benwood, West Virginia.

tral Railroad of New Jersey; Lehigh & Hudson River; New York Central; Baltimore & Ohio; Elgin, Joliet & Eastern; Katy; Santa Fe; and Southern Pacific. Any hope of even cracking the huge market represented by AT&SF and SP was largely dashed by the strong commitments of both roads to the EMD F unit (Alco was never successful in breaking EMD's hold, either). The Sharks' visit to SP, for example, was primarily a courtesy call on an established customer with an eye toward sales of other models. On the SP in February 1950, the DR-4-4-1500 team was put through rugged workouts in California and Oregon, running as far north as Eugene. The tests in California included several runs over Tehachapi.

The tour of Baldwin 6001 did not spawn any new DR-4-4-1500 production, but did undoubtedly influence several orders for the unit's successor in the 1950 line, the RF-16. And the demonstrators did find a home for themselves — the Elgin, Joliet & Eastern. Entering EJ&E service under a lease-purchase agreement in December 1950, the quartet traded its company colors for orange and green, took road numbers 700A-701A (cabs) and 700B-701B (boosters), and joined the VO-660 and VO-1000 switchers and DT-6-6-2000 transfer units based out of Joliet, Illinois.

With the start of delivery of Pennsy's second order of DR-4-4-1500s (cabs 9700A-9707A, boosters 9700B-9707B) in April 1950, design changes were revealed which were precursors of the RF-16. Visually, the changes were subtle. Panel-type air filters replaced air intake louvers, and the locomotive was lengthened ever so slightly, to 54'-8" for the cab and 53'-2" for the booster. The nose of the unit, meanwhile, was actually shortened by 1' to allow an equal gain in the length of the engine compartment. This was done to allow better maintenance access to the electrical cabinet. A thicker exterior frame side sill was also employed (all DR-4-4-1500 sharknose units were built with fabricated frames). Pennsy 9700A was the first to feature these changes, and all subsequent units followed suit until DR-4-4-1500 production ceased with delivery of Pennsylvania 9706A-9707A, 9706B-9707B in June 1950.

THE DR-4-4-1500 IN SERVICE

DR-4-4-1500 deliveries spanned 32 months and totaled 105 units sold to five customers. Once away from Eddystone, Baldwin's first streamlined freight units varied considerably in years of service; some were retired early, others lived relatively long lives. The DR-4-4-1500 babyfaces simply were not reliable locomotives, troubled as they were with haphazard wiring and plumbing and their air intake problems, as well as the piston and turbocharger failures that afflicted many early 608SC-powered units.

CNJ's 15 units enjoyed the longest tenure, working in freight service well into the mid-1960s — but the financially distressed road had little choice but to work the units until they literally dropped. Scrapping began in 1965, and by early 1966 three cabs (71, 72, and 77) were working out their final days. Through the years, the CNJ babyfaces exchanged their tangerine-and-blue livery for deep sea green and yellow (as had the DRX-6-4-2000 dual-cabs) and finally ended their days in a drab, solid-green scheme. NYC's six DR-4-4-1500s were originally assigned to mainline duties out of Cleveland, Ohio, but the units were unpopular and as early as 1952 some were banished from the high iron and relegated to hump service at Selkirk (Albany), New York. The cab units were renumbered 3800-3803 in June 1951. In October 1957, NYC 3803 was repowered with an EMD 567-series V-16 power plant and rebuilt with EMD electric throttle and m.u., but the project was never duplicated. The repowered unit was retired in February 1963 and scrapped in July 1964, but at that it outlasted its pure-Baldwin sisters which were retired in December 1960 and scrapped in 1961 and 1962. The youngest babyface DR-4-4-1500s — the MoPac units — were the first to die. MoPac's 12 DR-4-4-1500s operated primarily south and west from St. Louis —

Four thousand five hundred Baldwin horses work past St. Louis Union Terminal in the summer of 1952. MoPac's DR-4-4-1500s survived little more than a decade on the MP roster.

Final stop for the much-traveled ex-demonstrator DR-4-4-1500 set was the Baltimore & Ohio, which bought the quartet from the Elgin, Joliet & Eastern in 1955. B&O No. 4200 is ex-B&O 847, ex-EJ&E 700A, and first saw the light of day as Baldwin Locomotive Works No. 6001.

to Little Rock and Texarkana, Arkansas, and Kansas City. They did not even survive to be caught up in Missouri Pacific's massive non-EMD-power purge of the early 1960s; they were scrapped in September 1959, a few months short of their eleventh birthdays.

As for the DR-4-4-1500 sharknoses, PRR's 68 units served what in first-generation diesel terms were considered average life-spans. The first 52-unit batch was originally placed in service at Crestline and Columbus, Ohio, and Altoona

and Enola, Pennsylvania. The second group of 16 units got its start at Renovo, Pennsylvania. Through the years, PRR's Sharks worked the core of Pennsy territory in Pennsylvania and Ohio, and their lugging potential was put to good use on coal, ore, and heavy, slow freights. In December 1959, after being wrecked near Pittsburgh, one DR-4-4-1500B (PRR 9583B, ex-EJ&E B) was repowered by Alco at Schenectady, New York, with an 1800-h.p. 251-series engine and renumbered 9632B. It was retired in May 1965. The rest of the

White wheel rims contribute to the stylish appearance of NYC RF-16 set 3807-3703-3806, shiny and new at Eddystone in 1951. NYC rostered 18 RF-16 cabs and 8 boosters. Below, a foggy day at Eddystone in the summer of 1951 finds Pennsylvania RF-16s 2005A-2004B-2004A posing for the camera of Baldwin photographer Fred Haines. Soon, the trio would depart to begin their revenue-producing days at Enola, Pennsylvania.

PRR DR-4-4-1500s were retired between 1963 and 1965.

Elgin, Joliet & Eastern found the streamlined, full-width carbody of the DR-4-4-1500 ill-suited to its operations, and as a result the units were not popular and were not provided with the best of maintenance. In 1954 the quartet was leased to one of the J's sister U. S. Steel roads, the Duluth, Missabe & Iron Range. On the DM&IR, only two of the four units (a cab-and-booster set) were found to be operable. While on the DM&IR the two operable units were assigned road numbers 728-729, but were not relettered. At this same time, DM&IR was also operating a set of Bessemer & Lake Erie EMD Fs. In head-to-head competition, the Sharks proved they could easily out-pull the F units, but because of their poor condition, the Baldwins recorded maintenance costs three times those of the EMDs. When the DM&IR's lease on the Sharks expired in 1955 the EJ&E sold the quartet to the B&O. Once on B&O property and renumbered 847-847X-849X-849 (later renumbered 4200-5200-5201-4201), the well-traveled A-B-B-A set found itself in the company of younger, more potent Baldwin siblings — the RF-16s.

FINAL REFINEMENT OF THE SHARK

As part of the 1950 horsepower increase and model revision, the streamlined freight model was transformed from the DR-4-4-1500 to the RF-16. Nestled into the redesigned shark-nose carbody which had appeared during late DR-4-4-1500 production was Eddystone's new 608A engine. The 1600-h.p. figure tagged on the 608A put the RF-16 right in step with its competition. In 1950, Alco-GE introduced its 1600-h.p. FA2 and newcomer Fairbanks-Morse unveiled its 1600-h.p. CFA16-4. EMD, on the other hand, stayed with the 1500-h.p. F7 (introduced in February 1949) through the end of 1953.

Electrical equipment and controls for the RF-16 came, as usual, from Westinghouse, with 471-series main generators and 370-series traction motors being employed (as they had been in the DR-4-4-1500). The infinite-position air throttle and no-transition electrical operation continued to be major elements of the Baldwin-Westinghouse control system. To enhance electrical reliability, all electrical cables were run through conduits and all were mounted underneath the frame on the opposite side from oil and water piping. Roller bearing trucks were standard, and to suit the RF-16 to specific customer needs, major options included a front coupler cover, "Titelock" couplers, dynamic brakes, and electrical throttles and m.u. control to allow operation with non-Baldwin locomotives. Customers could select from 15:68, 15:63, and 17:62 gear ratios which provided maximum speeds of 65, 70, and 80 mph, respectively. Options offered only on the RF-16 booster were a hostler's control stand and a steam generator.

The first RF-16 order came in July 1950. Baltimore & Ohio, already an operator of VO-1000 and DS-4-4-1000 switchers, signed for its first Baldwin diesel road power. The B&O order was for 14 locomotives, all cab units. Eddystone's old reliable diesel buyer, the PRR, was next, placing an order for 44 cabs and 16 boosters in August 1950. Both Pennsy and B&O planned to use the units in heavy-duty service, so the RF-16 — dubbed the "hauling fool" by Baldwin in its sales literature — was a natural purchase. Another strong selling point for both roads was undoubtedly a promise of fast delivery, and B&O's RF-16s (851/851A-863/863A, odd numbers only) were shipped in November and December 1950; all 14 were placed in service at Benwood, West Virginia. Shipments of PRR units (numbered in the 9500- and 9700-series, see production list for specifics, page 148) began in December 1950 and concluded in May 1951. The 60 1600-h.p. cabs and boosters were placed in service at seven locations — Crestline, Canton, and Columbus, Ohio, and Conway, Shire Oaks, Altoona, and Enola, Pennsylvania.

In March 1951 Baldwin completed a sweep of the East's

Baltimore & Ohio RF-16 4215 and an AS-16 head a southbound train of empty hoppers out of Lorain, Ohio, in October 1958. B&O 4215 originally carried number 863A.

traditional "Big Three" roads when New York Central issued an order for 26 RF-16s (18 cabs and 8 boosters). Pennsy returned with an order for 42 more (28 cabs, 14 boosters) in May 1951, and B&O placed a follow-up order for two cabs and seven boosters in 1951. From these orders, PRR units (cabs 2000A-2027A, boosters 2000B-2026B even numbers only) were shipped between June 1951 and April 1952 and placed in service in Crestline, Canton, and Enola. NYC's Sharks (cabs 3804-3821, boosters 3702-3709) began departing Eddystone in December 1951 and deliveries ended in February 1952. Originally, the NYC "lightning-stripe"-clad Baldwins were assigned from DeWitt (Syracuse), New York. Sharks in B&O's second group of RF-16s (cabs 865-865A, boosters 851X-865X, odd numbers only) were shipped in May 1952. The two cab units were placed in service out of Grafton, West Virginia. Of the seven boosters, six went to Benwood to be matched up with cab units already there, while the seventh went to Grafton with the new cabs.

In 1952 the B&O placed its third order for the RF-16 (3 cab units and 6 boosters). In March through May of 1953 the elegant B&O blue, gray, black, and gold graced Eddystone as the RF-16s emerged from the paint shop and were shipped. This time, all units (cabs 867-871, odd numbers only; boosters 867X/867AX-871X/871AX, odd numbers only) went into service at Grafton, West Virginia.

Delivery of these units, which brought B&O's RF-16 ownership to 32, proved to be the finale for the RF-16. American railroads were discovering the many advantages of the road-switcher over streamlined units in freight service, and with the EMD GP7 of 1949 and the Alco RS3 of 1950, the changeover had begun in earnest. Not only were road-switchers more versatile, they were less expensive — an

At Cleveland, Ohio, the Pennsylvania puts on a display befitting a road which operated 68 DR-4-4-1500s and 102 RF-16s. Sharks 2016A and 9570A in five-stripe dress bracket 9709A and 9715A in the latter-day single-stripe Pennsy livery.

125

A 608A power plant is eased into Pennsylvania RF-16 No. 9735A early in 1951.

AS-16 cost $16,000 less than a similarly equipped RF-16. As the market for streamlined freight units disappeared, Baldwin's already slim piece of the pie disappeared with it. In 1954, with little prospect of further RF-16 orders, Baldwin dropped the streamlined freight unit from its catalog. Final production count for the RF-16: 160 units.

A FEW HEARTENING CASES OF LONGEVITY

In the RF-16 Baldwin had a diesel locomotive that proved rugged and powerful — a diesel that did, indeed, live up to its "hauling fool" nickname. Mechanically, it represented the zenith of Baldwin streamlined road power, either passenger or freight. The combination of the 608A power plant and the improvements in layout of electrical and piping systems had made the RF-16 a locomotive that was both more reliable and easier to maintain than the DR-4-4-1500, but the unit's status as a minority-builder model on all roads that had purchased it, plus the general trend of retirement of middle-aged freight cabs that began in the mid-1960s, precluded the RF-16s from establishing extraordinary

Bob Lorenz

The "hauling fool" hard at work. Pennsy RF-16 9740A and two boosters lug an ore train westbound through Tyrone, Pennsylvania, on August 8, 1958. Wearing Pennsy's single-stripe livery, the lead Shark is a veteran of more than seven years' duty since being placed in service at Crestline, Ohio, in 1951.

The clean roof lines of Baldwin's RF-16 are apparent as a pair of New York Central Sharks moves a string of freight through Bellefontaine, Ohio, in 1955.

Bob Lorenz

Scott Hartley

In 1967 the Monongahela rescued nine ex-NYC RF-16s (seven cabs, two boosters) from death's door. Sharks 1205 and 1216 proved to be the final survivors of Monongahela's fleet, but when they were photographed at Brownsville, Pennsylvania, in September 1971 their careers were far from over.

Louis R. Saillard

All odds were against finding a Baldwin RF-16 still in service on October 10, 1978, but alive, indeed, was Castolite-owned RF-16 No. 1216, leading a Michigan Northern freight at Oden, Michigan. Remarkably, 1216 and sister 1205 would move again, to the Escanaba & Lake Superior.

records of longevity — except in a few heartening cases.

On the B&O, the Sharks were denizens of coal territory, lugging black diamonds on B&O's Wheeling and Monongah Divisions. In the late 1950s and early 1960s B&O Sharks (cabs renumbered into the 4200-series, boosters into the 5200-series) worked — often in the company of AS-16s — out of Pittsburgh, Pennsylvania, to Rochester, New York (the old Buffalo, Rochester & Pittsburgh), and also migrated to the road's Lorain, Ohio, branch, again working in the company of AS-16s. By 1962, one RF-16 (B&O 4215, ex-863A) and three of B&O's four secondhand DR-4-4-1500s were retired. The remaining DR-4-4-1500 (4201, ex-849) was traded to EMD in 1963. After periods in storage (mostly at Glenwood, Pennsylvania), B&O's RF-16s were retired en masse beginning in 1965. By 1967 the RF-16 was gone from B&O, all but the already-scrapped 4215 traded to EMD for second-generation high-horsepower road-switchers.

Pennsy's 102 RF-16s were legion in the middle of the system — in Pennsylvania and Ohio, in particular — during the 1950s and on into the early 1960s. Crestline remained a haunt for RF-16s through the years (the decrepit roundhouse there was often full of Sharks), and during their final days the Pennsy Sharks were often found at Conway, Pennsylvania. Like the DR-4-4-1500 Sharks on the Pennsy, the RF-16s were assigned to heavy coal, ore, transfer, and slow freight hauling. A pair of PRR RF-16s (9726A, 2001A) was repowered in 1959 with Alco engines in the style of the DR-4-4-1500B mentioned previously (these two units had also been involved in the Pittsburgh-area accident). Renumbered 9632A and 9633A respectively, the units were retired by the end of 1966, the same year the last standard RF-16s were purged from the PRR roster.

After their original assignment out of DeWitt, the NYC's RF-16s were — early in their careers — transferred to Beech Grove, Indiana (near Indianapolis), and from that base spent most of their lives working on NYC's "Big Four" lines. They frequented runs from Indianapolis to Cincinnati, and also worked regularly to Columbus, Toledo, and Detroit (as a rule, NYC Sharks did not work west of Indianapolis to St. Louis). Almost regularly, many of the 26 units went into storage during the slow summer business periods; however, during several summers in the late 1950s some NYC RF-16s were leased to the Rock Island for grain movements. The cab units were renumbered 1204-1221 in April 1966, and serviceable Sharks spent their final days at Cincinnati (Sharonville, Ohio). From there, the Sharks — tired and timeworn in Central's latter-day "cigar-band" liv-

ery — worked transfers, locals, and as helpers. NYC began officially retiring RF-16s in September 1966 (although some had been stored for some time previous to that) and by May of the following year the sharknose was only history on the Central.

Logic would imply that the story of Baldwin streamlined freight units should end with NYC's retirement of its RF-16s. But logic loses. In the winter of 1967, the power-hungry Monongahela Railway purchased (via GE) seven ex-NYC RF-16 cabs (1205, 1207, 1209, 1210, 1211, 1213, and 1216) and two boosters (3708 and 3709) for $6000 each. Working out of Brownsville, Pennsylvania (except 1211 and 3709, which were held for parts), the old Baldwins were right at home on the Monongahela, lugging long coal drags. As might be expected of such elderly, orphaned diesels, attrition took its toll (as did the arrival of EMD GP38s beginning in 1969) and by February 1, 1972, only two units — 1205 and 1216 — remained in service. In 1974, the road retired its last S-12 switchers (a process that had been going on for several years) and the remaining RF-16s; EMD Geeps (new GP38s plus ex-P&LE GP7s) then ruled the Monongahela. But again the RF-16 refused to become extinct.

Monongahela Sharks 1205 and 1216, sold to scrap dealer David Joseph of Bulter, Pennsylvania, were rescued by the Delaware & Hudson in mid-1974 (in trade for derelict freight cars of equal scrap value). The D&H, then under the stewardship of C. B. Sterzing Jr., was something of a refuge for uncommon diesels (D&H also harbored four Alco PAs, Nos. 16-19, all of AT&SF origin). The two Sharks were sent through the D&H's Colonie Shops (Watervliet, New York), and in the process received a new blue, yellow, and silver "warbonnet" paint scheme patterned after that worn by the D&H PAs (which in turn was patterned after the PA's original AT&SF livery). The RF-16s were not mere curios on the D&H; they were put to work. Early on, the Sharks worked transfers at Colonie and as pushers on Richmondville Hill, then they powered freights from Whitehall, New York. Later, they tended D&H's Binghamton (New York)-Sayre (Pennsylvania) operation, worked as pushers out of Binghamton on Belden Hill, and then returned to Whitehall to handle trains on the Washington and Rutland branches. In a manner far removed, though, from their labors of lugging hoppers on the NYC and Monongahela, the Sharks were coupled to one excursion passenger train, a Colonie-West Rutland circle trip (via Eagle Bridge, the Washington branch, and return via Whitehall).

At the end of 1977, following a management shakeup on

William S. Christopher

Ex-Delaware & Hudson RF-16 No. 1216 hauls two cars from Channing toward Wells, Michigan, on the Escanaba & Lake Superior, November 5, 1982. The unit last operated on the E&LS on November 9, 1982, and has been stored (with sister 1205) since.

the Delaware & Hudson, the Sharks were again out of service and for sale — at a minimum bid of $35,000 a copy. John Kunzie's Castolite Corporation of Woodstock, Illinois, purchased the duo and the units were leased to the Michigan Northern. Based at Cadillac, Michigan, the Sharks remained on the Michigan Northern for approximately one year; No. 1205 worked only briefly before falling to a crankshaft problem, No. 1216 operated through December 1978. In the spring of 1979 Castolite's Sharks were ferried to Diesel Electric Services in Minneapolis, Minnesota, for repairs. That August No. 1216 was transferred to another short line, Upper Michigan's Escanaba & Lake Superior, where it saw occasional use as late as November 9, 1982. Diesel Electric Services closed its doors in Minneapolis before restoring 1205 to serviceable condition, and the Shark was stored for approximately a year and a half by the Minneapolis, Northfield & Southern. The RF-16 was then moved to the E&LS to join its sister, and was placed in storage. Today, the much-traveled 1205 and 1216 are the only surviving Baldwin streamlined diesels in North America.

Saved from extinction by the Delaware & Hudson in mid-1974, warbonnet-dressed RF-16s 1216 and 1205 roll through Castleton, Vermont, at sunset on May 16, 1977.

Scott Hartley

On a sunny day in 1948, Baldwin's first domestic light road-switcher, TC DRS-4-4-1000 No. 75, poses at Eddystone. Along with sister No. 76, it entered service on July 13, 1948.

YARD GOATS WITH ROAD-SWITCHERS' SHOES

Light road-switchers

IN THE LATE 1930s when North America's diesel builders looked to release their new breed from the confines of yard and passenger service, an easy step was to build and market a "light road-switcher." In essence, such a locomotive would be little more than a stretched switcher with equipment such as road trucks and a steam generator to make it suitable for road duties or — in many cases — passenger terminal switching.

Unencumbered by any attachment to steam, not surprisingly Electro-Motive was the first builder to experiment with light road-switchers. In 1938 EMC constructed a pair of Winton-powered, 12-cylinder, 900-h.p. units for the Missouri Pacific. Designated NW4s, these locomotives were based on EMC's contemporary NW1 switcher but incorporated stretched frames, steam generators, and road trucks (taken from EMC's boxcab demonstrators 511-512). The

PRR 5592 was completed early in 1950. All six of Pennsy's DRS-4-4-1000s had steam generators and were originally assigned to Chicago, primarily to work the coach yards there.

units were a custom job for MoPac and were never duplicated, but in 1939 EMC began building another custom model for the Great Northern — the NW3. It, too, was little more than an elongated endcab switcher with road trucks and steam generator, but it was one step closer to being a production model, employing the same 12-cylinder, 1000-h.p., 567-series engine used in EMC's popular NW2 switcher and riding on the same Blomberg road trucks used under EMC's FT. However, following the delivery of the last GN NW3 in early 1942 (seven were built), Electro-Motive could not introduce another light road-switcher until after World War Two due to WPB restrictions.

Although EMC premiered the light road-switcher, Alco-GE was the builder that brought it to the forefront — with the RS1 of 1941. During WWII the RS1 was produced in standard form and in a six-axle military version, the RSD1, and after the war Alco-GE began chalking up enviable sales of the RS1. Meanwhile, Electro-Motive continued to dabble. In 1946-47 La Grange built the NW5, a 1000-h.p. model which accounted for 13 sales to three customers.

THE DRS-4-4-1000

Baldwin's first light road-switcher (and its first road-switcher of any size) was the export model DRS-6-4-660. From 1946 to 1948 Eddystone built and delivered 106 such units. The similar 606SC-powered DRS-6-4-1000 was constructed for export sales in 1948-49 (see page 141), and it seemed only natural for Baldwin to enter the chase for domestic light road-switcher sales. The company's 1000-h.p. switchers were earning a good reputation, and Eddystone had production tooling on hand — from construction of its switchers, the export light road-switchers, and domestic heavy road-switchers — that could be used to build domestic light road-switchers. Enter the DRS-4-4-1000, a four-axle, 1000-h.p. light road-switcher.

For its first domestic light road-switcher Baldwin mated the 606SC engine to Westinghouse's 480-series main generator and 362-series traction motors. The cab, short hood,

W. Gibson Kennedy

Above, CP DRS-4-4-1000 8012 makes an appearance on the mainland, in the yards at Vancouver, British Columbia, in May 1949. At left, CP 8001 ushers varnish across the Arbutus Canyon bridge on Vancouver Island in May 1950.

W. Warner

GSC Commonwealth Type B truck, and GSC cast underframe were, for all intents and purposes, identical to those of the DRS-4-4-1500 heavy road-switcher (first delivered in July 1947), and the long hood and cooling system were borrowed from the DS-series switcher line. Inside coupler knuckles, the DRS-4-4-1000 would measure 58' even. Eddystone offered its usual range of options, including m.u. control, steam generator, roller bearing trucks, and a 1000-gallon underbelly fuel tank between the trucks (the standard fuel tank position was in the short hood).

The first order, for three DRS-4-4-1000s, came from the Tennessee Central Railway in June 1947. At the time, the TC had only two diesel switchers: an Alco HH660 and an Alco S1. The second DRS-4-4-1000 buyer came forth in January 1948. The Canadian Pacific was committed to dieselizing its Esquimalt & Nanaimo Railway (a wholly owned subsidiary) on Vancouver Island. It was no secret that CP would have preferred to dieselize the E&N with Alco or EMD units, but the wait for delivery from either builder would have been lengthy. Canadian Locomotive Company, through an agreement with Baldwin, offered CP reserved positions on Eddystone's production line, and CP responded with an order for 13 DRS-4-4-1000s. A third DRS-4-4-1000 buyer joined the gathering in 1948 when the Pennsylvania reserved two units.

On July 13, 1948, Tennessee Central DRS-4-4-1000s 75-76 were placed in service. The road's third unit — No. 77 — entered service on August 3, 1948. Attired in maroon and yellow, the locomotives went to work out of Nashville, Tennessee. As 1948 drew to a close Eddystone was finishing Canadian Pacific's DRS-4-4-1000s. Because of Canadian Locomotive Company's role in the sale, and to facilitate their importation into Canada, the CP DRS-4-4-1000s

(8000-8012) carried both Baldwin and Canadian Locomotive Company construction numbers, even though the units had been built entirely at Eddystone. Unfortunately, several of the units were shipped with water in the cooling systems and steam generators (CP 8000-8004 carried steam generators and had underbelly tanks). The water froze during shipment, causing damage which had to be repaired when the units reached their destination. The CP DRS-4-4-1000s were finally placed in service at Victoria, B. C., between January 11 and February 28, 1949, replacing 20 oil-burning Ten-Wheelers of the D-3, D-4, and D-10 classes. The steam generator-equipped units were used to protect E&N Train 1/2, while the remainder tended to freight on the E&N's 139 miles of mainline and 64 miles of branches.

A close look at the CP DRS-4-4-1000s revealed a minor design change made after delivery of the three Tennessee Central units. The long hood of the CP units (and all subsequent units) was slightly longer, and as a result the rather gangly front platform of the TC units was gone.

Pennsy became the third DRS-4-4-1000 operator on February 24, 1949, when it placed DRS-4-4-1000s 9276-9277 in service at Chicago. PRR soon issued a repeat order, this time for four units. The results of that order, Nos. 5591-5594, were placed in service at Chicago in March 1950. All six of the PRR units carried steam generators, but lacked m.u. or roller bearing trucks. The diminutive Baldwins were used to switch the Chicago coach yards, and were known to handle the local passenger run to Valparaiso, Indiana. With production of the 1950 line of locomotives set to begin later in the year, PRR 5594 proved to be the last DRS-4-4-1000. The tally for the model ended at 22 units produced over 21 months.

A SMALL BUT LONG-LIVED CONTINGENT

Despite being few in number the DRS-4-4-1000s did not disappear quickly. In fact, all three owners of the model operated it more than 15 years — more than the "average" diesel life expectancy. Through the 1950s and into the 1960s the three Tennessee Central DRS-4-4-1000s toiled in central Tennessee, working the yard at Nashville, serving the road's Old Hickory branch, and pushing freights bound for TC's Western Division on the Nashville belt line. Although the road became a bastion of Alco power after its DRS-4-4-1000 purchase, TC ran its Baldwins into 1966 and the railroad itself survived only two years longer. After their Chicago days, Pennsy's DRS-4-4-1000s eventually migrated to Camden, New Jersey, where their duties included

131

Cadillacs of the RS-12s were the 17 built for NYC in 1951. Number 5828 helped dieselize the road's Putnam Division.

Milwaukee RS-12 No. 970 rode GSC Commonwealth switcher trucks, as did later sister No. 971. Although only the second RS-12 built, this unit was the last with a cast underframe.

John Coniglio

Martin Zak

Michael Wilkie

Top, Tennessee Central DRS-4-4-1000 No. 77 works near Nashville in the late 1950s. Middle, renumbered 8050 in anticipation of the PC merger, PRR's first DRS-4-4-1000 (ex-9276) works eastbound at Camden, New Jersey, April 29, 1967. Above, seven CP DRS-4-4-1000s congregate at Wellcox engine terminal at Nanaimo, Vancouver Island, in June 1971.

Camden-Pemberton and Camden-Trenton passenger jaunts. PRR's first DRS-4-4-1000 retirement occurred when No. 9277 was stricken from the roster in May 1966, and No. 5594 followed in February 1967. The remaining four units served Penn Central (renumbered first into the 8050-series, then into the 8300-series), but none survived to work for Conrail. PC DRS-4-4-1000s 8300-8303 (ex-PRR 9276, 5591, 5592, 5593) were officially retired in March 1976, although they had been stored for some time before that.

Canadian Pacific's 13 DRS-4-4-1000s became venerable institutions on the E&N, and saw some use on the mainland in British Columbia. From 1961 through 1967 all had m.u. capability added. In early 1973 CP 8012 became the first unit removed from the roster, and four more — 8006, 8007, 8008, and 8011 — met their fate in a head-on collision on the Victoria Subdivision in June 1973. The rest of the CP units were retired by May 1975, but No. 8000 has been retained by the railroad for preservation. In 1983 it was repainted in an approximation of its original paint scheme.

THE RS-12

When Baldwin's 1950 line was announced in June 1950 the DRS-4-4-1000 was replaced by the 1200-h.p., 606A-powered RS-12. Options included Farr air filters, dual controls, steam generators (from Vapor Car Heating Co., or Elesco), flange oilers, hump control, Gardner-Denver 6-cylinder water-cooled air compressor, and roller bearing trucks (choice of Hyatt, SKF, or Timken). The Pennsy was the first road to order the RS-12, reserving one unit in August 1950. In October 1950 New York Central placed a more pleasing order — 17 units — and in November 1950 the Milwaukee Road matched Pennsy's request with a one-unit order.

The RS-12 first appeared in April 1951 when PRR 8975 was shipped to Cleveland, Ohio. Externally, the unit was nearly identical to PRR's DRS-4-4-1000s. It had a cast frame and carried a steam generator, but did not employ m.u. or roller bearing trucks. One visible difference was that the RS-12 wore Pennsy's distinctive radio-phone antenna system.

Milwaukee Road's first RS-12 — No. 970 — was shipped in May 1951. CMStP&P had become a Baldwin diesel operator in May 1940 when it put a single VO-660 into service, and in the decade that followed had added VO-1000s, DS-4-4-1000s, and S-12s to its switcher fleet. For the Milwaukee, the RS-12 was merely an addition to that switcher fleet; the road needed a unit to shuffle passenger equipment at the Minneapolis depot and coach yards, and the RS-12 — equipped with a steam generator — fit the mold perfectly. The unit's pseudo-switcher status could have been illustrated no better than by its use of GSC switcher trucks instead of the GSC Type B road trucks standard on the RS-12.

Built in 1952, Kaiser Bauxite RS-12 No. 102 had optional safety lights and dynamic brakes.

Attractively dressed in SAL's red and black and equipped with a steam generator, RS-12 No. 1469 took up duties at Charlotte, North Carolina, in 1952.

Equipped with steam generator, SKF roller bearings, and weighing 242,800 pounds, CNJ 1207 was one of four RS-12s shipped to Jersey City in January 1953.

Although only the second RS-12 delivered, No. 970 was the last built with a cast underframe. Future units would employ welded frames, a change that went along with the evolution of frame construction in the switcher and heavy roadswitcher lines.

In November and December 1951 Eddystone shipped NYC's 17 RS-12s. Like Milwaukee 970, these 1200-h.p. Baldwins were built to lock couplers with passenger equipment, but they would do so on the high iron. NYC used nine of the RS-12s (5820-5828) to dieselize its Putnam Division between Brewster, New York (on the Harlem Division), and the Bronx; the remaining units (5829-5836) were used on the West Shore line from Weehawken, New Jersey, to Albany, New York. The NYC locomotives were the Cadillacs of RS-12 production. Clothed in the Central's "lightning stripe" livery, they had a variety of optional equipment: Elesco steam generators, eight-notch electric throttles, m.u., Timken roller bearing trucks, 14:68 (60 mph) gearing,

H. H. Harwood Jr.

In April 1954 Central Railroad of New Jersey RS-12 No. 1208 rattles across the diamond at Elizabethport, New Jersey, as it arrives with a passenger shuttle from Newark.

special classification lamps, and oval-shaped side cab windows. Each NYC RS-12 weighed 248,000 pounds.

A SHRINKING MARKET

When 1951 shipments of RS-12s were totaled, the tally — 19 units — was far from spectacular. That total DRS-4-4-1000 production had run to only 22 units made the RS-12 figure more palatable, and there was another factor to be considered — one which caused both pleasure and pain to Baldwin. While the Alco-GE RS1 had sold well through the 1940s, it, too, was selling slowly in the early 1950s — in 1951 Alco delivered only 30 RS1s. So the RS-12 was cornering a good share of the light road-switcher market; unfortunately, though, that market was shrinking.

Slim market or not, by the time Eddystone completed the Pennsy, Milwaukee, and NYC RS-12s in 1951 Baldwin's salesmen had obtained three more orders. In May Kaiser Bauxite Co., a subsidiary of Kaiser Aluminum & Chemical Corp., ordered two RS-12s for its new 12-mile bauxite ore railroad in Jamaica. In September Seaboard Air Line ordered six, and in November 1951 PRR again ordered a single RS-12. All these orders were for 1952 delivery.

The first RS-12s shipped in 1952 were Kaiser Bauxite 101-102. They featured dynamic brakes (installed in the short hood), dual head lamps, and m.u. The pair was delivered to Port Kaiser, Jamaica (also known as Little Pedro Point), and went to work battling ore cars — and grades of up to 2.2 percent. Seaboard's order (SAL 1466-1471) was shipped in May 1952. SAL's six RS-12s were earmarked primarily for passenger terminal switching and therefore carried steam generators but lacked m.u. SAL 1466 and 1471 were assigned to Hamlet, North Carolina, 1467 and 1470 to Birmingham, 1468 to Atlanta, and 1469 to Charlotte, North Carolina. Pennsy's second RS-12 — No. 8776 — was shipped in September 1952. Equipped with steam generator, trainphone system, SKF roller bearing trucks, and m.u., PRR 8776 was placed in service at Baltimore, Maryland.

Rounding out Eddystone's shipments of RS-12s in 1952 was another single-unit order — this one a repeat from the Milwaukee Road. In January 1952 the road had ordered a twin for RS-12 No. 970, and RS-12 No. 971 was the result — in October 1952. Differing from No. 970 only in its welded frame (and a new paint scheme), No. 971 went to work at Minneapolis.

Shipped on February 15, 1954, No. 8110 was Pennsy's last RS-12, and one of the last three Baldwins delivered to the road. It has the tall rear hood of RS-12s built from 1954 onward.

134

On the last day of 1952 Baldwin could look at its RS-12 production total for the year — 10 units — and reason that it had outperformed Alco (only four RS1s were delivered in 1952). But a look at the production schedule for 1953 left little cause for celebration. In addition to Milwaukee's single-unit January 1952 order (which had already been filled), Central Railroad of New Jersey had ordered four RS-12s in March 1952, and Seaboard had returned with an order for four more in September. Production of RS-12s in 1953 would cease after eight units were constructed unless other buyers were found — and quickly. But none was.

Jersey Central Lines' four RS-12s — CNJ 1206-1209 — were shipped in January 1953. Equipped with steam generators and SKF roller bearing trucks, each unit weighed in at 242,800 pounds and offered 60,700 pounds of tractive effort. The locomotives were assigned to light passenger trains and were placed in service at Jersey City. Seaboard's second order of RS-12s — SAL 1472-1475 — was also shipped in January. Equipped with steam generators, the units went into service at Hamlet, North Carolina (1472), Portsmouth, Virginia (1473), and Richmond, Virginia (1474-1475). Then, only one month into 1953, RS-12 production came to a stop.

The drought in RS-12 orders was not broken until June 1953, when Baldwin's most reliable customer, Pennsy, ordered six units as part of its final Baldwin order. Then, 57-mile short line Durham & Southern ordered three RS-12s in November. Pennsy's units — 8105-8110 — were shipped in February 1954 and brought PRR's roster of RS-12s to eight. The PRR locomotives incorporated several design changes that had been developed during the 13-month pause in RS-12 production. Most noticeable was that the rear hood was taller than the front hood, a carry-over from the heavy road-switcher line (the change been introduced on B-L-H AS-616 demonstrator/test-bed No. 1601). The same tooling was used to make rear hoods for all road-switcher models. A second modification was the use of Baldwin's final frame design. Of welded construction like the preceding RS-12 frame, the new frame featured bolt-on stairwells and pilots to facilitate repairs in the field. The frame was also 6" longer than those previously used, in preparation for the switch to GE electrical equipment (as it turned out, all RS-12s were completed with Westinghouse electrical components).

Durham & Southern's three RS-12s — 1200-1202 — were shipped in March 1954. Like the Pennsy units, these had all the new design changes. Equipped with Hyatt roller bearing trucks for road work, the locomotives went to work out of Dunn, North Carolina, sounding the death knell for steam on the D&S.

Soon after D&S received its RS-12s another short line — California's McCloud River Railroad — ordered two. The road ordered the locomotives primarily for use on its rugged Burney (California) extension, and they were to be equipped with dynamic brakes (to be compatible with McCloud River DRS-6-6-1500 No. 29), and m.u. To bring the units' speed of continuous tractive effort down to 6 mph, thereby making them more compatible with McCloud's DRS-6-6-1500s (28 and 29) and S-12 (alias S-8) No. 31, the RS-12s were ordered with Westinghouse 370-series traction motors instead of the standard 362-series. Shipped in April 1955, McCloud River 32-33 each weighed 240,000 pounds and was capable of 57,700 pounds of tractive effort.

As Eddystone's diesel-electric business wound down in 1955 only one RS-12 order was received. On November 23, 1955, Kaiser Bauxite ordered two more RS-12s. Numbered 103-104 and equipped with dynamic brakes (a la Nos. 101-102), the two RS-12s departed Eddystone on May 15, 1956, and were loaded aboard the S. S. *Belocean* at the Port of Baltimore. The pair arrived at Port Kaiser, Jamaica, on June 5, 1956. Kaiser Bauxite 103 was placed in service on June 18, No. 104 in July. The Kaiser Bauxite RS-12s were the last road-switchers of any model built at Eddystone. A postscript to RS-12 production occurred in 1957 when Kai-

In March 1966 Durham & Southern's three RS-12s (1200-1202), along with DRS-4-4-1500 No. 362, provide ample horsepower for two cars and a caboose at Apex, North Carolina.

ser Bauxite expressed an interest in purchasing four more. Baldwin considered preparing four RS-12 "kits" which Kaiser could assemble, but the plan was eventually dismissed.

LONG MAY THEY RUN

Essentially an S-12 switcher perched on an AS-16 frame and trucks, the RS-12 enjoyed many of the qualities of the former, and accordingly survived long and served its owners well. The Pennsy used its RS-12s in Pennsylvania and western New York state. Numbers 8105-8109 had been placed in service at Oil City, Pennsylvania, and these units frequented Buffalo and Olean, New York, working to Emporium, Pennsylvania, and Rochester, New York. Following service debuts at Cleveland and Baltimore, PRR 8975 and 8776 were used around Conway and Pitcairn, Pennsylvania. PRR 8110, originally assigned to Philadelphia, spent

At top, the first RS-12, PRR 8084 (ex-8975), stands at Pemberton, New Jersey, on November 20, 1966, with the local from Camden. Above, carrying new numbers assigned in 1953, New York Central RS-12s 6222 and 6225 hustle a mail-express at Spuyten Duyvil, New York, in May 1955.

William S. Christopher

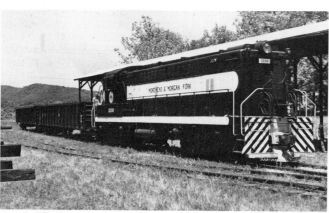

William J. Husa Jr.

Above, Escanaba & Lake Superior RS-12 No. 300 on a passenger extra in November 1982. Below, two of Oregon, California & Eastern's RS-12s at Klamath Falls, Oregon, in May 1980.

David Lustig

Left, Morehead & Morgan Fork RS-12 No. 1200 (ex-Durham & Southern 1200), at Clearfield, Kentucky, July 25, 1976.

Warren Calloway

SCL RS-12 No. 208 (ex-SAL 1467) with S-12 No. 206 at Hamlet, North Carolina. SCL did not retire its RS-12s until 1977.

most of its years there, usually working race specials out of 30th Street Station. As the Penn Central era neared, the RS-12s gravitated to Camden, New Jersey (along with their older DRS-4-4-1000 kindred). The units were renumbered into the PC 8084-8091 number slot; No. 8084 (ex-PRR 8975) was again renumbered PC 8306, and 8088 (ex-PRR 8108) was renumbered 8307 in 1972. These two RS-12s survived into the mid-1970s but did not find a place on the Conrail roster in 1976.

New York Central's RS-12s worked through the 1950s in New York state, where they appeared on the Putnam and Harlem Divisions, the West Shore Line, and the Hudson River Division. In May 1953 they were renumbered 6220-6236. In their latter days, they gained a certain notoriety among train-watchers as part of NYC's Lima-Hamilton and Baldwin gathering (which included the RF-16 Sharks) that

worked at Cincinnati through the mid-1960s. NYC's RS-12s received road numbers 8067-8083 for the Penn Central merger, but most were soon retired (because of their electric throttles they could not be m.u.ed with the ex-PRR air throttle-equipped units). Two ex-NYC RS-12s, 8073 (ex-NYC 6226) and 8082 (ex-NYC 6235), were renumbered PC 8304 and 8305 in 1972. Both were assigned to Camden, like their ex-PRR kindred. None survived to serve Conrail.

Milwaukee Road's RS-12s, which were renumbered 926-927, were members in good standing of the road's Twin Cities Baldwin enclave for more than two decades. When their passenger switching duties ended the two were used as freight-toting yard goats. Milwaukee 927 (ex-971) was retired in June 1974, but No. 926 remained active through late 1975 and was not scrapped until the spring of 1976.

The careers of CNJ's RS-12s in passenger service out of Jersey City were short-lived, but the units found employment in freight service and wound up their days knocking around Jersey City and Elizabethport, New Jersey. Retirements began in the early 1970s, and by late 1972 only 1207-1208 remained at work. By January 1973 all of the CNJ's RS-12s were stilled.

In Jamaica, Kaiser Bauxite's RS-12s patiently lugged 12-car trains of bauxite ore on the 12-mile journey from mine to rotary dumper, working in relative obscurity for years. It was reported that the operation (60 miles west of Kingston) still called two of the RS-12s to duty in 1984.

On the Seaboard Air Line, Baldwin's 1200-h.p. light road-switchers found favor with both operating crews and shopmen, and the RS-12s prospered. In 1955, when SAL

Both photos, Henry W. Brueckman

opened its new Hamlet, North Carolina, yard, RS-12 1467 was reassigned there. In December 1957 the unit was equipped with m.u. so that it could work the yard in tandem with SAL S-12s 1462-1465. Following that, all SAL RS-12s received m.u. By this time, all except 1467 had been moved into Florida where they worked around Baldwin, Mulberry, Tampa, and Wildwood, primarily in phosphate service. In 1966 SAL's GP40s arrived, releasing the road's first-generation Geeps for secondary services, and the RS-12s were bumped to yard duty at Hamlet, Jacksonville, Baldwin, and Hermitage (Richmond).

With the merger of SAL and ACL into Seaboard Coast Line in 1967, SAL 1466-1475 were renumbered SCL 207-216. Under SCL most of the RS-12s congregated at Jacksonville (SCL 208, ex-SAL 1467, meanwhile continued its lonely vigil at Hamlet). Retirements came in 1977, but still not ready for the scrapper's torch, eight SCL RS-12s moved on. Four units — SCL 207, 209-211 — went to the Oregon, California & Eastern at Klamath Falls, Oregon, in November 1977 and became OC&E 7908-7911, where they remained on the roster, but were for sale, in 1984. A trio — SCL 212, 213, and 215 — headed for the Michigan Northern in the summer of 1978. On the MN the three RS-12s operated only briefly and were afflicted by a number of ailments. The three units were sold to the Escanaba & Lake Superior in 1980. On the E&LS, No. 213 immediately went into service while No. 215 entered the shop at Wells, Michigan, for a complete rebuild which was finished early in 1982. The rebuilt unit was also renumbered E&LS 300 and painted in the road's Great Northern-inspired livery. E&LS 213 and 300 were in service in 1984; number 212 was on the property but not operational in 1984. The eighth ex-SCL RS-12 to move on was No. 214, originally sold to Birmingham Rail for leasing, then, in 1983, sold to the Escanaba & Lake Superior, where it remained in 1984.

Durham & Southern's RS-12s, joined by secondhand Baldwin heavy road-switchers from Norfolk Southern and Soo, worked in North Carolina into the 1970s. The arrival of EMD GP38-2s in 1972 soon brought their days on the D&S to an end. In February 1974 the D&S RS-12s were acquired by the Morehead & Morgan Fork, a four-mile coal road with trackage from Morehead to Clearfield, Kentucky. In 1984 the M&MF was still in existence but operation was rare. RS-12s 1200 and 1202 remained on the property in serviceable condition; No. 1201 was also on the property, but served only as a source of parts.

Another — and more successful — case of RS-12s exchanging duties on one short line for those on another oc-

Following a January 1970 accident which claimed most of its Baldwin fleet, California Western purchased McCloud River RS-12s 32-33 (shown below working the McCloud's Pondosa branch on May 9, 1969). Displaced on the McCloud River by EMD SD38s, the pair of dynamic-brake-equipped units became Cal Western 55-56, shown above at Fort Bragg, California, in the company of CW switcher No. 53.

curred in California. McCloud River employed its RS-12s until May 9, 1969; on the following day, Electro-Motive SD38s took over. But McCloud River 32-33 were far from dead. Purchased in September 1970 by the California Western, the RS-12s were earmarked to replace CW Baldwin DS-4-4-750s 51-52 and S-12 54, which had been wrecked. As California Western 55-56, the ex-McCloud River RS-12s prospered. In 1984 the Baldwins were slated to haul CW's summer excursion trains from Fort Bragg to Willits, California. For train-watchers, few tonics could be better.

The first Baldwin diesel road-switcher, DRS-6-4-660 No. 040-DA-1 bound for France, is lifted off American soil and swung on board a ship for the North Atlantic crossing. The historic locomotive was placed in service at Marseilles-Arenc, France, on April 15, 1946.

BOUND FOR FOREIGN SHORES

Baldwin export-model diesels

WHARF 251 AT EDDYSTONE was a monument to Baldwin's success as locomotive builder to the world — the point of embarkation from which countless steam locomotives bearing the builder's plates of Baldwin Locomotive Works had begun journeys to distant lands. Wharf 251 was evidence in concrete and timber and steel of the importance Baldwin placed on export sales. Even in the late 1940s and early 1950s when other builders were ready to call it quits, Baldwin still exported scores of steam locomotives. Not until 1955, when Eddystone shipped 50 2-8-2s to India, did this tradition end.

Though minor in comparison to the volume of diesel export business eventually achieved by Alco or Electro-Motive, Baldwin also earned a niche in the diesel export market. In 12 years — 1945 through 1956 — Eddystone exported 401 diesel locomotives, comprising 18 different models, to four continents. Export sales accounted for approximately 12.5 percent of Baldwin's total diesel production.

For all intents and purposes, export diesels fell into three categories: stock domestic models, domestic models modified for foreign conditions, and models sold only as exports. Locomotives in the first two categories have already been documented in the domestic locomotive chapters; this chapter is the story of those models built exclusively for export.

FOR RUSSIA: THE 0-6-6-0 1000/1 DE

Given today's political climate it seems incongruous that the Soviet Union was the recipient of Baldwin's first export-model diesels, but Baldwin was a longtime supplier of Russian motive power, dating back to 1872 when the company exported six 2-6-0s and four 4-4-0s for the Veronej-Rostoff Railway. At the close of World War Two in Europe the restoration of Russia's war-torn rail system was an important aspect of U. S.-Soviet relations, and the U. S. armed services arranged for Baldwin to design and manufacture 30 road freight locomotives for service in the U. S. S. R. Eddystone's design was a 1000-h.p., six-axle (C-C), streamlined diesel weighing 280,000 pounds — the 0-6-6-0 1000/1 DE.

In building the 0-6-6-0 1000/1 DEs Baldwin used proven components wherever possible. The 8-cylinder normally aspirated VO was the power plant, Westinghouse electrical controls, main generator, and traction motors were employed, and the throttle control was Baldwin's standard electropneumatic system. General Steel Castings provided a cast underframe, and the power plant was placed on top of it with the main generator toward the cab. To keep water from freezing in the engine when the locomotive was shut down a water heater was installed at the rear of the unit; if

Baldwin's first diesel-electric model built exclusively for export was the 0-6-6-0 1000/1 DE constructed for use in the Soviet Union. Built to ride the 5' gauge of the Russian railways, the 30 0-6-6-0 1000/1 DEs were capable of 60 mph speeds. Each of the C-C units weighed in at 280,000 pounds.

Its paint job incomplete, one of the French DRS-6-4-660s is put through its paces on the Eddystone test track on January 4, 1946. Delivery of the units began in April 1946.

SNCF 040-DA-14 reveals the internal arrangement of the DRS-6-4-660, with the 606NA power plant the centerpiece. Note the porch-like walkway at the front of the unit.

Leaving Petitjean for Tangier on May 27, 1951, DRS-6-4-660 No. 040-DB-403 drums along with nary a hint of smoke from its four exhaust stacks. The unit was one of six DRS-6-4-660s assigned to service in Morocco.

William D. Middleton

necessary, this heater could also be used to warm the diesel fuel. Twin radiators for engine cooling were also placed at the rear of the locomotive. Cooling air would be drawn in through ducts in the sides of the carbody and exhausted out the roof, with thermostatically controlled radiator shutters providing temperature regulation. To package the mechanical equipment, Baldwin used a full-width carbody similar to that introduced on the 0-6-6-0 1000/2 DE passenger demonstrators of 1944-45. The Russian 0-6-6-0 1000/1 DEs also debuted one important new component: the GSC Commonwealth C-type truck later used on hundreds of Baldwin domestic heavy road-switchers and transfer units. These first Commonwealth C-type trucks were nonstandard in one important respect — they were constructed to the 5' gauge of the Russian railroad system.

Finishing touches included m.u. fixtures (on the rear of the units only), and Russian-style couplers and buffers. When completed the 0-6-6-0 1000/1 DEs measured 58' inside coupler knuckles, exerted a starting tractive effort of 84,000 pounds (at 30 percent adhesion), and maintained a continuous tractive effort of 49,300 pounds (at 5.6 mph). A 14:68 gear ratio allowed these rather handsome diesels a top speed of 60 mph. Before departing Eddystone in mid-1945, the 30 units were lettered "U. S. A." and given road numbers 2460-2489 (they also carried Russian numbers 20-71 to 20-100).

After crossing the North Atlantic, the 0-6-6-0 1000/1 DEs

were placed in service between June 15 and August 24, 1945. Assigned class Db on the Soviet system, the Baldwins were employed on two routes. The first was the Tuapse-Sukhumi-Samtredia route along the resort-lined eastern shore of the Black Sea, where the diesels were bracketed by steam and electric motive power — northeast of Tuapse the line was operated by steam, south of Samtredia it was electrified. The streamlined Baldwins were also based at Gudermes and worked south along the west shore of the Caspian Sea to Baku. Baku is a Soviet oil field center and use of diesels there was natural considering the readily available fuel. Today, both routes are electrified, but the electrification was completed after 1970, so it seems likely that the 0-6-6-0 1000/1 DEs spent their entire careers working the two lines. Retirement dates are unknown, but the Baldwins were apparently not overly popular, reportedly requiring major overhauls after approximately 400,000 kilometers of service, while the Russian-built equivalents — the TE1 and TE2 — could attain up to 600,000 kilometers between major overhauls. Of course, the Baldwin units could receive no factory support once the cold war began.

THE LIBERATION MIKE —
IN DIESEL TERMS

When France was liberated from German occupation in 1944 the SNCF (French National Railways) was faced with a horrible statistic — 82 percent of the country's locomo-

Algeria was the destination to which Baldwin shipped 20 DRS-6-4-1000s in 1948-49. Above, equipped with roller bearing trucks and steam generator, 040-DC-14 was placed in service at Algiers in June 1948. At right, the lone DRS-6-4-750 operated in Morocco for the Office Cherifien des Phosphates. With a seemingly endless string of phosphate hoppers in tow, OCP No. 6 moves through the yards at Kourigha, Morocco.

Above, an artist's conception of the never-built 1600-h.p. C-C R-616E included a Baltimore & Ohio-like livery. The final export model to be built was the similar R-615E, shown below. A total of 51 of the 1500-h.p. six-axle units were shipped to the Argentine State Railways between June 1953 and October 1954. All entered service at Bahía Blanca, Argentina.

tives were either destroyed or out of service. To replace the ravaged locomotives France would accept 1440 new locomotives from builders in the U. S., Great Britain, and Canada. The "Liberation Mikes" — 2-8-2s constructed by Alco, Baldwin, Lima, and Montreal Locomotive Works — came to be symbolic of the rehabilitation of French railroads, but not all the immediate postwar orders from France were for steam. As the rejuvenation of the French railways progressed through the 1940s and into the early 1950s, France became one of Baldwin's best diesel customers.

In August 1945 Eddystone received an order for 30 660-h.p. diesels through the French Supply Council. The resulting units — which were given the designation DRS-6-4-

GENERAL ROCA

5001

On a foggy day one of the snub-nosed Argentine State Railways R-615Es is eased aboard ship for the long journey across the North and South Atlantic to Argentina.

660 — became Baldwin's first diesel road-switchers. Before deliveries even began, a second order — for 70 more locomotives — was received in January 1946. Together, these orders were hailed by Baldwin officials as the largest export diesel requirement ever placed with a U. S. builder.

The heart of the DRS-6-4-660 was the 6-cylinder, 660-h.p. 606NA engine. This was the first locomotive application for the 606NA, predating its use in a domestic unit by approximately one month. Westinghouse provided the electrical controls, main generator, and traction motors, and GSC furnished cast underframes and Commonwealth A1A-type trucks. The new model marked Baldwin's first use of this A1A-type truck, which later became standard on the domestic DRS-6-4-1500 and AS-416 road-switchers and DR-6-4-1500 passenger locomotive. The 11′-6″ wheelbase of the A1A truck, plus the need for space to fit an underbelly fuel tank, required a frame length of 58′ (the same as the DRS-6-4-1500). Ample space remained even after the inline 6-cylinder engine and its attendant equipment, cab, and a short hood were arranged on the frame, so the DRS-6-4-660 displayed a porch-like end platform on the front. The carbody and many mechanical components — such as the cooling and exhaust systems — were modifications of the equipment used in the Baldwin switcher line. To satisfy French clearance requirements the DRS-6-4-660 was built with a low-clearance cab, requiring that the locomotive's batteries be placed in the base of the rear hood instead of under the cab floor (which was standard Baldwin practice).

Deliveries to France of the first 30 DRS-6-4-660s began in April 1946 (040-DA-1 was assigned to the depot at Marseilles-Arenc on April 15, 1946) and were completed that

December; the DRS-6-4-660s from the 70-unit order were delivered from January to October 1947. The diminutive road-switchers were assigned throughout France, with noteworthy concentrations found at Marseilles, Lyons, Paris, and La Chapelle.

Baldwin received a third order for DRS-6-4-660s in January 1947. This time, however, the order was for six units — and this time the diesels were to be delivered to Morocco. There, the 660-h.p. road-switchers would join the Baldwin DRS-6-4-1500s being constructed on behalf of the French Supply Council (see page 80). The final six DRS-6-4-660s were delivered in January 1948; three were placed in service at Safi and three at Casablanca, Morocco.

The DRS-6-4-660s proved themselves hearty and capable, performing services in France ranging from switching to branch line runs to occasional duty on passenger trains. In 1962 the French units were renumbered into the 62000-series, and in mid-1983 93 of the units remained, with the largest concentrations based at Thionville and Lens, France. SNCF found that the Baldwins were capable of 700,000 kilometers between major overhauls. In 1984, however, heavy repairs were no longer being performed on the venerable Baldwins and the units were to be retired at a rate of approximately 12 per year. Some may remain in service until 1990.

ALGERIA AND THE DRS-6-4-1000

Two months after Baldwin had received its order for DRS-6-4-660s for Morocco, another French-sponsored order — for 15 units of a new model — was logged at Eddystone. Like Morocco, Algeria was at the time benefit-

Richard Campbell

Bound for Buenos Aires with 1500 tons of general merchandise, sun-visored R-615E No. 7041 rolls over wide-gauge track nearly hidden in the grass of the Argentine pampas.

ing from the French Supply Council's purchases of DRS-6-4-1500s. However, a lighter, lower-horsepower unit was also needed on the Algerian railways. The answer was the DRS-6-4-1000, essentially a DRS-6-4-660 equipped with the 1000-h.p. 606SC power plant instead of the normally aspirated 606NA. When constructed, the new DRS-6-4-1000s also displayed a few other differences from their 660-h.p. kindred. They were equipped with steam generators and Timken roller bearings on all truck journals, and the steam generator and its water supply were carried in the short hood, which in turn required that the batteries be located in front of the cab.

The 15 DRS-6-4-1000s were delivered from April to June 1948 and were assigned duty out of Algiers and Constantine, Algeria. In April 1949 the Algerian Railway placed a follow-up order for five more DRS-6-4-1000s, which joined their elder sisters in October and November of that same year. Some DRS-6-4-1000s may still be extant in Algeria.

ONE-OF-A-KIND, NONE-OF-A-KIND

The third — and last — exclusively export road-switcher model was the DRS-6-4-750. Like the DRS-6-4-1000, it was developed from the DRS-6-4-660. In May 1949 the Office Cherifien des Phosphates of Morocco placed an order for a single A1A-A1A road-switcher. By this time the 606NA power plant used in the DRS-6-4-660 had been upgraded to 750 h.p. for use in the domestic DS-4-4-750 switcher, and as a result the DRS-6-4-660 became the DRS-6-4-750. The unit was numbered 6 and delivered in December 1949. It was employed to switch and assemble phosphate trains from the mines near Kourigha for shipment to Casablanca.

The lone DRS-6-4-750 marked the end of production of the DRS-series export road-switchers. When the revised 1950 domestic line was introduced Baldwin cataloged a 1200-h.p. A1A-A1A export road-switcher designated the AS-412E. A logical progression of the design begun with the DRS-6-4-660, the AS-412E was adaptable to track gauges ranging from 39⅜″ to 66″, and its weight in working order could range between 175,000 and 178,000 pounds (with from 116,600 to 118,000 pounds on drivers). Regardless of the merits of the design, none was ever produced. From 1950 on, foreign customers in need of road-switchers were satisfied to take either stock or modified domestic models.

FOREIGN FINALE

Along with the AS-412E road-switcher of 1950 Baldwin also cataloged a streamlined, six-axle (C-C), 1600-h.p. dual-

service locomotive designated the R-616E. As originally designed the R-616E never reached production, but a similar model — the R-615E — was ordered by the Argentine State Railways (General Roca) in February 1952. The order called for 51 units.

In design, the R-615E closely followed conventional Baldwin practices of the period. Power came from a 608A power plant, although at the customer's request it was derated to 1500 h.p. Frames were welded, and the power plant was placed with main generator toward the cab. The cooling system was located in the rear of the locomotive, with side air intakes and roof exhaust. Space was provided for a steam generator, although the Argentine units were not to be equipped for passenger service. Westinghouse provided the electrical gear, including a 471-series main generator and 561A-series traction motors. Outwardly, though, the R-615E looked different from any domestic Baldwin diesel ever built. General Steel Castings supplied 12′-6″ wheelbase swing-bolster C-type trucks, built to conform to 5′-6″ gauge. Measuring only 52′ long (nearly 3′ shorter than an RF-16), the locomotive looked like a kid in grown-ups' shoes, an appearance reinforced by the little 650-gallon fuel tank nestled between the lanky trucks. The finishing touch was a squat carbody with little more than a hint of Baldwin's sharknose design up front. Weighing 231,000 pounds in working order, the R-615E was a lightweight compared to the domestic RF-16 (248,000 pounds) or the AS-616 (up to 377,000 pounds).

Following completion of the first R-615E, Argentine State Railways 5001, Baldwin displayed the unit at the Atlantic City Railroad Exhibition in June 1953. There it joined Baldwin AS-616 test-bed/demonstrator 1601. The specifications of the R-615E were close to those of Alco-GE's 1600-h.p. "World Locomotive," which was also displayed at Atlantic City. With many foreign railroad executives attending the event, Baldwin hoped the R-615E's presence would generate interest — and orders. But the Argentine order proved to be both the first and last Baldwin would write for its R-616E/R-615E.

The 51 R-615Es of the Argentine State Railways were completed by the end of October 1954, and all were originally based at Bahía Blanca, on the east coast of Argentina south of Buenos Aires. The units, eventually renumbered into the 7000-series, enjoyed lengthy careers; in February 1978, 46 were still in serviceable condition and 28 were in service. In early 1984 approximately 20 of the gallant Baldwins remained at work.

PRODUCTION LIST

EXPERIMENTAL BOXCABS 12 (OE) 1000-1-CC,1

No.	C/N	Date
BALDWIN LOCOMOTIVE WORKS 1		
58501	58501	6/25

8-OE-1000-1-CC,1

No.	C/N	Date
BALDWIN LOCOMOTIVE WORKS 1		
61000	61000	5/29

YARD SWITCHERS 80E 660/1

No.	C/N	Date
ATCHISON, TOPEKA & SANTA FE 1		
2200	62000	10/36 1

VO-660

No.	C/N	Date
AKRON & BARBERTON BELT 1		
25	64244	3/42
AMERICAN SMELTING & REFINING CO. 4		
1950	72813	11/45
1951	72814	10/45
1952-1953	72815-72816	11/45
AMERICAN STEEL & WIRE CO. 3		
1	62491	4/41
11	72820	1/46
23-1	64387	7/42
BALDWIN LOCOMOTIVE WORKS 1		
299	62299	4/39 2
BASIC MAGNESIUM INC. 1		
101	64250	4/42
CENTRAL OF GEORGIA 1		
5	62337	10/40 2,3
CENTRAL RAILROAD OF NEW JERSEY 4		
1040-1043	64235-64238	1/42
CHICAGO & EASTERN ILLINOIS 1		
110	64992	8/42
CHICAGO & NORTH WESTERN 10		
1237-1238	71514-71515	4/45
1239	71516	5/45
1240-1242	71519-71521	6/45
1243-1245	71569-71571	6/45
1246	71575	8/45
CHICAGO, MILWAUKEE, ST. PAUL & PACIFIC 1		
1635	62393	5/40 2
CHICAGO, ST. PAUL, MINNEAPOLIS & OMAHA (C&NW) 3		
58-59	71572-71573	6/45
68	71574	6/45
DENVER & RIO GRANDE WESTERN 9		
66	62496	5/41
67-68	62501-62502	7/41
69-72	64183-64186	8/41
73	64187	9/41
74	64188	8/41
ELGIN, JOLIET & EASTERN 3		
270	62336	5/40 2
271-272	62488-62489	3/41
FRANCISCO SUGAR CO. 1		
45	72818	6/46
IOWA ORDNANCE PLANT 1		
2-100	62495	6/41
KANSAS CITY SOUTHERN 1		
1150	72829	5/46
LA SALLE & BUREAU COUNTY 1		
6	72828	1/46
LONG ISLAND 1		
403	71578	10/45
LOUISVILLE & NASHVILLE 4		
20	64230	11/41
21-23	64231-64233	12/41
MINNEAPOLIS, NORTHFIELD & SOUTHERN 1		
600	62394	6/40 2
MINNESOTA WESTERN 1		
1	64394	9/42
MISSOURI PACIFIC 4		
9009-9010	62397-62398	9/40 2
9012	62500	7/41
9206	62498	6/41
NASHVILLE, CHATTANOOGA & ST. LOUIS 1		
10	64197	11/41
NEW ORLEANS PUBLIC BELT 3		
41	64196	12/41
42-43	64241-64242	3/42
NEW YORK CENTRAL 12		
501	62494	5/41
502	64234	1/42
752	64396	10/42
753-754	64397-64398	11/42
755-761	70327-70333	1/45
NORTHERN PACIFIC 3		
128	62392	5/40 2
129-130	64245-64246	4/42
PATAPSCO & BACK RIVERS 3		
63	64189	8/41
64-65	64251-64252	4/42
PENNSYLVANIA 12		
5907	64247	1/42
5908	64393	9/42
5909	64395	9/42
5932-5934	64401-64403	9/42
5935-5937	64404-64406	10/42
5941-5942	72821-72822	10/45
5943	72827	11/45
PICKENS 1		
2	72824	11/45
PROCTER-GAMBLE CO. 1		
125	72819	12/45
READING 11		
36	62300	6/39 3
61	62399	9/40 2
62-63	62400-62401	10/40 2
64	64190	9/41
65-66	64192-64193	9/41
67	64194	10/41
68-69	64390-64391	7/42
70	64399	9/42
ST. LOUIS-SAN FRANCISCO 2		
600-601	64253-64254	5/42
SEABOARD AIR LINE 1		
1202	62490	2/41
SOUTHERN PACIFIC 2		
1021-1022	62492-62493	4/41
SOUTHERN RAILWAY 1		
DS-2005	64195	10/41
STANDARD STEEL DIV.-BLW 1		
12	62335	2/40 2
TERMINAL RAILROAD ASSOC. OF ST. LOUIS 4		
531-532	62395-62396	7/40 2
533	64239	2/42
534	64240	3/42
UNION TERMINAL RY. OF MEMPHIS (MoPac) 2		
9090-9091	64248-64249	4/42
U. S. NAVY DEPARTMENT 6		
10-11	72002-72003	4/45
15-16	70324-70325	12/44
18	70326	12/44
31	72004	5/45
UPPER MERION & PLYMOUTH 2		
51	62499	7/41
52	64243	8/42
WABASH 1		
200	62497	7/41
WARNER COMPANY 1		
11	72817	11/45
WESTERN MARYLAND 4		
101	64191	10/41
103-104	64388-64389	7/42
105	64400	9/42
WESTINGHOUSE ELECT. & MFG. CO. 1		
10	64747	6/42 3
WYANDOTTE TERMINAL 3		
101	72823	10/45
102-103	72825-72826	11/45
YOUNGSTOWN SHEET & TUBE 8		
600	71759	2/45
601	71760	3/45
602-603	71512-71513	4/45
604-605	71517-71518	5/45
606	71576	8/45
607	71577	9/45

DS-4-4-660

No.	C/N	Date
AMERICAN CYANAMID CO. 1		
13	72830	6/46
ARMCO STEEL CORP. 1		
1001	73041	10/46
CHESAPEAKE WESTERN 3		
661	73045	12/46
662-663	73359-73360	12/46
CHICAGO & NORTH WESTERN 3		
1259-1261	73901-73903	3/49
CHICAGO, ST. PAUL, MINNEAPOLIS & OMAHA (C&NW) 1		
71	73904	3/49
ERIE 5		
381-382	73043-73044	11/46
383	73366	10/47
384-385	73898-73899	2/49
ESCANABA & LAKE SUPERIOR 1		
101	73367	11/47
GEORGIA RAILROAD 1		
172	73368	1/48
LONG ISLAND 4		
409-412	73628-73631	5/48
MORRISSEY, FERNIE & MICHEL RAILWAY 1		
1	73042	11/46
NEW ORLEANS PUBLIC BELT 6		
44-45	73038-73039	11/46
46	73040	12/46
47-49	73895-73897	2/49
NORFOLK SOUTHERN 3		
661-662	73361-73362	1/47
663	73365	5/47
PATAPSCO & BACK RIVERS 4		
306-307	73034-73035	10/46
308-309	73036-73037	11/46
PENNSYLVANIA 99		
5957-5963	73618-73624	3/48
5964-5965	73625-73626	4/48
5966	73627	5/48
9000-9006	73905-73911	3/49
9007	73912	4/49
9008	73913	3/49
9009-9010	74236-74237	3/49
9011-9018	74238-74245	4/49
9019-9029	74246-74256	5/49
9030-9049	74410-74429	5/49
9110	73632	7/48
9111-9115	73633-73637	8/48
9116	73641	8/48
9117-9119	73638-73640	8/48
9120	73642	8/48
9121	73803	8/48
9210-9215	73805-73810	11/48
9216-9222	73811-73817	12/48
9223-9230	73818-73825	1/49
9231-9232	73826-73827	2/49
9233-9236	73889-73892	2/49
SLOSS SHEFFIELD STEEL & IRON CO. 1		
30	73893	9/48
TENNESSEE VALLEY AUTHORITY 1		
100	73900	2/49
WABASH 2		
201	73363	3/47
202	73364	4/47
WYANDOTTE SOUTHERN 1		
D-100	73804	9/48
WYANDOTTE TERMINAL 1		
104	73894	1/49

DS-4-4-750

No.	C/N	Date
AMERICAN CYANAMID CO. 1		
14	74784	3/50
AMERICAN STEEL & WIRE CO. 1		
20	74674	8/49
ATCHISON, TOPEKA & SANTA FE 9		
525-533	74394-74402	7/49
BALDWIN LOCOMOTIVE WORKS 1		
301	74813	9/50 4
CALIFORNIA WESTERN 2		
51-52	74408-74409	8/49
ERIE 4		
386-389	74430-74433	8/49
PENNSYLVANIA 24		
5595-5598	74720-74723	5/50
5599-5618	74724-74743	6/50
TEXAS-MEXICAN RAILWAY 2		
509-510	74594-74595	7/49
WARNER CO. 1		
14	74785	4/50
WEYERHAEUSER TIMBER 2		
101	74814	10/50 5
102	74815	11/50 5
YOUNGSTOWN SHEET & TUBE 6		
608-610	74405-74407	8/49
700-702	73657-73659	2/51

S-8

No.	C/N	Date
ARMCO STEEL CORP. 3		
1151	75527	12/51
1152	74988	10/52
1201	75834	1/54
CHICAGO, ROCK ISLAND & PACIFIC 5		
802-806	75683-75687	9/52
COLUMBIA GENEVA STEEL 1		
13	75399	7/53
ESCANABA & LAKE SUPERIOR 1		
102	75700	8/52
LA SALLE & BUREAU COUNTY 1		
8	75429	10/51
MEDFORD CORP. 1		
8	75481	3/52
NEW ORLEANS PUBLIC BELT 2		
50-51	75251-75252	5/51
OLIVER IRON MINING CO. 18		
1200A-1201A	75243-75244	7/51
1202A-1203A	75245-75246	8/51
1200B-1201B	75247-75248	7/51
1202B-1203B	75249-75250	8/51
1204A	75488	10/51
1205A-1206A	75489-75490	11/51
1204B	75491	10/51
1205B-1206B	75492-75493	11/51
1214A-1215A	75692-75693	6/52
1214B-1215B	75696-75697	6/52
PENNSYLVANIA 6		
8994-8997	75117-75120	3/51
8998-8999	75121-75122	4/51
PENNSYLVANIA-READING SEASHORE LINES 1		
6006	75253	5/51
SHARON STEEL CORP. 8		
3	75421	3/52
4	75422	7/52
5-6	75423-75424	8/52
7-8	75425-75426	2/53
9-10	75427-75428	8/53
SLOSS SHEFFIELD STEEL & IRON CO. 4		
33-34	75520-75521	12/51
35-36	75522-75523	3/52
UNITED RAILWAY OF HAVANA 2		
8001-8002	75719-75720	6/52
UNITED STATES PIPE & FOUNDRY 1		
37	75836	12/54
WEYERHAEUSER TIMBER 2		
103, 105	75254-75255	6/51
YOUNGSTOWN SHEET & TUBE 7		
703	75430	11/51
800-803	75494-75497	3/52
804	75163	2/53
805	75332	2/53

8DE 900/1

No.	C/N	Date
NEW ORLEANS PUBLIC BELT 3		
31-33	62135-62137	12/37

VO-1000

No.	C/N	Date
AMERICAN STEEL & WIRE CO. 1		
12	71560	1/46
ATCHISON, TOPEKA & SANTA FE 59		
2201-2202	62302-62303	12/39 6,7
2203	62304	11/39 6,7
2204	62305	1/40 6,7
2205	62306	2/40 6,7
2206	62535	6/41 6,7
2207	64432	11/42
2208-2209	64734-64735	2/43
2210	64740	2/43
2211-2212	64748-64749	4/43
2213-2216	67713-67716	5/43
2217-2218	67724-67725	6/43
2219-2220	67728-67729	7/43
2221	67744	8/43
2222-2223	69640-69641	8/43
2224-2226	70122-70124	12/43
2227	70146	2/44
2228-2229	70162-70163	3/44
2230	70864	5/44
2231-2234	70865-70868	6/44
2235-2241	70872-70878	6/44
2242	71927	7/44
2243	71928	6/44
2244	71929	7/44
2245-2247	70848-70850	5/44
2248-2249	72029-72030	7/45
2250-2252	72031-72033	8/45
2253-2254	72042-72043	9/45
2255-2256	72048-72049	9/45
2257-2259	71530-71532	10/45
ATLANTIC COAST LINE 9		
606-607	64266-64267	1/42
608	64415	8/42
609	64417	8/42
616-617	69667-69668	10/43
619	70156	3/44
621	70157	3/44
623	70158	3/44
BALTIMORE & OHIO 25		
413-416	69649-69652	8/43
417-418	70112-70113	11/43
419-420	70114-70115	12/43
421-422	70858-70859	5/44
423	70879	6/44
424-427	71930-71933	7/44
428-430	71989-71991	1/45
431-432	71426-71427	1/45
433-437	71733-71737	2/45
BELT RAILWAY OF CHICAGO 2		
401	64412	7/42
402	70303	11/44
BINGHAM & GARFIELD 2		
801	64731	1/43
803	64743	3/43
CANTON 2		
30-31	70132-70133	1/44
CENTRAL OF GEORGIA 3		
22	62333	10/40 6
26	69653	9/43
27	70174	4/44
CENTRAL RAILROAD OF NEW JERSEY 5		
1062	70176	4/44
1063	70851	4/44
1064	70852	7/44
1065	71936	7/44
1066	71937	8/44
CHICAGO & NORTH WESTERN 12		
1024	71941	8/44
1037-1038	71746-71747	3/45
1039-1040	72009-72010	5/45
1041	72015	3/45
1042	72016	5/45
1043	72022	7/45
1044-1045	71561-71562	12/45
1046-1047	71563-71564	1/46
CHICAGO, BURLINGTON & QUINCY 30		
9350-9351	69778-69779	11/43
9352-9355	70103-70106	12/43
9356-9357	70119-70120	12/43
9358-9363	70294-70299	11/44
9364	70305	11/44
9365-9373	70306-70315	12/44
9374-9377	70317-70319	12/44
9378-9379	71977-71978	12/44
CHICAGO, MILWAUKEE, ST. PAUL & PACIFIC 12		
1680	62406	10/40 6
1681	62407	11/40 6
1682	64434	11/42
1683-1684	69642-69643	8/43
1685	70121	1/44
1686	70142	2/44
1687	70857	5/44
1688-1691	72044-72047	9/45
CHICAGO, ROCK ISLAND & PACIFIC 5		
760-761	70107-70108	12/43
762-764	70129-70131	1/44
CHICAGO, ST. PAUL, MINNEAPOLIS & OMAHA (C&NW) 3		
87	70149	3/44
88-89	72027-72028	7/45
CHICAGO SHORT LINE 3		
100	64268	1/42
101	70175	4/44
102	71729	2/45
COLORADO & WYOMING 3		
1107-1108	69654-69655	9/43
1109	70016	12/43
DEFENSE PLANT CORP. (for Carbon County) 2		
262-1	69773	11/43
262-2	69774	11/43
DETROIT TERMINAL 2		
101	71558	4/45
102	72005	4/45
ELGIN, JOLIET & EASTERN 10		
475	62410	12/40 6
476-477	64207-64208	9/41
478	70884	7/44
479-480	71938-71939	8/44
481-482	71954-71955	9/44
483	71961	10/44
484	70304	11/44
ESCANABA & LAKE SUPERIOR 1		
100	72227	6/46
GREAT NORTHERN 10		
5332-5333	64211-64212	10/41
5334	69785	11/43
5335	70109	12/43
139-140	71942-71943	8/44
141-144	71944-71947	9/44
INTERNATIONAL-GREAT NORTHERN (MoPac) 3		
9150-9152	70167-70169	4/44
IOWA ORDNANCE PLANT 1		
1-120	62411	5/41 6
KENTUCKY & INDIANA TERMINAL 4		
44	64419	8/42
45	64424	10/42
46	64430	10/42
47	70117	12/43
LEHIGH VALLEY 5		
135-139	70843-70847	4/44
LITCHFIELD & MADISON 1		
100	64274	2/42
LOUISVILLE & NASHVILLE 9		
2202-2205	67740-67743	8/43
2206-2208	70171-70173	4/44
2209-2210	70854-70855	5/44
MACON, DUBLIN & SAVANNAH 1		
1000	64275	2/42
MINNEAPOLIS & ST. LOUIS 2		
D-145	70302	11/45
D-340	62334	4/40 6
MINNEAPOLIS, ST. PAUL & SAULT STE. MARIE 1		
310	71554	11/45
MISSOURI PACIFIC 6		
9103	62301	11/39 6,7
9117	71750	4/45
9118	72012	5/45
9119	72026	7/45
9198-9199	71526-71527	9/45
NASHVILLE, CHATTANOOGA & ST. LOUIS 6		
15	64210	10/41
30-31	69644-69645	8/43
32-34	69646-69648	9/43
NEW YORK CENTRAL 8		
8600-8602	71958-71960	10/44
8603-8604	70300-70301	11/44
8605-8607	71730-71732	2/45
NORTHERN PACIFIC 28		
108-109	62503-62504	6/41
111-112	64428-64429	10/42
119-121	70139-70141	2/44
122	70153	3/44
123	70861	6/44
124	71926	8/44
153	70842	5/44
154	70860	6/44
159-160	71751-71752	4/45
161	72011	5/45
162-164	72023-72025	7/45
165-166	72036-72037	8/45
167	71541	11/45
168	71545	10/45
169-174	71546-71551	11/45
OLIVER IRON MINING CO. 15		
907	62419	7/40 6
908-909	62420-62421	8/40 6
910-911	64276-64277	3/42
912-913	64278-64279	4/42
914-915	64408-64409	7/42
918	64746	4/43
919	67712	5/43
922	67721	6/43
923-925	67734-67736	8/43
PATAPSCO & BACK RIVERS 4		
70	62408	10/40 6
71	62409	12/40 6
72	62505	8/41
73	64416	8/42
PENNSYLVANIA 8		
5913-5916	69662-69665	9/43
5917	69666	10/43
5918	69784	11/43
5919-5920	71552-71553	10/45
PHELPS-DODGE CORP. 2		
9-10	64729-64730	2/43
PHILADELPHIA, BETHLEHEM & NEW ENGLAND 2		
251-252	72007-72008	4/45
PITTSBURGH & WEST VIRGINIA 1		
30	69656	9/43
READING 24		
55-57	71948-71950	8/44
58-59	71956-71957	9/44
71-73	67731-67733	6/43
74-75	70110-70111	11/43
76-79	70134-70137	1/44
80	62402	8/40 6
81	62403	9/40 6
82	64431	10/42
83-84	67722-67723	5/43
85	67730	6/43
86-88	70164-70165	3/44
89	70138	1/44
ST. LOUIS, BROWNSVILLE & MEXICO (MoPac) 5		
9153-9154	70160-70161	3/44
9155	70170	4/44
9160-9161	71565-71566	5/46
ST. LOUIS-SAN FRANCISCO 38		
200	64258	11/41
201-202	64259-64260	12/41
203	64261	1/42
204	64262	12/41
205	64411	7/42
206	64433	11/42
207-208	69669-69670	10/43
209	69675	10/43
210-213	69780-69783	11/43
214-217	70125-70128	1/44
218-219	70869-70870	6/44
220-221	70882-70883	7/44
222	71951	9/44
223-224	71743-71744	3/45
225-227	71755-71757	4/45
228	72013	5/45
229	72017	6/45
230-235	71533-71538	10/45
236-237	71567-71568	6/46
ST. LOUIS SOUTHWESTERN 23		
1000	64410	7/42
1001	64427	10/42
1002	64435	11/42
1003	64750	4/43
1004	69658	9/43
1005	69673	10/43
1006	70158	3/44
1007	71934	8/44
1008	71935	1/44
1009-1010	71741-71742	3/45
1011	72014	5/45
1012	72018	6/45
1013-1015	72019-72021	7/45
1016-1017	72038-72039	8/45
1018	71555	11/45
1019-1022	71556-71559	12/45
SEABOARD AIR LINE 7		
1400	64209	9/41
1401-1402	64256-64257	11/41
1413	71979	12/44
1414	71980	1/45
1415	71981	12/44
1416	71982	1/45
SOUTHERN PACIFIC 25		
1320-1321	62506-62507	7/41
1322-1324	64198-64200	7/41
1325-1329	64269-64273	3/42
1371-1372	70154-70155	3/44
1373	70853	5/44
1374	70862	6/44
1375-1376	64736-64737	2/43
1377	67717	5/43
1378	69657	9/43
1379	70118	1/44
1380-1382	70143-70145	2/44
1383	70863	6/44
1384-1385	70880-70881	7/44
SOUTHERN RAILWAY 1		
DS-2205	64255	11/41
SPOKANE, PORTLAND & SEATTLE 5		
30	62307	12/40 6,8
31	62332	12/40 6,8
32	64426	10/42
33-34	71539-71540	10/45
TENNESSEE COAL IRON & RAILROAD 4		
800-801	72230-72231	6/46
802-803	72789-72790	7/46
TENNESSEE EASTMAN CORP. 1		
4	72228	6/46
TERMINAL RAILROAD ASSOC. OF ST. LOUIS 11		
591-592	64201-64202	8/41
593	64263	12/41
594-595	64264-64265	1/42
596	64418	8/42
597-598	71952-71953	9/44
599-601	71962-71964	10/44
UNION PACIFIC 6		
1055	69672	10/43
1056-1058	69775-69777	10/43
1059-1060	70147-70148	2/44
UNION RAILROAD 6		
500-501	62404-62405	10/40 6
502-505	64203-64206	8/41
U. S. NAVY DEPARTMENT 40		
BREMERTON, WASHINGTON		
6	70886	7/44
11	70290	12/44
12	70291	12/44
13	70292	12/44
14	70293	12/44
18	71983	2/45
19	71984	2/45
BURNS CITY, INDIANA		
3	64423	9/42
5	64422	9/42
CHEATHAM ANNEX, VIRGINIA		
35	71524	11/45
36	71525	9/45
CRANE, INDIANA		
7	64738	3/43
8	64739	3/43
9	72006	4/45
10	71970	10/44
EARLE, NEW JERSEY		
3	69659	10/43
4	70102	4/44
8	71940	8/44

No.	C/N	Date
o	71969	10/44
0	71968	10/44
3	71428	2/45
4	71429	2/45
9	71430	2/45

AWTHORNE, NEVADA

No.	C/N	Date
	64733	2/43
5	71897	2/45
6	71899	2/45

NDIAN HEAD, MARYLAND

No.	C/N	Date
	64732	2/43

MC ALESTER, OKLAHOMA

No.	C/N	Date
	71738	2/45
	67737	8/43
	71748	3/45
	71749	3/45
2	72034	8/45
3	72035	8/45

ORT CHICAGO, CALIFORNIA

No.	C/N	Date
1	71986	2/45
2	71753	5/45
3	71754	5/45

CHUMAKER, OKLAHOMA

No.	C/N	Date
	71739	3/45
7	72040	9/45
8	72041	9/45

TOCKTON, CALIFORNIA

No.	C/N	Date
	71985	2/45

U. S. WAR DEPARTMENT 26

No.	C/N	Date
-1800	71740	4/45
-1801	71745	4/45
126	64741	3/43
127	64744	3/43
128	64745	4/43
129-7130	67710-67711	5/43
137-7138	67718-67719	6/43
139-7140	67726-67727	7/43
143	67739	8/43
225	70856	5/44
226	70871	6/44
227	70885	7/44
453	64407	7/42
454	64413	7/42
455	64414	8/42
456-7457	64420-64421	8/42
461	64436	12/42
462-7463	64727-64728	12/42
464	64742	3/43
466	67720	6/43
467	67738	8/43

WABASH 4

No.	C/N	Date
00	64425	9/42
01	70151	3/44
02	70152	2/44
03	72229	6/46

WESTERN MARYLAND 5

No.	C/N	Date
28-129	69660-69661	9/43
30-131	69786-69787	11/43
32	70150	2/44

WESTERN PACIFIC 5

No.	C/N	Date
81-582	71528-71529	10/45
83-585	71542-71544	11/45

WESTERN RAILWAY OF ALABAMA 4

No.	C/N	Date
21-623	71965-71967	10/44
24	70316	12/44

DS-4-4-1000 (608NA-Powered)

BELT RAILWAY OF CHICAGO 1

No.	C/N	Date
05	73841	7/47

COLUMBIA GENEVA STEEL 6

No.	C/N	Date
21-22	72851-72852	7/47
23-26	72853-72856	12/47

COPPER RANGE 2

No.	C/N	Date
00-101	72839-72840	4/47

DETROIT TERMINAL 1

No.	C/N	Date
03	72812	1/47

ERIE 2

No.	C/N	Date
00	72808	11/46
01	72809	12/46

MISSOURI-KANSAS-TEXAS 11

No.	C/N	Date
000-1003	72795-72798	8/46
004-1005	72799-72800	9/46
006-1009	72834-72837	2/47
010	72838	3/47

NEW YORK, CHICAGO & ST. LOUIS 2

No.	C/N	Date
100-101	72849-72850	10/47

NORFOLK SOUTHERN 2

No.	C/N	Date
1001-1002	72832-72833	1/47

READING 14

No.	C/N	Date
26	72841	4/47
27	72842	5/47
28	72843	8/47
29-32	72844-72847	9/47
33	72848	10/47
34	72232	6/46
35	72234	6/46
36-37	72793-72794	7/46
38-39	72801-72802	8/46

ST. LOUIS SOUTHWESTERN 5

No.	C/N	Date
1023	73482	12/47
1024-1027	73483-73486	1/48

SEABOARD AIR LINE 8

No.	C/N	Date
1417	72233	6/46
1418-1419	72791-72792	7/46
1420-1423	72803-72806	9/46
1424	72807	10/46

WESTERN MARYLAND 2

No.	C/N	Date
133-134	72810-72811	12/46

DS-4-4-1000 (606SC-Powered)

AKRON & BARBERTON BELT 1

No.	C/N	Date
26	73605	3/48

AMERICAN SMELTING & REFINING CO. 2

No.	C/N	Date
101	73954	9/48
102	74637	2/50

ATCHISON, TOPEKA & SANTA FE 41

No.	C/N	Date
2200	74223	6/49
2260-2263	73576-73579	2/48
2264-2265	73580-73581	3/48
2266-2269	73789-73792	9/48
2270-2278	73793-73801	10/48
2279-2288	74073-74082	3/49
2289-2297	74206-74214	6/49
2298	74222	6/49
2299	74224	6/49

ATLANTA & WEST POINT 2

No.	C/N	Date
676-677	74596-74597	4/49

BALTIMORE & OHIO 49

No.	C/N	Date
376	74778	7/50
377-381	74788-74792	7/50
382-383	74799-74800	8/50
384-385	74881-74882	8/50
386-391	74937-74942	8/50
392-393	74943-74944	9/50
394-399	74945-74950	10/50
438-440	73839-73841	10/48
441-458	73842-73859	11/48
459-462	73860-73863	12/48

BESSEMER & LAKE ERIE 1

No.	C/N	Date
282	73958	3/49

CALUMET & HECLA 2

No.	C/N	Date
201-202	73956-73957	8/48

CANADIAN PACIFIC 11

No.	C/N	Date
7065	73802	3/48 9
7066-7069	73943-73946	10/48 9
7070-7072	73947-73949	11/48 9
7073	73950	10/48 9
7074-7075	73951-73952	11/48 9

CARNEGIE ILLINOIS STEEL CORP. 3

No.	C/N	Date
74-76	73613-73615	6/48

CENTRAL OF GEORGIA 2

No.	C/N	Date
36	74194	8/49
37	74195	10/49

CENTRAL RAILROAD OF NEW JERSEY 3

No.	C/N	Date
1072-1074	74774-74776	4/50

CHICAGO & NORTH WESTERN 5

No.	C/N	Date
1018-1021	74083-74086	3/49
1022	74087	4/49

CHICAGO GREAT WESTERN 10

No.	C/N	Date
32-33	73914-73915	2/49
34-41	74225-74232	7/49

CHICAGO, MILWAUKEE, ST. PAUL & PACIFIC 10

No.	C/N	Date
1692-1697	73920-73925	11/48
1901-1904	74632-74635	10/49

CHICAGO, ST. PAUL, MINNEAPOLIS & OMAHA (C&NW) 2

No.	C/N	Date
99-100	74088-74089	3/49

COLUMBIA GENEVA STEEL 6

No.	C/N	Date
27-31	73606-73610	6/48
32	73611	7/48

ERIE 15

No.	C/N	Date
602	73568	1/48
603-604	73569-73570	2/48
605-606	73766-73767	6/48
607-608	73959-73960	3/49
609-610	74203-74204	6/49
611	74616	8/49
612-614	74617-74619	7/49
615	74620	8/49
616	74196	9/49

GEORGIA RAILROAD 1

No.	C/N	Date
921	74205	6/49

IRONTON RAILROAD 2

No.	C/N	Date
750	73953	10/48
751	74600	7/49

KENTUCKY & INDIANA TERMINAL 2

No.	C/N	Date
53	73926	10/48
54	73927	9/48

LEHIGH VALLEY 9

No.	C/N	Date
140-141	74234-74235	6/49
142-143	74598-74599	6/49
144-147	74627-74630	1/50
148	74631	2/50

LONG ISLAND 1

No.	C/N	Date
450	73612	4/48

MINNEAPOLIS, ST. PAUL & SAULT STE. MARIE 2

No.	C/N	Date
311-312	74186-74187	6/49

MISSOURI PACIFIC 17

No.	C/N	Date
9120-9122	73582-73584	2/48
9123	73963	3/49
9124	74090	3/49
9125	74091	4/49
9126	74092	3/49
9127	74093	4/49
9133-9138	74765-74770	3/50
9139-9141	74771-74773	4/50

OAKLAND TERMINAL 1

No.	C/N	Date
101	73773	7/48

OLIVER IRON MINING CO. 5

No.	C/N	Date
928-930	74188-74190	6/49
931-932	74191-74192	7/49

PATAPSCO & BACK RIVERS 8

No.	C/N	Date
337-341	73571-73575	3/48
342-344	74648-74650	12/49

PENNSYLVANIA 137

No.	C/N	Date
5550	74759	3/50
5551-5552	74638-74639	2/50
5553-5557	74641-74645	2/50
5558-5564	74651-74657	2/50
5565	74658	3/50
5566-5570	74198-74202	1/50
5571-5576	74621-74626	1/50
5577	74636	1/50
5578-5584	74659-74665	4/50
5585	74197	1/50
5586	74666	2/50
5587-5590	74704-74707	2/50
5967-5977	73585-73595	4/48
5978-5979	73603-73604	5/48
9050-9055	74100-74105	3/49
9056	74106	4/49
9057-9059	74107-74109	3/49
9060-9072	74110-74122	4/49
9073-9077	74179-74183	4/49
9078	74184	5/49
9079	74185	4/49
9122-9123	73616-73617	6/48
9124-9125	73753-73754	6/48
9126-9135	73755-73764	7/48
9136	73765	8/48
9177-9181	73596-73600	4/48
9182-9183	73601-73602	5/48
9251-9252	73864-73865	12/48
9253	73866	1/49
9254	73867	12/48
9255-9259	73868-73872	1/49
9260	73873	12/48
9261-9267	73874-73880	1/49

No.	C/N	Date
9268-9269	73881-73882	2/49
9270	73883	1/49
9271-9272	73884-74885	2/49
9273	73886	1/49
9274	73887	2/49
9275	73888	1/49
9429-9434	74708-74713	5/50

READING 30

No.	C/N	Date
700-710	73774-73784	9/48
711-714	73785-73788	10/48
715-720	74601-74606	7/49
721-725	74607-74611	9/49
726-729	74612-74615	7/49

ST. LOUIS, BROWNSVILLE & MEXICO (MoPac) 8

No.	C/N	Date
9148-9149	74763-74764	3/50
9162-9165	74094-74097	3/49
9166-9167	74098-74099	4/49

ST. LOUIS-SAN FRANCISCO 4

No.	C/N	Date
238-241	73916-73919	12/48

SEABOARD AIR LINE 27

No.	C/N	Date
1435-1437	74760-74762	2/50
1438-1443	74793-74798	8/50
1444-1451	74883-74890	8/50
1452-1454	75098-75100	10/50
1455-1456	75101-75102	11/50
1457-1458	75103-75104	12/50
1459-1461	75105-75107	1/51

SOUTHERN PACIFIC 10

No.	C/N	Date
1393-1402	73933-73942	9/48

SOUTHERN RAILWAY 5

No.	C/N	Date
2285-2289	73928-73932	11/48

TERMINAL RAILROAD ASSOC. OF ST. LOUIS 2

No.	C/N	Date
602-603	73961-73962	3/49

UNION PACIFIC 5

No.	C/N	Date
1206-1210	73768-73772	9/48

USA (CORPS OF ENGINEERS) 2

No.	C/N	Date
L-4	74777	5/50
W-8380	74193	8/49

WABASH 1

No.	C/N	Date
304	73955	1/49

WESTERN RAILWAY OF ALABAMA 1

No.	C/N	Date
630	74233	11/48

S-12

AKRON & BARBERTON BELT 2

No.	C/N	Date
27	75028	5/51
28	75316	7/52

AMERICAN SMELTING & REFINING CO. 2

No.	C/N	Date
1954-1955	75544-75545	4/52

APACHE RAILWAY 1

No.	C/N	Date
600	75616	6/52

ARMCO STEEL CORP. 1

No.	C/N	Date
706	76091	2/55

ATLANTA & WEST POINT 1

No.	C/N	Date
678	75280	7/51

BALTIMORE & OHIO 5

No.	C/N	Date
463-467	75961-75965	11/53

CALUMET & HECLA 1

No.	C/N	Date
203	75141	9/51

CENTRAL OF GEORGIA 4

No.	C/N	Date
311-312	75814-75815	3/53
313-314	75816-75817	4/53

CENTRAL RAILROAD OF NEW JERSEY 7

No.	C/N	Date
1053-1055	75025-75027	6/51
1056-1059	75058-75061	6/51

CHICAGO & NORTH WESTERN 16

No.	C/N	Date
1073-1076	75064-75067	7/51
1106-1108	75194-75196	9/52
1109	75682	9/52
1117-1121	75394-75398	6/53
1126-1128	76025-76027	7/54

CHICAGO, MILWAUKEE, ST. PAUL & PACIFIC 21

No.	C/N	Date
1905-1909	75007-75011	11/50
1910-1914	75146-75150	11/51
1915-1916	75278-75279	11/51
1917	75701	10/52
1918-1921	75967-75970	12/53
1922-1925	75971-75974	1/54

No.	C/N	Date
CHICAGO, ROCK ISLAND & PACIFIC 2		
758-759	75935-75936	7/53 [10]
COLUMBIA GENEVA STEEL 3		
33-35	76138-76140	8/56 [11]
COPPER RANGE 1		
200	75068	7/51
ERIE 12		
617-618	74875-74876	2/51
619-620	75672-75673	4/52
621-628	75674-75681	5/52
ERIE MINING 4		
400-402	76116-76118	10/55
403	76125	10/56 [12]
GREAT NORTHERN 5		
24-28	75818-75822	2/53
INTERNATIONAL-GREAT NORTHERN (MoPac) 3		
9230-9232	75528-75530	4/52
KANSAS CITY SOUTHERN 4		
1160-1163	75054-75057	4/51
LEHIGH VALLEY 14		
230-233	74952-74955	9/50
234-236	74960-74962	9/50
237-239	74963-74965	10/50
240-243	74956-74959	10/50
MC CLOUD RIVER 2		
30-31	75912-75913	10/53
MICHIGAN LIMESTONE 2		
116	75959	11/53
117	75960	12/53
MINNEAPOLIS, ST. PAUL & SAULT STE. MARIE 2		
313-314	75617-75618	3/52
MISSOURI-KANSAS-TEXAS 15		
1201	75504	9/51
1202-1206	75505-75509	10/51
1207-1210	75510-75513	12/51
1211-1212	75183-75184	6/52
1213-1215	75191-75193	6/52
MISSOURI PACIFIC 27		
9200-9207	75033-75040	5/51
9208-9216	75041-75049	6/51
9217	75050	7/51
9218-9219	75051-75052	9/51
9220-9223	75531-75534	3/52
9224-9226	75535-75537	4/52
MONONGAHELA 27		
400-406	75797-75803	11/52
407-408	75838-75839	5/53
409-410	75840-75841	6/53
411-418	75842-75849	7/53
419-422	76010-76013	3/54
423-425	76014-76016	6/54
426	76017	7/54
NEW ORLEANS PUBLIC BELT 2		
61-62	76120-76121	12/55
NEW YORK CENTRAL 21		
9308-9310	75275-75277	10/51
9311-9321	75546-75556	6/52
9322-9328	75557-75563	7/52
OLIVER IRON MINING CO. 1		
933	75053	6/51
PATAPSCO & BACK RIVERS 4		
335	74640	2/53 [13]
345-347	75234-75236	9/51 [14]
PENNSYLVANIA 87		
8100-8104	75945-75949	2/54
8732-8739	75631-75638	9/52
8740-8750	75639-75649	10/52
8751-8768	75650-75655	10/52
8769-8772	75659-75662	12/52
8773-8775	75656-75658	12/52
8777-8779	75292-75294	12/51
8780-8787	75295-75302	1/52
8788-8796	75303-75311	2/52
8976-8981	74857-74862	1/51
8982-8987	74863-74868	2/51
8988-8993	74869-74874	3/51
PENNSYLVANIA-READING SEASHORE LINES 11		
6017-6020	75930-75933	6/53
6021	75934	7/53
6028-6033	76126-76131	4/56 [11]

No.	C/N	Date
RAYONIER INC. 2		
201-202	76136-76137	7/56 [11]
ST. LOUIS, BROWNSVILLE & MEXICO (MoPac) 3		
9227-9229	75313-75315	4/52
SEABOARD AIR LINE 10		
1462-1465	75142-75145	1/52
1476-1481	75759-75764	1/53
SHARON STEEL CORP. 2		
1	75032	5/51
10	75140	7/51
SIERRA 2		
40	76092	2/55
42	76093	2/55
SOUTHERN PACIFIC 56		
1442-1445	74877-74880	1/51
1446-1448	74970-74972	1/51
1449-1455	74973-74979	2/51
1456-1457	75017-75018	3/51
1458-1463	75019-75024	4/51
1492-1494	75774-75776	10/52
1495-1499	75777-75781	11/52
1500-1506	75782-75788	12/52
1507-1513	75789-75795	2/53
1539-1546	75914-75921	9/53
1547-1550	75922-75925	9/53
SOUTHERN RAILWAY 10		
2290-2299	75603-75612	7/52
TENNESSEE COAL IRON & RAILROAD 8		
1200-1204	75012-75016	10/50
1205-1207	75029-75031	5/51
TENNESSEE VALLEY AUTHORITY 4		
1-2	75601-75602	7/52
3	75937	7/54
200	75312	1/52
TERMINAL RAILROAD ASSOC. OF ST. LOUIS 4		
1250-1253	75688-75691	8/52
TEXAS & NEW ORLEANS (SP) 3		
105-107	75613-75615	2/52
UNION TERMINAL RY. OF MEMPHIS (MoPac) 7		
9233-9236	75827-75830	4/53
9237-9239	75831-75833	5/53
U. S. AIR FORCE 2		
1841-1842	75703-75704	12/52
U. S. NAVY DEPARTMENT 14		
65-00292	75289	12/51
65-00293	75290	12/51
65-00315	75291	12/51
65-00365	75705	11/52
65-00366	75706	11/52
65-00367	75707	11/52
65-00368	75708	11/52
65-00369	75709	11/52
65-00370	75710	12/52
65-00371	75711	12/52
65-00372	75712	12/52
65-00373	75713	12/52
65-00374	75714	12/52
65-00391	75796	2/53
UNITED STATES STEEL CORP. 10		
GE-1/GE-2	75281-75282	7/51
GE-3	75283	8/51
GE-4/GE-5	75284-75285	9/51
GE-6/GE-8	75286-75288	3/52
GE-17/GE-18	75542-75543	2/52
WABASH 5		
305-306	75062-75063	4/51
307-309	75823-75825	2/53

1. AT&SF 2200 was completed as BLW 62000 in 10/36, was purchased by AT&SF in 6/37.
2. All known oval-grille VO-660s include: BLW 299, CMStP&P 1635, CofG 5, EJ&E 270, MN&S 600, MP 9009-9010, NP 128, RDG 61-63, Standard Steel 12, TRRA 531-532.
3. All known VO-660s built with Baldwin switcher trucks include: CofG 5, RDG 36, Westinghouse 10.
4. BLW 301 was placed in service in 9/50 as a plant switcher. In 1/56 the unit was rebuilt with a new 606 800-h.p. power plant and sold as Weyerhaeuser 301.
5. Weyerhaeuser 101-102 were built as B-L-H DS-4-4-750 demonstrators 750-751 in 5/50.
6. All known oval-grille VO-1000s include: AT&SF 2201-2206, CofG 22, CMStP&P 1680-1681, EJ&E 475, Iowa Ordnance 1-120, M&StL D-340, MP 9103, P&BR 70-71, RDG 80-81, SP&S 30-31, OIM 907-909, Union 500-501.
7. All known VO-1000s delivered with the Baldwin switcher trucks include: AT&SF 2201-2206, MP 9103.
8. SP&S 30-31 were built as BLW VO-1000 demonstrators 307 and 332 in 5/40.
9. CP 7065 carried Canadian Locomotive Co. C/N 2519. CP 7066-7075 carried CLC C/Ns 2520-2529. Actual construction took place at Eddystone.
10. RI 758-759 were built as B-L-H S-12 demonstrators 1200-1201. As demonstrators they were m.u. equipped; however, this equipment was removed prior to delivery to the RI in 7/53.
11. A total of 11 S-12s were built with GE electrical equipment as follows: CGS 33-35, PRSL 6028-6033, Rayonier 201-202.
12. Erie Mining 403 was actually constructed in late 1955.
13. The locomotive which became P&BR 335 was constructed as a DS-4-4-1000 which was used in a test program to develop the 600-series engine into a dual-fuel power plant (burning either diesel fuel or natural gas). The unit was used basically to transport the test engine; the dual-fuel 600-series engine would have been applied to stationary applications only. Upon sale to P&BR it was repowered with a 606A engine.
14. P&BR 345 was shipped from Eddystone without a power plant. The customer installed the engine at its Sparrows Point (Maryland) shops.

STREAMLINED PASSENGER-SERVICE UNITS

4-8-8-4 750/8 DE

No.	C/N	Date
BALDWIN LOCOMOTIVE WORKS 1		
6000	64639	4/43 [1]

DR-12-8-3000

No.	C/N	Date
BALDWIN LOCOMOTIVE WORKS 2		
6000A-6000B	73129-73130	3/48 [2]
NATIONAL RAILWAYS OF MEXICO 14		
6400	72672	4/47 [3]
6401	72673	1/48
6402	72674	4/48
6403-6407	72675-72679	5/48
6408	72680	6/48
6409-6413	72681-72685	7/48
PENNSYLVANIA 24		
5823A1-5823A2	73131	4/47
5824A1-5824A2	73377	5/47
5825A1-5825A2	73378	6/47
5826A1-5826A2	73379	9/47
5827A1-5827A2	73380	10/47
5828A1-5828A2	73381	11/47
5829A1-5829A2	73382	12/47
5830A1-5830A2	73383	1/48
5831A1-5831A2	73384	1/48
5832A1-5832A2	73385	2/48
5833A1-5833A2	73386	2/48
5834A1-5834A2	73387	2/48
SEABOARD AIR LINE 14		
4500	71579	12/45
4501	73141	3/47
4502-4503	73142-73143	4/47
4504-4505	73144-73145	5/47
4506	73388	6/47
4507	73389	7/47
4508-4509	73390-73391	9/47
4510	73392	11/47
4511-4512	73393-73394	12/47
4513	73395	1/48

0-6-6-0 1000/2 DE

No.	C/N	Date
NATIONAL RAILWAYS OF MEXICO 3		
6000	70320	12/44 [4]
6001	70321	3/45 [4]
6002	72621	8/46

DRX-6-4-2000

No.	C/N	Date
WHARTON & NORTHERN (CNJ) 6		
2000	73060	11/46
2001	73061	12/46
2002	73062	2/47
2003	73750	8/48
2004-2005	73751-73752	9/48

DR-6-4-2000 (608NA-Powered)

No.	C/N	Date
GULF, MOBILE & OHIO 2		
280	71580	1/47
281	71581	2/47

DR-6-4-2000 (606SC-Powered)

No.	C/N	Date
PENNSYLVANIA (A Units) 18		
5770A-5771A	73505-73506	6/48
5772A-5773A	73507-73508	8/48
5774A-5775A	73509-73510	9/48
5776A-5777A	73511-73512	10/48
5778A-5779A	73513-73514	10/48
5780A-5781A	73515-73516	10/48
5782A-5783A	73517-73518	11/48
5784A-5785A	73519-73520	11/48
5786A-5787A	73521-73522	12/48
PENNSYLVANIA (B Units) 9		
5770B	73523	6/48
5772B	73524	8/48
5774B	73525	9/48
5776B	73526	10/48
5778B	73527	10/48
5780B	73528	10/48
5782B	73529	11/48
5784B	73530	11/48
5786B	73531	12/48

DR-6-2-1000

No.	C/N	Date
CHICAGO & NORTH WESTERN 1		
5000A	73464	11/48

DR-6-4-1500

No.	C/N	Date
NEW YORK CENTRAL (A Units) 4		
3200-3201	73132-73133	11/47
3202-3203	73134-73135	5/48
NEW YORK CENTRAL (B Units) 2		
3300	73136	11/47
3301	73137	5/48
SEABOARD AIR LINE (A Units) 3		
2700	73396	11/47
2701-2702	73397-73398	1/48

RP-210

No.	C/N	Date
NEW YORK CENTRAL 1		
20	76108	5/56
NEW YORK, NEW HAVEN & HARTFORD 2		
3000-3001	76109-76110	10/56

1. The construction plate on BLW 6000 read 194(
2. BLW DR-12-8-3000 demonstrator 6000A-6000 was ordered as Union Pacific 998-999 but the o der was canceled prior to delivery.
3. Prior to delivery, National Railways of Mexic 6400 was lettered as BLW 6400. It is not believe that the unit was ever employed as a demonstra tor.
4. National Railways of Mexico 6000-6001 were e: BLW demonstrators 2000-2001, and were deli ered to the NdeM in 8/45.

HEAVY TRANSFER UNITS

DT-6-6-2000 (608NA-Powered)

No.	C/N	Date
ELGIN, JOLIET & EASTERN 1		
100	72831	5/46 [1]

DT-6-6-2000 (606SC-Powered)

No.	C/N	Date
ATCHISON, TOPEKA & SANTA FE 7		
2600	73748	6/48
2601	74434	8/49
2602	74435	7/49
2603-2605	74436-74438	11/49 [2]
2606	73980	3/50 [3]
DULUTH, SOUTH SHORE & ATLANTIC 4		
300-302	74668-74670	10/49
303	74672	8/50

No.	C/N	Date

LGIN, JOLIET & EASTERN 26

No.	C/N	Date
01-104	73709-73712	3/48
05	73713	4/48
06	73714	3/48
07-110	73715-73718	4/48
11-113	73719-73721	5/48
14-116	73722-73724	6/48
17-119	73725-73727	7/48
20-122	73728-73730	8/48
23-125	73731-73733	9/48
26	74671	11/50 4

MINNEAPOLIS, NORTHFIELD & SOUTHERN 5

0-21	74137-74138	12/48
2-24	74139-74141	1/49

T. LOUIS SOUTHWESTERN 1

60	73532	5/48

RONA 2

0-51	74123-74124	4/49

RT-624

MINNEAPOLIS, NORTHFIELD & SOUTHERN 1

5	75393	7/53

ENNSYLVANIA 23

13	75958	2/54 5
724-8727	75664-75667	10/52 5
728-8729	75668-75669	11/52 5
730-8731	75670-75671	12/52 5
952-8953	75123-75124	8/51
954-8957	75125-75128	9/51
958-8959	75129-75130	10/51 6
960-8965	75131-75136	11/51 6

EJ&E 100 was the only DT-6-6-2000 equipped ith 608NA engines.

AT&SF 2603-2605 were the only DT-6-6-2000s uilt with dynamic brakes.

AT&SF 2606 was built in 12/48 as BLW demon-trator 2000. The unit was turned over to AT&SF in /50.

EJ&E 126 was completed in 2/50 and demon-trated as BLW 2001. Ownership was transferred o the EJ&E in 11/50.

PRR 8113, 8724-8731 were built with outside-qualized trucks.

PRR 8958-8965 were the only RT-624s built ith dynamic brakes.

HEAVY ROAD-SWITCHERS
DRS-4-4-1500

RIE 6

100	73652	11/49
101-1102	74289-74290	11/49
103-1105	74291-74293	12/49

RON MINES CO. OF VENEZUELA 3

	73138	10/47 1,2
	73139	7/49 1,2
	73140	3/48 1,2

EHIGH VALLEY 1

00	73651	12/48 3

MINNEAPOLIS, ST. PAUL & SAULT STE. MARIE 8

60-363	73497-73500	12/47
64-365	73501-73502	1/48
66-367	73503-73504	2/48

EW YORK CENTRAL 2

300-8301	73479-73480	7/48 3

ORTHERN PACIFIC 2

75-176	73645-73646	9/48 3

PENNSYLVANIA-READING SEASHORE LINES 6

000-6005	74752-75757	4/50 3

T. LOUIS, BROWNSVILLE & MEXICO (MoPac) 4

112-4113	73647-73648	2/49
114-4115	73649-73650	3/49

WESTERN MARYLAND 3

70	73399	7/47
71-172	73643-73644	7/48

DRS-6-4-1500

CHICAGO & NORTH WESTERN 1

504	73478	7/48

COLUMBUS & GREENVILLE 5

No.	C/N	Date
601	72624	10/46
602-603	72625-72626	12/46
604-605	72627-72628	1/47

FRENCH SUPPLY COUNCIL 55
ALGERIA

040-DA-1	72630	12/46
040-DA-2 to		
040-DA-6	72632-72636	1/47
040-DA-7 to		
040-DA-9	72641-72643	1/47
040-DA-10	72644	2/47
040-DB-1 to		
040-DB-4	73327-73330	7/47
040-DB-5 to		
040-DB-6	73331-73332	8/47
040-DB-7 to		
040-DB-8	73333-73334	10/47
040-DB-9 to		
040-DB-10	73335-73336	11/47
040-DB-11 to		
040-DB-12	73337-73338	1/48
040-DB-13	73339	12/47
040-DB-14	73340	1/48
040-DB-15 to		
040-DB-17	73341-73343	12/47
040-DB-18 to		
040-DB-19	73344-73345	1/48
040-DB-20	73346	3/48
040-DB-21	73347	2/48
040-DB-22	73348	1/48
040-DB-23 to		
040-DB-25	73465-73467	2/48
040-DA-101	72631	12/46 4
040-DA-102 to		
040-DA-104	72637-72639	1/47 4
040-DA-105	72640	12/47 4

MOROCCO

040-DA-11 to		
040-DA-12	72645-72646	4/47
040-DA-13	72647	3/47
040-DA-14 to		
040-DA-15	72648-72649	4/47
040-DA-201 to		
040-DA-204	72650-72653	5/47 4
040-DA-205	73349	10/47 4
040-DA-206	73350	11/47 4

TUNISIA

040-DA-301	73216	2/47
040-DA-302	73217	12/46
040-DA-303 to		
040-DA-304	73218-73219	1/47

KENNECOTT COPPER CO. 1

901	73474	3/48 5

MOROCCAN RAILWAY 7

040-DA-306 to		
040-DA-307	74287-74288	12/49 4
040-DA-308 to		
040-DA-309	75108-75109	7/51 4
040-DC-331 to		
040-DC-333	75524-75526	7/52 6

NORFOLK SOUTHERN 10

1501	73487	10/47
1502-1506	73488-73492	2/48
1507-1510	73493-73496	3/48

SAVANNAH & ATLANTA 8

100-103	73660-73663	5/48
104-107	73664-73667	6/48

SOUTHERN PACIFIC 3

5200	73654	8/48
5201-5202	73655-73656	12/48

UNION PACIFIC 1

1250	72629	1/48 7

DRS-6-6-1500

BESSEMER & LAKE ERIE 7

401	73988	2/49
402	73989	1/49
403	74715	5/50
404-407	74933-74936	7/50

CHESAPEAKE & OHIO 3

5530-5532	74701-74703	11/49

CHICAGO & NORTH WESTERN 8

1500-1502	73475-73477	2/48

No.	C/N	Date
1505-1506	74452-74453	8/49
1507-1509	74279-74281	8/49

DULUTH, SOUTH SHORE & ATLANTIC 4

200-202	74693-74695	11/49
203	74716	8/50 8

ERIE 12

1150	74714	4/50
1151-1152	74717-74718	6/50
1153	74719	9/50 9
1154-1158	74779-74783	9/50 9
1159-1161	74930-74932	9/50 9

KAISER STEEL CO. 2

1010A	73749	8/48 9
1010B	74751	8/49 9

MC CLOUD RIVER 2

28	73653	11/48
29	74812	7/50 9

MINNEAPOLIS, NORTHFIELD & SOUTHERN 1

15	74758	3/50

NORTHERN PACIFIC 1

177	73838	8/48

SOUTHERN PACIFIC 25

5203	74257	3/49
5204-5205	73258-73259	4/49
5206-5208	73260-73262	5/49
5209-5212	73263-73266	6/49
5213-5216	74678-74681	12/49 9
5217-5227	74682-74692	1/50 9,10

TENNESSEE COAL IRON & RAILROAD 2

1500	73746	5/48
1501	73747	6/48

TEXAS & NEW ORLEANS (SP) 4

187	74267	3/49
188	74268	4/49
189	74667	12/49
190	74677	12/49

UNION RAILROAD 12

613-614	74220-74221	2/49
615-619	74215-74219	2/49
620-624	74696-74700	10/49

AS-16

BALTIMORE & OHIO 16

890-894	76096-76100	5/55
895-898	76101-76104	6/55
899	75996	2/54
900-903	75498-75501	5/52
904	75502	6/52
905	75420	3/53

ERIE 16

1106-1107	74903-74904	5/51
1108-1110	74980-74982	7/51
1111-1112	74986-74987	11/51
1113-1116	75516-75519	3/52
1117-1120	75538-75541	1/52 ·
1140	74983	7/51 11

INTERNATIONAL-GREAT NORTHERN (MoPac) 2

4195-4196	75161-75162	11/51

MINNEAPOLIS, ST. PAUL & SAULT STE. MARIE 2

379-380	74984-74985	8/51

MISSOURI-KANSAS-TEXAS 18

1571-1573	74891-74893	9/50
1574	74894	10/50
1575	74895	9/50
1576-1578	74896-74898	10/50
1579-1584	75431-75436	10/51
1585-1586	75341-75342	1/51
1787-1788	75694-75695	1/53 11

NEW YORK, CHICAGO & ST. LOUIS 4

320-321	75943-75944	11/53
322-323	76028-76029	6/54

PENNSYLVANIA-READING SEASHORE LINES 16

6007-6010	75804-75807	3/53 11
6011-6012	75850-75851	3/53 11
6013-6016	75852-75855	4/53 11
6022-6023	75979-75980	12/55
6024-6027	75975-75978	2/56 11

READING 43

530	75151	7/51
531-533	75152-75154	8/51

No.	C/N	Date
534-535	75155-75156	9/51
536-537	75317-75318	9/51
538-539	75319-75320	10/51
540-550	75321-75331	11/51
551-553	75926-75928	10/53 12
554	75929	11/53 12
560-563	75157-75160	9/51 11
576-581	75591-75596	6/52 12
582-585	75597-75600	7/52 12
586-589	75715-75718	7/52 12

ST. LOUIS, BROWNSVILLE & MEXICO (MoPac) 6

4326-4327	76004-76005	6/54
4328-4331	76006-76009	7/54

WESTERN MARYLAND 4

173-174	74899-74900	5/51
175-176	74901-74902	6/51

AS-416

ALGERIAN RAILWAY 4

040-DF-1 to		
040-DF-4	75094-75097	9/51

COLUMBUS & GREENVILLE 1

606	75273	9/51

NORFOLK SOUTHERN 17

1601	75237	5/51
1602	75238	6/51
1603-1605	75239-75241	7/51
1606	75699	9/52
1607-1608	75721-75722	9/52
1609-1610	75723-75724	10/52
1611-1613	75938-75940	1/54
1614-1615	76037-76038	3/55
1616	76112	12/55
1617	76114	12/55

SAVANNAH & ATLANTA 3

108	75111	12/50
109	74675	7/52
110	76107	8/55

AS-616

BESSEMER & LAKE ERIE 2

408-409	75757-75758	7/52

CENTRAL OF BRAZIL 32

3371-3372	75725-75726	6/52 13,14,15
3373	75727	7/52 13,14,15
3374	75728	8/52 13,14,15
3375-3378	75729-75732	10/52 13,14,15
3379-3380	75733-75734	11/52 13,14,15
3381-3382	75735-75736	12/52 13,14,15
4371-4374	75737-75740	1/53 14,15,16
4375-4379	75741-75745	2/53 14,15,16
4380-4384	75746-75750	3/53 14,15,16
4385-4389	75751-75755	4/53 14,15,16
4390	75756	5/53 14,15,16

CHESAPEAKE & OHIO 39

5528-5529	75391-75392	7/53 15
5533-5536	74917-74920	11/50
5537-5543	74921-74927	12/50
5544-5545	74928-74929	1/51
5546	74951	1/51
5547-5550	74966-74969	1/51
5551-5552	75171-75172	7/51
5553-5555	75173-75175	8/51
5556-5558	75176-75178	9/51
5559-5564	75345-75350	2/52
5565-5569	75351-75355	3/52

CHICAGO & NORTH WESTERN 3

1560-1561	75333-75334	1/52
1604	75182	9/52

CHICAGO, MILWAUKEE, ST. PAUL & PACIFIC 8

2100A-2101A	75085-75086	4/51 17
2100B-2101B	75232-75233	4/51 17
2104-2105	75907-75908	8/53
2106-2107	75909-75910	9/53

DULUTH, SOUTH SHORE & ATLANTIC 8

204-208	75071-75075	2/51
209-210	75180-75181	8/52
211	74676	3/52 14,15,18

HOUSTON BELT & TERMINAL 1

32	75179	3/52

KAISER STEEL 2

1012A-1012B	75356-75357	6/52

No.	C/N	Date
NATIONAL RAILWAYS OF MEXICO 20		
6800-6807	75981-75988	3/54 14,15
6808-6814	75989-75995	4/54 14,15
6815-6819	75996-76000	5/54 14,15
OREGON & NORTHWESTERN 1		
1	75826	1/55 14,15,19
ORINOCO MINING CO. 10		
1001-1002	75437-75438	6/52 14
1003-1004	75439-75440	11/52 14
1005-1006	75441-75442	6/53 14
1007-1009	75443-75445	7/53 14
1010	75942	7/53 14,20
PARAÑA-SANTA CATARINA 5		
60	75769	1/54 14,15,16
61	75770	2/54 14,15,16
62-64	75771-75773	1/54 14,15,16
PENNSYLVANIA 11		
8111-8112	75956-75957	2/54 15
8966	75076	5/51
8967-8968	75077-75078	6/51
8969-8971	75082-75084	6/51 21
8972-8974	75079-75081	5/51
PITTSBURGH & WEST VIRGINIA 1		
40	75164	5/51
SOUTHERN PACIFIC 56		
5228-5239	74905-74916	9/50 14
5240-5242	75087-75089	2/51 14
5243-5246	75090-75093	3/51 14
5247-5248	75137-75138	3/51 14
5249	75139	4/51 14
5250-5252	75226-75228	10/51 14
5253-5255	75449-75451	3/52 14
5256-5262	75452-75458	4/52 14
5263-5271	75459-75467	2/52 14
5272	75468	3/52 14
5273-5278	75469-75474	5/52 14
5501-5502	75224-75225	4/51 14,22
5503-5505	75229-75231	10/51 14,22
TENNESSEE COAL IRON & RAILROAD 5		
1502-1503	75069-75070	10/50
1504	75168	5/51
1505	75169	2/51
1506	75170	5/51
TEXAS & NEW ORLEANS (SP) 8		
177-181	75335-75339	1/52
182-183	75343-75344	1/52
184	75340	1/52
TRONA 1		
52	75835	3/54 14,15
UNION PACIFIC 6		
1260-1263	75185-75188	12/51
1264-1265	75189-75190	1/52
UNION RAILROAD 3		
625-627	75165-75167	6/51

1. Iron Mines Co. of Venezuela 1-3 had raised cabs to allow installation of special air reservoirs.
2. Iron Mines Co. of Venezuela 1-3 were the only DRS-4-4-1500s equipped with dynamic brakes.
3. DRS-4-4-1500s equipped with steam generators included: LV 200, NP 175-176, NYC 8300-8301, PRSL 6000-6005.
4. Equipped with Roto-Clone air filter equipment.
5. Kennecott Copper Co. 901 was built as BLW DRS-6-4-1500 demonstrator 1501 in 2/48. Ownership transferred to KCC in 10/48. Unit was steam generator-equipped when built.
6. Steam generator-equipped.
7. Union Pacific 1250 was built as BLW DRS-6-4-1500 demonstrator 1500 in 11/46. Unit was turned over to UP in 1/48. Unit was equipped with a steam generator.
8. Built as BLW DRS-6-6-1500 demonstrator No. 1500 about 3/50. To the DSS&A no. 203 in August 1950.
9. DRS-6-6-1500s equipped with dynamic brakes included: Kaiser Steel 1010A-1010B, Erie 1153-1161, McCloud 29, Southern Pacific 5213-5227.
10. Southern Pacific 5227 was a cabless booster.
11. Steam generator-equipped AS-16s included: Erie 1140, M-K-T 1787-1788 , PRSL 6007-6016, 6026-6027, Reading 560-563.
12. Dynamic brake-equipped AS-16s included: Reading 551-554, 576-589.
13. Central of Brazil 3371-3382 were built to operate on 5'-3" gauge.

14. Dynamic brake-equipped AS-616s included: CofB 3371-3382, 4371-4390, DSS&A 211, Kaiser Steel 1012A-1012B, NdeM 6800-6819, O&NW 1, Orinoco 1001-1010, PSC 60-64, SP 5228-5278, 5501-5505, Trona 52.
15. Outside-equalized Type C trucks were installed on the following AS-616s: CofB 3371-3382, 4371-4390, C&O 5528-5529, DSS&A 211, NdeM 6800-6819, PSC 60-64, PRR 8111-8112, Trona 52, O&NW 1.
16. Central of Brazil 4371-4390 and Paraña-Santa Catarina 60-64 were modified export models, designated AS-616E. All were built to operate on meter gauge.
17. Milwaukee Road 2100B, 2101B were cabless boosters.
18. Built as B-L-H AS-616 demonstrator 1600 in 3/52. To DSS&A 211 about 8/52.
19. Built as B-L-H demonstrator/test-bed 1601 in 1953. To O&NW 1 in 1/55.
20. Orinoco 1010 was a rebuild of No. 1008.
21. The only steam generator-equipped AS-616s were PRR 8970-8971.
22. Southern Pacific 5501-5505 were cabless boosters.

STREAMLINED FREIGHT-SERVICE UNITS
DR-4-4-1500 Babyface

CENTRAL RAILROAD OF PENNSYLVANIA (CNJ)
A Units 10

No.	C/N	Date
70-71	73114-73115	11/47
72-73	73116-73117	7/48
74-75	73118-73119	8/48
76-77	73120-73121	9/48
78-79	73122-73123	9/48
B Units 5		
K	73124	11/47
L	73125	7/48
M	73126	8/48
R	73127	9/48
S	73128	9/48

MISSOURI PACIFIC
A Units 8

No.	C/N	Date
201A,205A	73734-73735	12/48
202A,206A	73736-73737	12/48
203A,207A	73738-73739	12/48
204A,208A	73740-73741	12/48
B Units 4		
201B	73742	12/48
202B	73743	12/48
203B	73744	12/48
204B	73745	12/48

NEW YORK CENTRAL
A Units 4

No.	C/N	Date
3400-3401	73676-73677	10/48
3402-3403	73678-73679	10/48
B Units 2		
3700	73680	10/48
3701	73681	10/48

DR-4-4-1500 Sharknose

ELGIN, JOLIET & EASTERN
A Units 2

No.	C/N	Date
700A	73981	6/49 1
701A	73984	6/49 1
B Units 2		
700B	73982	6/49 1
701B	73983	6/49 1

PENNSYLVANIA
A Units 34

No.	C/N	Date
9568A-9569A	73697,73700	2 /49
9570A-9571A	73701,73704	3 /49
9572A-9573A	73705,73996	3 /49
9574A	73985	3/49
9575A	74142	3/49
9576A	74143	4/49
9577A-9578A	74146-74147	4/49
9579A	74150	4/49
9580A	74151	5/49
9581A-9582A	74154-74155	5/49
9583A-9584A	74158-74159	5/49
9585A	74162	5/49
9586A	74163	6/49
9587A-9588A	74166-74167	6/49
9589A	74170	6/49
9590A	74171	7/49
9591A-9592A	74174-74175	7/49
9593A	74177	7/49
9700A-9701A	74441-74442	4/50
9702A-9703A	74444-74445	5/50
9704A-9705A	74439,74447	5/50
9706A-9707A	74448,74450	6/50
B Units 34		
9568B-9569B	73698-73699	2/49
9570B-9571B	73702-73703	3/49
9572B-9573B	73964-73965	3/49
9574B-9575B	73986-73987	3/49
9576B-9577B	74144-74145	3/49
9578B-9579B	74148-74149	4/49
9580B-9581B	74152-74153	5/49
9582B-9583B	74156-74157	5/49
9584B-9585B	74160-74161	5/49
9586B-9587B	74164-74165	6/49
9588B-9589B	74168-74169	6/49
9590B-9591B	74172-74173	7/49
9592B-9593B	74176,74178	7/49
9700B	74440	4/50
9701B	74443	4/50
9702B	74446	5/50
9703B	74449	5/50
9704B	74748	5/50
9705B	74749	5/50
9706B	74750	6/50
9707B	74751	6/50

RF-16

BALTIMORE & OHIO
A Units 19

No.	C/N	Date
851-851A	74801-74802	11/50
853-853A	74803-74804	11/50
855-855A	74805-74806	11/50
857-857A	74807-74808	11/50
859-859A	74809-74810	11/50
861-861A	74811,74816	11/50
863-863A	74817-74818	12/50
865-865A	75386-75387	5/52
867	75388	3/53
869	75389	4/53
871	75390	5/53
B Units 13		
851X	75414	5/52
853X	75415	5/52
855X	75416	5/52
857X	75417	5/52
859X	75418	5/52
861X	75419	5/52
865X	75413	5/52
867X-867AX	75808-75809	3/53
869X-869AX	75810-75811	4/53
871X-871AX	75812-75813	5/53

NEW YORK CENTRAL
A Units 18

No.	C/N	Date
3804-3811	75360-75367	12/51
3812-3819	75368-75375	1/52
3820-3821	75376-75377	2/52
B Units 8		
3702-3705	75401-75404	12/51
3706-3709	75405-75408	1/52

PENNSYLVANIA
A Units 72

No.	C/N	Date
2000A-2003A	75197-75200	6/51
2004A-2005A	75201-75202	7/51
2006A-2007A	75203-75204	9/51
2008A-2009A	75205-75206	10/51
2010A-2015A	75207-75212	2/52
2016A-2017A	75213-75214	3/52
2018A-2019A	75358-75359	3/52
2020A-2021A	75378-75379	3/52
2022A-2027A	75380-75385	4/52
9594A-9599A	74849-74854	4/51
9708A-9709A	74819-74820	12/50
9710A-9715A	74821-74826	1/51
9716A-9727A	74995-75006	3/51
9728A-9731A	74991-74994	2/51
9732A-9733A	74847-74848	4/51
9734A-9735A	74855-74856	5/51
9736A-9739A	75112-75115	5/51
9740A-9743A	74827-74830	2/51
9744A-9745A	74989-74990	2/51
B Units 30		
2000B, 2002B	75215-75216	6/51
2004B	75217	7/51
2006B	75218	9/51
2008B	75219	10/51
2010B, 2012B,		
2014B	75220-75222	2/52
2016B	75223	3/52
2018B	75400	3/52
2020B	75409	3/52
2022B, 2024B,		
2026B	75410-75412	4/52
9594B, 9596B,		
9598B	74841-74843	4/51
9708B	74831	12/50
9710B, 9712B,		
9714B	74832-74834	1/51
9728B, 9730B	74838-74839	2/51
9732B	74840	4/51
9734B, 9736B,		
9738B	74844-74846	5/51
9740B, 9742B,		
9744B	74835-74837	2/51

1. EJ&E 700A, 700B, 701B, 701A were built i 6/49 as BLW DR-4-4-1500 demonstrator set 600 In 12/50 the EJ&E signed a lease agreement, fo lowed by actual purchase on 1/1/51.

LIGHT ROAD-SWITCHERS
DRS-4-4-1000

CANADIAN PACIFIC 13

No.	C/N	Date
8000-8006	73967-73973	1/49 1
8007-8012	73974-73979	2/49 1
PENNSYLVANIA 6		
5591-5594	74744-74747	3/50 2
9276-9277	74403-74404	2/49 2
TENNESSEE CENTRAL 3		
75-76	73706-73707	7/48
77	73708	8/48

RS-12

CENTRAL RAILROAD OF NEW JERSEY 4

No.	C/N	Date
1206-1208	75446-75448	1/53 3
1209	75698	1/53 3
CHICAGO, MILWAUKEE, ST. PAUL & PACIFIC 2		
970	75242	5/51 3,4
971	75702	10/52 3,4
DURHAM & SOUTHERN 3		
1200-1202	76001-76003	3/54
KAISER BAUXITE 4		
101-102	75486-75487	4/52 5
103-104	76133-76134	5/56 5
MC CLOUD RIVER 2		
32	76024	4/55 5
33	76105	4/55 5
NEW YORK CENTRAL 17		
5820-5829	75256-75265	11/51 3
5830-5836	75266-75272	12/51 3
PENNSYLVANIA 8		
8105-8110	75950-75955	2/54 3
8776	75663	9/52 3
8975	75116	4/51 3
SEABOARD AIR LINE 10		
1466-1471	75475-75480	5/52 3
1472-1475	75765-75768	1/53 3

1. CP 8000-8012 were constructed at Eddystone however, they also carried Canadian Locomotiv Company builder plates. Construction numbers as signed by CLC were 2531-2543. CP 8000-800 were steam generator equipped.
2. All PRR DRS-4-4-1000s were steam generato equipped.
3. RS-12s built with steam generators included CNJ 1206-1209; MILW 970-971; NYC 5820-5836 PRR 8110, 8776, 8975; SAL 1466-1475.
4. Equipped with GSC switcher trucks.
5. RS-12s built with dynamic brakes included: Kai ser Bauxite 101-104; McCloud River 32-33.

EXPORT MODELS
0-6-6-0 1000/1 DE

U. S. A. (For Russia) 30

U. S. A. No.	Russ. No.	C/N	Date
2460-2468	20-71/20-79	72173-72181	6/45
2469-2481	20-80/20-92	72182-72194	7/45

U.S.A. No.	Russ. No.	C/N	Date
2482-2489	20-93/20-100	72195-72202	8/45

DRS-6-4-660

FRENCH SUPPLY COUNCIL (France) 100

No.	C/N	Date
040-DA-1	72898	4/46
040-DA-2	72899	6/46
040-DA-3 to 040-DA-4	72900-72901	5/46
040-DA-5	72902	8/46
040-DA-6 to 040-DA-7	72903-72904	6/46
040-DA-8 to 040-DA-13	72905-72910	8/46
040-DA-14 to 040-DA-17	72911-72914	9/46
040-DA-18 to 040-DA-25	72915-72922	10/46
040-DA-26 to 040-DA-27	72923-72924	11/46
040-DA-28 to 040-DA-30	72925-72927	12/46
040-DA-31 to 040-DA-32	73146-73147	1/47
040-DA-33 to 040-DA-35	73148-73150	2/47
040-DA-36	73151	12/46
040-DA-37	73152	1/47
040-DA-38	73153	12/46
040-DA-39	73154	3/47
040-DA-40	73155	12/46
040-DA-41	73156	1/47
040-DA-42	73157	12/46
040-DA-43 to 040-DA-47	73158-73162	1/47
040-DA-48	73163	2/47
040-DA-49	73164	4/47
040-DA-50	73165	5/47
040-DA-51 to 040-DA-53	73166-73168	3/47
040-DA-54	73169	6/47
040-DA-55 to 040-DA-56	73170-73171	2/47
040-DA-57	73172	4/47
040-DA-58	73173	2/47
040-DA-59	73174	3/47
040-DA-60 to 040-DA-63	73175-73178	4/47
040-DA-64 to 040-DA-66	73179-73181	5/47
040-DA-67	73182	6/47
040-DA-68 to 040-DA-69	73183-73184	5/47
040-DA-70 to 040-DA-72	73185-73187	6/47
040-DA-73 to 040-DA-80	73188-73195	7/47
040-DA-81	73196	8/47
040-DA-82 to 040-DA-83	73197-73198	7/47
040-DA-84	73199	8/47
040-DA-85	73200	7/47
040-DA-86	73201	8/47
040-DA-87	73202	9/47
040-DA-88	73203	8/47
040-DA-89 to 040-DA-90	73204-73205	9/47
040-DA-91	73206	10/47
040-DA-92 to 040-DA-95	73207-73210	9/47
040-DA-96	73211	8/47
040-DA-97 to 040-DA-99	73212-73214	9/47
040-DA-100	73215	8/47

FRENCH SUPPLY COUNCIL (Morocco) 6

No.	C/N	Date
040-DB-401 to 040-DB-406	73468-73473	1/48

DRS-6-4-750

CHERIFIEN DES PHOSPHATES (Morocco) 1

No.	C/N	Date
6	74673	12/49

DRS-6-4-1000

ALGERIAN RAILWAY 5

No.	C/N	Date
040-DC-16 to 040-DC-18	74282-74284	10/49
040-DC-19 to 040-DC-20	74285-74286	11/49

FRENCH SUPPLY COUNCIL (Algeria) 15

No.	C/N	Date
040-DC-1 to 040-DC-6	73682-73687	4/48
040-DC-7 to 040-DC-13	73688-73694	5/48
040-DC-14 to 040-DC-15	73695-73696	6/48

R-615E

ARGENTINE STATE RAILWAYS (General Roca) 51

No.	C/N	Date
5001	75856	6/53
5002-5004	75857-75859	5/53
5005-5006	75860-75861	6/53
5007-5010	75862-75865	7/53
5011	75866	9/53
5012-5013	75867-75868	5/53
5014-5015	75869-75870	6/53
5016-5017	75871-75872	7/53
5018-5021	75873-75876	9/53
5022-5023	75877-75878	10/53
5024	75879	11/53
5025	75880	12/53
5026-5029	75881-75884	1/54
5030-5031	75885-75886	2/54
5032-5033	75887-75888	3/54
5034-5035	75889-75890	4/54
5036-5038	75891-75893	5/54
5039-5041	75894-75896	6/54
5042-5044	75897-75899	7/54
5045-5046	75900-75901	8/54
5047-5048	75902-75903	9/54
5049-5051	75904-75906	10/54

Authors' note: This production list was compiled from Baldwin Locomotive Works records. Original owners and original road numbers are shown. The dates shown are when the locomotive warranties went into effect. From 1925 through 1949, this date (in most cases) represents the date the units were placed in service. From early 1950 on the date is representative of when the units were shipped from Eddystone.

INDEX

A

Alaska Railroad, 38
Alco, 7, 12, 13, 14, 15, 17, 19, 22, 23, 24, 26, 35, 40, 46, 47, 52, 53, 55, 59, 61, 64, 65, 71, 75, 82, 107, 110, 112, 114, 119, 123, 124, 125, 128, 131, 135, 138, 140
Alco-GE, 33, 80, 82, 83, 90, 101, 118, 125, 130, 134, 142
Algerian Railway, 98, 99, 142
Allied Chemical, 44, 51
Alton, 64
Amador Central, 50, 51
American Car & Foundry, 12, 25
American Cyanamid, 38, 39
American Smelting & Refining Co., 43, 51
American Steel & Wire, 31
American Steel Foundries, 13
Arcata & Mad River, 43
Argentine State Railways, 23, 140, 141, 142
Armco Steel, 38, 48
AS-16, 21, 22, 25, 98, 99, 101, 102, 103, 105, 106, 107, 108, 109, 110, 111, 112, 113, 114, 115, 126, 128, 135
AS-412E, 22, 142
AS-416, 21, 24, 98, 99, 101, 103, 107, 109, 110, 111, 112, 141
AS-616, 21, 22, 24, 75, 77, 78, 92, 93, 97, 98, 99, 100, 101, 102, 103, 104, 105, 106, 107, 108, 109, 110, 115, 116, 117, 135, 142
AS-616E, 108, 109
Atchison, Topeka & Santa Fe, 9, 11, 12, 13, 27, 28, 29, 30, 31, 32, 33, 35, 37, 40, 41, 43, 44, 61, 73, 74, 75, 76, 123, 128
Atlantic Coast Line, 37, 38, 56, 58, 137
Austin-Western Co., 22, 23, 24, 25
Auto-Train, 38, 50, 51
Avondale Shipyards, 50, 51

B

Baldwin, Matthias W., 4
Baldwin-Lima-Hamilton Industrial Line, 2, 23, 25
Baldwin-Westinghouse Standard Line, 22, 23, 24, 98
Baltimore & Ohio, 4, 11, 14, 25, 35, 38, 40, 43, 44, 53, 56, 57, 59, 61, 101, 102, 103, 107, 108, 109, 112, 114, 122, 123, 124, 125, 128
Benson-Quinn Terminals, 44
Bessemer & Lake Erie, 59, 61, 86, 88, 90, 92, 96, 103, 115, 125
Bethlehem Mines, 38, 51
Bethlehem Steel, 26, 82
Birmingham Rail, 137
Birmingham Southern, 115
Blairsville & Indiana, 51
Boston & Maine, 11, 57
Boston Metals, 37, 38
Brinley, Charles E., 13, 15
Broadway Limited, The, 60, 61, 66
Buckeye Cellulose, 38, 44
Budd Co., 11
Buffalo, Rochester & Pittsburgh, 115, 128
Burlington (see Chicago, Burlington & Quincy)
Burlington Northern, 38, 95, 96
Busch-Sulzer, 70

C

California State Railroad Museum, 97
California Western, 43, 44, 51, 86, 137
Canadian Locomotive Company, 131
Canadian Pacific, 43, 44, 83, 131, 132
Canton Railroad, 38
Carbon County Railway, 75, 101
Cargill, Inc., 38, 51
Castolite Corporation, 128, 129
Central of Brazil, 101, 103, 104, 108, 109
Central of Georgia, 29, 32, 56, 94, 111
Central Railroad of New Jersey, 7, 17, 18, 19, 32, 44, 53, 54, 57, 61, 63, 64, 65, 66, 74, 75, 81, 82, 118, 119, 121, 122, 123, 133, 134, 135, 136
Central Railroad of Pennsylvania, 17, 118

Charleston & Hamburg, 4
Chesapeake & Ohio, 21, 25, 88, 89, 90, 92, 96, 98, 99, 101, 106, 107, 108, 115
Chesapeake Western, 39
Chicago, Burlington & Quincy, 11, 35, 36, 39, 52, 56
Chicago & Eastern Illinois, 56
Chicago, Milwaukee, St. Paul & Pacific, 9, 29, 48, 49, 98, 99, 101, 106, 107, 108, 115, 116, 132, 133, 134, 135, 136
Chicago & North Western, 21, 35, 36, 37, 38, 41, 44, 48, 49, 50, 61, 64, 65, 66, 83, 85, 86, 87, 88, 89, 90, 94, 95, 96, 101, 103, 107, 111, 115, 116
Chicago, Rock Island & Pacific, 9, 46, 47, 50, 51, 64, 73, 128
Chicago, St. Paul, Minneapolis & Omaha, 35, 44
Coleman, Catherine, 59
Colonial, The, 57
Columbia Geneva Steel, 25, 47, 49, 51
Columbus & Greenville, 14, 17, 80, 81, 83, 85, 94, 98, 110, 111, 112
Conrail, 38, 44, 50, 112, 136
Consolidation Coal Co., 44
Cotton Belt (see St. Louis Southwestern)
Cramp Brass and Iron Foundries Division, 6

D

Davenport, 25
Davis, James J. (U. S. Secretary of Labor), 4
Day & Zimmerman, Inc., 33
Deitch Co., 38
DeKalb County Co-op, 44
De La Vergne, 10, 11
Delaware & Hudson, 128, 129
Delta Alaska Terminals, 44
Demonstrators (BLW and B-L-H):
    No. 1, 32, 37
    No. 299, 13, 14, 29, 30, 31, 32, 37, 39
    No. 301, 43, 48
    No. 307, 26, 31, 33, 35
    No. 332, 26, 31
    No. 750, 41, 43, 47
    No. 751, 41, 43, 47
    No. 1000, 7
    No. 1200, 47, 51
    No. 1201, 47
    No. 1500, 81, 85, 86, 92, 94
    No. 1501, 86, 87, 88, 94
    No. 1600, 101, 102, 103, 116
    No. 1601, 24, 105, 108, 109, 110, 117, 135, 142
    No. 2000, 16, 17, 54, 55, 56, 57, 58, 63, 74, 75
    No. 2001, 16, 17, 54, 57, 63, 74, 75
    No. 6000, 13, 15, 18, 52, 53, 55, 59
    No. 6000A/B, 59, 61, 63
    No. 6001, 21, 121, 122, 123
    No. 58501, 6, 7, 8, 9, 10
    No. 61000, 8, 9, 10, 12
    No. 62000, 11, 12, 13, 20, 26, 27, 28, 29, 31, 37
Denver & Rio Grande Western, 32, 56
Diesel Electric Services, 129
Dixie Flagler, The, 56
DR-4-4-1500, 17, 18, 19, 21, 66, 67, 118, 119, 120, 121, 122, 123, 124, 125, 126, 128
DR-6-2-1000, 21, 64, 65
DR-6-4-1500, 19, 22, 65, 66, 67, 141
DR-6-4-2000, 17, 18, 19, 20, 22, 40, 63, 64, 65, 66, 67, 121
DR-12-8-3000, 16, 18, 19, 22, 55, 56, 58, 59, 60, 61, 63, 64, 65, 66, 74, 118, 119
DRS-4-4-1000, 20, 24, 40, 130, 131, 132, 134, 136
DRS-4-4-1500, 17, 82, 83, 84, 85, 86, 87, 89, 90, 91, 92, 93, 94, 95, 98, 108, 131
DRS-6-4-660, 17, 20, 66, 130, 138, 139, 140, 141, 142
DRS-6-4-750, 21, 140, 142
DRS-6-4-1000, 20, 130, 140, 141, 142
DRS-6-4-1500, 14, 17, 23, 66, 80, 81, 82, 83, 84, 85, 86, 87, 88, 89, 90, 92, 93, 94, 98, 101, 106, 109, 111, 116, 120, 141, 142
DRS-6-6-1500, 17, 75, 78, 85, 87, 88, 89, 90, 91, 92, 93, 95, 96, 97, 98, 99, 106, 111, 115, 116, 135
DRX-6-4-2000, 18, 61, 64, 65, 66, 123
DS-4-4-660, 17, 20, 38, 39, 40, 41, 43, 44, 83

DS-4-4-750, 21, 40, 41, 43, 44, 47, 48, 137, 142
DS-4-4-1000, 15, 17, 19, 20, 21, 38, 39, 40, 41, 42, 43, 44, 82, 83, 107, 125, 132
DT-6-6-2000, 14, 18, 19, 20, 21, 40, 61, 71, 72, 73, 74, 75, 76, 77, 78, 79, 92, 93, 107, 111, 116, 123
Duluth, Missabe & Iron Range, 47, 74, 96, 125
Duluth, South Shore & Atlantic, 75, 78, 79, 83, 89, 90, 92, 93, 96, 98, 101, 102, 115, 116
Durham & Southern, 93, 94, 95, 112, 135, 136, 137

E

Eagle Mountain Railway, 85, 88, 90, 96, 97, 115, 117
8DE 900/1, 27, 28, 29, 32
8OE 660/1, 12, 26, 28, 32
8-OE-1000-1-CC, 1, 9
Electro-Motive Corporation, Division, 11, 14, 15, 17, 19, 23, 24, 25, 26, 33, 37, 38, 44, 46, 50, 52, 53, 55, 57, 59, 61, 64, 65, 67, 70, 71, 75, 76, 80, 82, 89, 90, 94, 95, 96, 101, 107, 110, 111, 112, 115, 116, 117, 118, 119, 123, 125, 128, 130, 131, 137, 138
Elgin, Joliet & Eastern, 14, 17, 18, 29, 31, 38, 71, 72, 73, 74, 75, 76, 96, 121, 122, 123, 124, 125
Elk Falls Pulp & Paper, 38
Erie, 40, 50, 57, 89, 90, 91, 92, 95, 96, 98, 99, 101, 112, 114
Erie Lackawanna, 95, 96, 112
Erie Mining, 25, 48, 49, 50, 51
Erman-Howell Co., 44
Escanaba & Lake Superior, 44, 47, 50, 128, 129, 136, 137
Esquimalt & Nanaimo, 131, 132,
Essl, Max, 52
Estrada De Ferro Central Do Brazil (see Central of Brazil)

F

Fairbanks-Morse, 21, 24, 55, 65, 67, 75, 79, 90, 95, 107, 125
Fairfield Works, 96, 115
Ferrocarril de Chihuahua al Pacifico, 94
Ferrocarril de Nacozari S.C.T., 93, 94
Ferrocarril del Pacifico, 94
4-8-8-4 750/8 DE, 15, 52, 53, 55, 58, 59
Francisco Sugar Co., 35
French National Railways, 139
French Supply Council, 80, 81, 85, 86, 140, 141, 142
Frisco (see St. Louis-San Francisco)

G

Gary Slag Co., 38
General Electric, 7, 11, 23, 24, 26, 38, 48, 49, 70, 87, 108, 110, 112, 128
General Motors, 25
General Steel Castings, 13, 26, 27, 40, 46, 55, 66, 71, 79, 80, 82, 102, 118, 131, 132, 138, 139, 141, 142
Georgetown Railroad, 38, 39, 51
Gettysburg Railroad, 51
Grace, W. R., 38
Great Northern, 52, 130, 137
Great Plains Railway, 38
Greenville & Northern, 69
Gulf Coast Rebel, The, 62, 64
Gulf, Mobile & Northern, 12
Gulf, Mobile & Ohio, 57, 62, 63, 64, 65, 66, 118

H

Haines, Fred, 124
Hamilton Corporation, 22
Hobet Mining Co., 94
Houston Belt & Terminal, 101, 103, 116

I

Illinois Central, 9, 11, 56, 70, 71
Illinois Central Gulf, 94, 111
Illinois Railway Museum, 39, 76
Indian Hill & Iron Range, 38
Indiana & Ohio, 44
Ingersoll-Rand, 7, 70
International-Great Northern, 98, 99, 111
International Harvester, 38
Iowa Ordnance Plant, 33
Iron Mines Company of Venezuela, 82, 84, 85, 111
Ironton Railroad, 44
ITT-Rayonier, 116

J

Jacksonville Port Authority, 44
Jawn Henry, The, 24
Jim Walter Resources, 50
Jones, James F., 69
Jones & Laughlin Steel, 38, 44

K

Kaiser Aluminum & Chemical Corp., 134
Kaiser Bauxite, 24, 25, 115, 116, 117, 133, 134, 135, 136
Kaiser Engineering Co., 85, 88
Kaiser Steel, 90, 96, 101, 103, 115, 117
Kansas City Railway Museum, 51
Kansas City Southern, 35
Katy (see Missouri-Kansas-Texas)
Katy Flyer, The, 108
Kelly, Ralph, 13, 20, 59
Kennecott Copper Co., 38, 51, 86, 87, 88, 94, 97
Kentucky & Indiana Terminal, 44
Keota Washington Transportation, 38
Ketchican Pulp, 51
Knudsen Motor Corporation, 7
Koppel Bulk Terminal, 97
Krupp, 8
Kunzie, John, 129

L

Lackawanna, 26
LaSalle & Bureau County, 38, 44, 50
Lehigh & Hudson River, 123
Lehigh Valley, 20, 40, 44, 87, 89, 94, 95
Lima-Hamilton Corporation, 22, 24, 67, 75, 78, 107, 136
Lima Locomotive Works, 22, 107, 140
Locomotive & Ordnance Division, 5
Loewy, Raymond, 21, 65
Long Island Railroad, 89
Louisville & Nashville, 35, 56

M

Magma Arizona, 50, 51, 97
Maine Central, 57
Marble Cliff Quarries, 25
Maybach, A. G., 24, 25, 68
McCloud River, 43, 48, 85, 86, 92, 97, 117, 135, 137
McGinnis, Patrick, 69
MD-655, 68
Medford Corp., 43, 46, 47, 50, 51
Metropolitan Stevedore Co., 51
Michigan Northern, 128, 129, 137
Middle Fork Railway, 38
E. L. Miller, The, 4
Milwaukee Road (see Chicago, Milwaukee, St. Paul & Pacific)
Minneapolis, Northfield & Southern, 31, 74, 75, 76, 77, 78, 79, 89, 90, 92, 96, 129
Minneapolis & St. Louis, 31
Minneapolis, St. Paul & Sault Ste. Marie, 76, 78, 79, 82, 85, 86, 94, 95, 96, 98, 111, 112, 116, 137

Minnesota Taconite Division, U. S. Steel, 50
Missouri-Kansas-Texas, 44, 49, 50, 51, 98, 101, 103, 108, 112, 123
Missouri Pacific, 29, 30, 31, 34, 39, 43, 47, 49, 50, 56, 57, 64, 87, 90, 94, 98, 99, 107, 109, 111, 113, 118, 119, 120, 121, 123, 124, 130
Missouri River Eagle, The, 56
Model VO, 10, 28, 43, 46
Monongahela Railway, 48, 49, 128
Montreal Locomotive Works, 140
Morehead & Morgan Fork, 94, 136, 137
Morgan, David P., 7
Moroccan Railway, 89, 90, 92, 93
Morocco-Algeria Express, The, 84
I. P. Morris & De La Vergne, Inc., 10
Morrison-Knudsen, 44, 115
Municipal Dock Railway, 44
Murray Hill, The, 57

N

Nashville, Chattanooga & St. Louis, 33
National Railways of Mexico, 16, 17, 18, 54, 58, 59, 60, 61, 63, 107, 109, 117
New England States, The, 67
New Hope & Ivyland, 38, 44, 51
New Orleans Public Belt, 13, 27, 28, 29, 32, 37, 39, 43, 48, 50
New York Central, 7, 17, 25, 31, 35, 36, 37, 50, 65, 67, 68, 69, 83, 94, 95, 118, 119, 120, 121, 122, 123, 124, 125, 127, 128, 132, 133, 134, 135, 136
New York, Chicago & St. Louis, 9, 22, 37, 107, 108, 109, 110, 112
New York Elevated Railroad, 6
New York & Long Branch, 64, 66
New York, New Haven & Hartford, 25, 26, 49, 57, 67, 68, 69, 81
Nicholson Terminal & Dock Co., 44
Nickel Plate Road (see New York, Chicago & St. Louis)
Norfolk Southern, 40, 83, 84, 85, 86, 93, 94, 98, 103, 107, 109, 111, 112, 137
Norfolk & Western, 24, 112
North Carolina State Ports Authority, 44, 51
Northern Pacific, 9, 31, 33, 35, 37, 38, 85, 86, 88, 89, 93, 95, 96
Northwestern Pacific, 43, 99
Nucor Steel, 44, 51

O

Oakland Terminal, 44
Office Cherifien des Phosphates, 140, 142
Office of Defense Transportation, 33
Ogden Union Railway & Depot, 116
Ohio Xplorer, The, 68, 69
Old Ironsides, 4, 5, 6
Oliver Iron Mining, 9, 31, 33, 47, 48, 49, 50
Oregon, California & Eastern, 136, 137
Oregon & Northwestern, 109, 110, 117
Orinoco Mining Co., 101, 103, 104, 109

P

Pacific Electric, 34, 43, 90, 97, 103, 104, 106, 116

Pacific Lumber, 38, 39, 41
Pan American Engineering, 115
Paraña-Santa Catarina Railway, 103, 108, 109
Patapsco & Back Rivers, 31, 33, 37, 38, 39, 44
Peabody Coal Co., 77, 78, 97, 109, 111, 113, 115
Peale, Franklin, 4
Peck Iron & Metals, 38
Pelton Water Wheel Company, 6
Penn Central, 44, 50, 79, 95, 112, 114, 115, 132, 136
Pennsylvania Railroad, 4, 6, 7, 9, 16, 18, 20, 21, 22, 23, 24, 25, 26, 31, 33, 35, 37, 40, 42, 43, 44, 47, 48, 49, 50, 52, 56, 58, 60, 61, 63, 64, 65, 66, 75, 78, 79, 89, 98, 99, 100, 101, 107, 109, 112, 115, 121, 122, 123, 124, 125, 126, 127, 128, 130, 131, 132, 134, 135
Pennsylvania-Reading Seashore Lines, 25, 49, 50, 89, 90, 92, 95, 103, 107, 108, 110, 111, 112
Pennsylvania's "State Road," 4
Perlman, Alfred E., 25
Philadelphia, Germantown and Norristown Railroad Company, 4
Philadelphia & Trenton, 4
Pickens Railroad, 44, 69
Pittsburgh, Chartiers & Youghiogheny Railroad, 101
Pittsburgh & Lake Erie, 101, 128
Pittsburgh & West Virginia, 35, 92, 98, 99, 115
Port of Los Angeles, 38
Powell, L. R. Jr., 59
Power plants:
    408, 12, 14, 52, 55
    412, 55
    547, 20, 21, 24
    600, 16, 21
    606, 21, 23, 24, 48, 91
    606A, 20, 21, 23, 24, 58, 76, 91
    606NA, 17, 21, 141, 142
    606SC, 19, 20, 21, 40, 65, 72, 73, 76, 130, 142
    608A, 21, 22, 23, 24, 91, 93, 98, 125, 142
    608NA, 15, 17, 20, 40, 65, 71, 72, 73
    608SC, 17, 19, 21, 66, 80, 91, 118, 120, 123
    2000, 19, 20
Pullman-Standard, 11, 13, 25

R

R-615E, 23, 24, 140, 142
R-616E, 22, 23, 140, 142
Rail-to-Water Transfer Corp., 94, 95
Railroad & Locomotive Historical Society (Pacific Coast Chapter), 97
Railroaders Memorial Museum, 39
Railway Club of Southern California, 97
Rayonier Lumber, 25, 48, 49, 51, 117
Reading Company, 4, 7, 14, 23, 28, 29, 31, 32, 35, 36, 37, 38, 39, 40, 43, 53, 55, 56, 57, 65, 98, 99, 101, 103, 105, 106, 107, 108, 110, 112, 114
Rêde Vicão Paraña-Santa Catarina, 103
Rentschler, George A., 23, 24
RF-16, 21, 24, 115, 118, 122, 123, 124, 125, 126, 127, 128, 129, 136, 142
Richmond, Fredericksburg & Potomac, 56
Rock Island (see Chicago, Rock Island & Pacific)
Roscoe, Snyder & Pacific, 117
Royal Blue, The, 11
RP-210, 25, 49, 67, 68, 69
RS-12, 21, 24, 25, 45, 132, 133, 134, 135, 136, 137
RT-624, 21, 23, 24, 75, 78, 79, 102

S

S-8, 21, 24, 40, 41, 43, 46, 47, 48, 49, 50, 135
S-12, 20, 21, 22, 24, 25, 40, 45, 46, 47, 48, 49, 50, 51, 128, 132, 135, 137
St. Louis, Brownsville & Mexico, 43, 87, 90, 94, 107, 109, 111, 113
St. Louis Car Co., 11, 70
St. Louis-San Francisco, 35, 37, 57
St. Louis Southwestern, 35, 37, 39, 40, 72, 73, 74, 76
San Diego & Arizona Eastern, 97
Santa Fe (see Atchison, Topeka & Santa Fe)
Savannah & Atlanta, 83, 87, 88, 94, 98, 101, 103, 109, 110, 111
Seaboard Air Line, 11, 15, 16, 18, 31, 33, 37, 38, 39, 40, 42, 43, 45, 55, 56, 58, 59, 60, 61, 63, 65, 66, 67, 119, 133, 134, 135, 136, 137
Seaboard Coast Line, 38, 39, 44, 136, 137
Seattle & North Coast, 44
Sharon Steel, 47, 49, 50
Sierra Railroad, 43, 47, 48, 51
Silver Meteor, The, 59
Smith, Marvin W., 20, 23
Soo Line (see Minneapolis, St. Paul & Sault Ste. Marie)
South Central Tennessee, 38
South Wind, The, 56
Southern Pacific, 14, 22, 23, 25, 33, 34, 35, 43, 46, 47, 48, 49, 50, 51, 57, 75, 77, 78, 86, 87, 88, 89, 90, 91, 92, 93, 94, 97, 98, 99, 100, 101, 102, 103, 104, 106, 107, 116, 117, 123
Southern Railway, 4, 33, 45, 94, 111
Southwark Division, 6
Southwest Lumber Mills, 51
Southwest Virginia, 38, 39
Spencer Shop Historic Site, 39, 111
Spirit of St. Louis, The, 61
Spokane, Portland & Seattle, 30, 31
Standard Gravel Co., 38
Standard Steel, 6, 28, 30, 31, 38, 39
Sterling, C. B. Jr., 128
Super Chief, 11
Swift Agricultural Chemicals, 38

T

Talgo, 25
Tennessee Central, 20, 130, 131, 132
Tennessee Coal & Iron Division, 96
Tennessee Coal Iron & Railroad, 35, 36, 85, 92, 96, 98, 99, 115
Tennessee Eastman, 38, 39
Tennessee Valley Authority, 38, 43, 44, 48, 51
Tennessee Valley Railroad Museum, 39
Terminal Railroad Association of St. Louis, 31, 33, 34
Texas Crushed Stone, 38, 44
Texas Export, 38
Texas & New Orleans, 49, 86, 87, 89, 90, 91, 92, 97, 101, 103, 104, 106, 116
Texas & Pacific, 57
Texas South-Eastern, 38, 44
Toledo, Peoria & Western, 22
Tooele Valley Railway, 86, 102
Trans-Kentucky Transportation, 38
Trayler, W. A., 80

Trona Railway, 61, 73, 74, 75, 76, 77, 78, 107, 109, 116
12 (OE) 1000-1-CC, 1, 7

U

U. S. Air Force, 39, 51
U. S. Army, 25, 37, 39
U. S. Navy, 21, 24, 35, 37, 39, 50, 51, 55
U. S. Steel, 44, 50, 51, 74, 86, 96, 97, 101, 103, 115, 125
U. S. Supply, Priorities and Allocation Board, 15
Union, The, 58
Union Pacific, 11, 52, 59, 61, 86, 94, 101, 116
Union Railway, 31, 86, 89, 90, 96, 98, 115
United Aircraft, 69
United Railway of Havana, 47
United States Pipe & Foundry, 47, 48, 50, 109, 111
Upper Merion & Plymouth, 37

V

Vauclain, Samuel Matthews, 2, 7, 8, 15
Veronej-Rostoff Railway, 138
VO-660, 12, 13, 14, 17, 28, 29, 30, 31, 32, 33, 34, 35, 36, 37, 38, 39, 40, 71, 78, 82, 85, 123, 132
VO-1000, 13, 14, 15, 17, 28, 29, 30, 31, 32, 33, 34, 35, 36, 37, 38, 39, 55, 71, 78, 82, 85, 123, 125, 132
VO engine, 11, 12, 13, 14, 16, 26, 27, 28, 29, 33, 37, 55, 58, 138

W

War Production Board, 15, 33, 35, 130
Webster, Dan'l, The, 69
Western Maryland, 39, 82, 83, 84, 85, 94, 98, 99, 112, 121
Western Pacific, 38, 86
Western Railroad, 38
Westinghouse Air Brake Co., 53
Westinghouse Electric & Manufacturing Co., 2, 6, 19, 20, 23, 24, 26, 28, 33, 35, 49, 55, 91, 107, 108, 109, 110, 125, 135, 138, 141
Weyerhaeuser Timber Co., 43, 44, 48, 50
Wharton & Northern, 61, 63, 65
Wheeling & Lake Erie, 108
White Pine Copper Co., 51
Whitcomb Locomotive Works, 2, 6, 23, 25
Wilmington & Northern, 107
Winton engine, 11, 26, 70, 130

Y

Young, Robert R., 25
Youngstown Sheet & Tube, 35, 39, 41, 43, 47
Yreka Western, 43

Z

0-6-6-0 1000/1 DE, 71, 138, 139
0-6-6-0 1000/2 DE, 13, 16, 17, 54, 55, 56, 58, 59, 63, 64, 139

ABOUT THE AUTHORS

GARY W. DOLZALL is an accomplished railroad author and photographer. His work has appeared in a variety of publications, including TRAINS magazine, *Extra 2200 South*, and *Railway Gazette International*. Since 1978, his railroad writing has appeared exclusively in TRAINS, and he has had more than a score of articles published in that respected magazine. Gary has also had articles and photos published in commercial aviation publications. A graduate of Indiana University, Gary is creative director/marketing for Kalmbach Publishing Co. He is a member of several railroad historical organizations, and his other interests include baseball (he is partial to the Milwaukee Brewers and Chicago Cubs), travel, auto racing, and photography. Gary, his wife Donnette, and son Paul live in Waukesha, Wisconsin. This is his first book.

STEPHEN F. DOLZALL has been interested in railroading since he was a youngster growing up in Bedford, Indiana, watching Milwaukee Road 2-8-0s and Mikados. He received a degree in business management from Indiana University in 1966, and has since worked for the Allison Division of General Motors Corporation in Indianapolis, Indiana, where he is now the superintendent of manufacturing for Allison's Electro-Motive Division Product Group. In addition to his interest in railroading, Stephen is an avid model railroader. He is also a student of automobile industry history (especially that of the Studebaker Corporation) and has owned several antique cars. Stephen, his wife Lana, and children Stephanie and Thad live in Brownsburg, Indiana. Stephen has written for TRAINS magazine; this is his first book.